THE NATURAL HISTORY OF
CANADA
R.D. LAWRENCE

THE NATURAL HISTORY OF
CANADA
R.D. LAWRENCE

KEY PORTER BOOKS

CANADIAN CATALOGUING IN PUBLICATION DATA
Lawrence, R. D. (Ronald Douglas), 1921-
    The natural history of Canada

Bibliography: p. 303
Includes index.
ISBN 1-55013-064-1 (bound) ISBN 1-55013-509-0 (pbk.)

1. Natural history - Canada. I. Title.

OH106.L3 1988   508.71   C87-095280-3

PAGE i: **Starfish or sea stars**, as they are also called, are common in the Pacific as well as the Atlantic Ocean. A variety of species are known, most of which possess five arms, but some have as many as twenty-four.

PAGES ii–iii **Totem Lake**, in British Columbia's Purcell Mountains, reflects the mountains, trees and sky in its still waters.

PAGE iv **The almost fluorescent hues** of a red maple contrast with the fresh green of a black spruce.

Key Porter Books Limited
70 The Esplanade
Toronto, Ontario
Canada M5E 1R2

Distributed in the United States of America by
National Book Network, Inc.

Cartography: James Loates Illustrating
Line drawings and silhouettes: Marie Gosling/Gosling Studios
Canada goose silhouette (chapter openings): Phyllis Black
Pastel illustrations: Nancy Gray Ogle
Design: Catherine Wilson for C. P. Wilson Graphic Communication
Typesetting: Compeer Typographical Services Limited

Printed and bound in Italy

94 95 96 97 98 5 4 3 2 1

This book is dedicated to Canada and
to the conservation of our natural heritage.

CONTENTS

▲ **Of the many species of trilliums** that grow in Canada, the red trillium is
probably the most spectacular. This wildflower grows in Quebec and Ontario.

PREFACE

In 1980 I received a letter from a young reader who asked: "What is life?" The query was simple and direct, but as I sought to find a definitive, understandable answer, the task proved beyond me until I realized that instead of seeking to define life, I had to characterize it, for definition must always be limiting and abstract. Characterization, conversely, is scientifically open-ended and tends to draw a researcher closer to the subject of enquiry. Life, I concluded, cannot be defined, but it can be characterized because every living entity is unique and has personality.

That child's letter and my reply were largely responsible for my desire to write this book, a project towards which, I suppose, I had been leaning for a long time.

Soon after completing four years of biological studies, during which I majored in mammalogy, I found myself frustrated by the restrictive foci of the science and especially by the fact that my tutors sought to push me towards a cloistered specialty. I wanted to be a generalist; I wanted to study life in the field — not in a classroom, not in a laboratory, not as a government biologist, and definitely not as an industrial adviser. So I turned to writing; however, I did not abandon biology. Instead, I became a sort of academic maverick, dedicating myself to field study and later interpreting my findings in language understandable to the layman.

I was not long in drawing criticism from a number of establishment biologists. I have persisted because I feel that it is vital to the well-being of the world to simplify biology for those who need, and want, to be informed, but who cannot grasp the meanings concealed in the jargon-ridden scientific texts and papers that are emerging in ever-increasing volume. *The Natural History of Canada* has therefore been written for the layperson.

In departing from the "scientific," I am aware that there are those who will want to quibble over my approach, who will see some of my writings as being biologically simplistic. To them, I say that such is my intent, my purpose being to characterize the nature of Canada and not to attempt a scientific text, albeit I stand behind the biology that this book contains. There may also be some critics within the scientific community who will accuse me of being anthropomorphic — of investing nature with human qualities. These individuals I answer with the words written by Dr. Marston Bates in his book, *The Forest and the Sea*:

"Students of behaviour make much of the sin of anthropomorphism, but I have never been able to get as upset about this as some of my colleagues. In fact, I think the effort to avoid the use of human terms in describing animal behaviour often produces not clarity and objectivity, but inhuman and unreadable prose."

My thanks are due to the following people for assistance given to me during the research and writing of this book:

Barry Kent MacKay, Wildlife Co-ordinator, the Toronto Humane Society, for reading the manuscript and making valuable suggestions; Michael Collins, my biochemist neighbour, for once again giving me a better understanding of some of the mysteries of his science; Hal W. Reynolds, wildlife biologist, Canadian Wildlife Service, Edmonton, for information on the present status of bison; Roxanne Masse-Proulx, Canadian Wildlife Service, Ottawa, for courteously and willingly pointing me towards those CWS biologists who could answer my questions; Jim Shearon, Director, Parks Information, Parks Canada, who has ever been helpful; Bert Tetreault, Assistant Deputy Minister — Operations, Ministry of the Environment, Sainte-Foy, Quebec, for assistance given in the past; Dr. Francis R. Cook, Curator, Department of Herpetology, National Museum of Natural Sciences, Ottawa, who helped me a lot!; Tina Harrison, Vancouver, British Columbia, who has kept me posted on the course of environmental despoliation in British Columbia; and staff members of the Royal Ontario Museum and the Ontario Science Centre.

Last, *but definitely not least*, I want to thank my wife, Sharon, and my editor, Laurie Coulter: the former because her love, patience and constant support always makes it possible for me to keep writing; the latter because her commitment to the project has contributed greatly to the quality of this book.

THE NATURAL HISTORY OF
CANADA

INTRODUCTION

WHEN CANADIAN WINTER BEGINS TO RETREAT before the subtle advance of spring, the gradual changes may easily be overlooked. For days, and in some areas even weeks, the cold continues and the snows are reluctant to melt. To the urban dweller, it might almost seem as if the country that occupies slightly more than one-half of the North American continent has been destined to remain in the embrace of the last great Ice Age.

The reality is, however, quite different and noticeable when observed in the wilderness of our land. Day by day, as the sun rises higher above the eastern horizon and sets later in the western skies, a new warmth filters downwards and the earth responds to its energy. Beneath and on top of the softening snow minute bits of life begin to stir. Some are invisible to the naked eye; others, such as the dot-sized springtails (or snowfleas, as they are also called), singly are almost impossible to detect as they hop about, but massed together can be observed on sunlit snow. At a casual glance they might be mistaken for a dusting of soot. Seeds of many kinds of plants are beginning to germinate; roots are absorbing the moisture that daily soaks into the soil. And as the stubborn snow continues to retreat and sunlight strikes more and more bare ground, small green plants thrust upwards and sap begins to rise, slowly changing the colour of deciduous trees and shrubs.

At such a time, a number of years ago, while walking through a wilderness glade in Ontario, my attention was drawn to a patch of grass the blades of which were greener and taller than those that surrounded them. In the middle of the clump, partly concealed by the lush stems, a whitish object caught the sun; it was unidentifiable from a distance but on closer scrutiny turned out to be the skull of a snowshoe hare (*Lepus americanus*), a not unusual find in a habitat where predators, disease, and starvation commonly reduce many animals to skeletal remains. As I was about to move away, I noticed that blades of grass were growing through the skull's eye-sockets. The new stems, the bleached bone, and the slanting sunshine suggested a photograph. Afterwards I examined the remains and their surroundings. What I found allowed me to determine the manner in which the hare had met its death.

Small bits of dehydrated tissue still clung to parts of the empty brain case. These suggested that the hare had died, or had been killed, only

◄ **Morning mists** are common in many parts of Canada, especially along our coasts. This aerial photograph shows two river valleys joining in a region west of Sept Iles, Quebec.

a few months before. Pieces of bone were scattered in and around the clump of grass, each segment bearing teeth marks. Just outside the perimeter of the skull site, the imprint of the right forefoot of a red fox (*Vulpes vulpes*) was nicely preserved in a patch of bare ground that had obviously been muddy when the small predator had stepped there. Having found a fox den but ten minutes earlier that showed signs of occupancy, I inferred that the hare had been killed by the fox some time during the previous autumn. To test my conclusion, I picked up the skull and returned to the lair, where a variety of small bones, clumps of old, matted fur, and the feathers of several ruffed grouse lay scattered at the entrance.

Poking through this debris, I collected a number of hare vertebrae. One of these, the first cervical, fitted exactly into the base of the skull I had found. There was no doubt that the hare whose relic I held had been killed by one of the foxes that occupied the den. It was also clear that the predator had been particularly hungry: it had eaten of the kill at or near the place where it was made, separating the head from the body while doing so, and then, partly sated, had carried the remains back to its home site, probably sharing the food with its mate.

The story that the early spring thaw had revealed was commonplace. The death of a plant eater had given life to a meat eater. But this was only the opening chapter of the wilderness narrative.

Posthumously, the hare had supplied solid nourishment as well to a number of birds, rodents, and insects, all of which had eaten bits of its leftover meat, skin, and bone marrow. The animal's body had released fluids — lymph, blood, urine — that had soaked into the ground, there to be converted into usable organic matter by a legion of invisible, but important decomposer organisms. Transformed, the hare's juices had fertilized the soil, giving new energy to the grasses that grew around and through their unwitting benefactor's skull. More distant places also profited from the kill when small patches of soil were enriched by the droppings and urine of the various animals that had consumed the hare.

In fact, the interaction of the fox and the hare illustrates in microcosm the cause-and-effect forces that have been regulating the wild environment since time immemorial, the whole based upon a fundamental biological dictum, which states: *Nature is careless of the individual, but careful of the species*. This is the first and most important law of conservation.

Viewed from the standpoint of persons who are consciously or subconsciously influenced by modern socio-religious doctrines, this biological dictum is often difficult to accept. Humans are most reluctant to think of themselves as being expendable (I am no exception in this

regard). Nevertheless, when examined more closely, and from the perspective of the natural environment, to which mankind is inexorably tied, a system that puts the well-being of the species — and thus the *whole environment* — ahead of the individual will continue to replicate itself successfully and will enjoy a longer span on the evolutionary time clock than a system that protects the individual at the expense of the species.

In practice, and in the absence of severe, widespread natural catastrophes, the first law of conservation safeguards the gene pools of *all* living things and by doing so ensures the continuation of life as it exists outside of man's influences. In effect, this system operates by means of a complex series of checks. Over the long term, these checks maintain population numbers in balance with the food resources. Somewhat like a farmer seeking to remove undesirable plants from his croplands, the primordial law ensures that the fittest will survive to pass on their genes to future generations and that, by dying, the inefficient will serve as food and, as earlier noted, will return organic matter by various

▲ **A Canada goose** defends its nest against a marauding skunk, which, like all of its kind, has a fondness for bird eggs. Because the skunk is the aggressor, it is not seeking to spray its noisome scent. Faced by the powerful wings of the goose, the skunk eventually retreated.

▲ **Red fox kits** enjoy vigorous wrestling matches.

means to the environment. To this end, nature long ago decreed that more living things must be produced every year than can be allowed to survive, a practice that at first glance would appear to be wasteful. In fact, this practice is sound economy. Many of the newcomers and a proportion of the old or inefficient adults will become the food of the surviving consumers: the predatory mammals and birds, the grazing and browsing animals, the rodents, seed-eating birds, fish, reptiles, insects, bacteria, and fungi. Within this complex scheme, the survivors continue to reproduce, be they animals or plants, but the numbers of the new populations will vary in accordance with the food resources. Thus, through the periods of feast and famine that affect different species in different locations and for varying periods of time, balance is attained over the long term.

Nature's checks and balances are known today because of the biological research that has been taking place most intensively during the last 50 years. But from personal contact with such environmentally aware people as the Bushmen of Africa's Kalahari Desert and the Pygmy folk of the Congo's Ituri forest, I postulate that a deep, inherent understanding of the workings of nature has existed in the world for a very long time. Agricultural/technological man, however, retreating behind urban bastions many centuries ago, gradually lost touch with the natural environment, although it is likely that at least some individuals in each urban generation remained attuned.

Stripped of its archaic terminology, the biblical story of Joseph's interpretation of the Pharaoh's dream — in which the Egyptian ruler saw fat cattle and good wheat crops followed by thin cattle and meagre wheat crops — is good biology delivered in symbolic language. Joseph forecasted seven "fat" and seven "lean" years. Then he advised the Egyptian ruler to set aside one-fifth of his croplands from which the food should be harvested and stored during the seven good years as reserves to be used during the seven bad years.

Apart from the timing, which in the wild environment varies in accordance with the size and longevity of the different species, Joseph clearly described the cycles of feast and famine that intermittently occur in nature, when, during lean times, a representative "fifth" of the animals and plants survive in order to ensure the continuity of life. Such interactions occur not just in Canada, but over the entire *biosphere*, or that part of the earth's environment that is the home of all living things as well as the repository of the non-living elements and energy forms that are vital to life.

The biosphere incorporates all of the planet's *ecosystems*. The latter are composed of communities (populations) of living things and of the geophysical environments in which they interact and on which all depend. The ecosystem concept can be applied to a drop of water in which microscopic organisms interact, to a pond, to natural areas as large as the Pacific or Atlantic oceans, or, ultimately, to the entire biosphere.

Even the smallest and simplest ecosystem is enormously complex; so much so that biologists have a long way to go before they can understand all of the forces that govern the continuity of life. Indeed, this goal may never be attained!

An ecosystem is, in effect, a co-operative unit wherein its living and non-living components combine to transform solar energy into the fuel that is the prerequisite of life, while at the same time changing inorganic materials into the essential organic compounds that are required for the development of living matter. In addition, such a system recycles

▲ **A male American robin** perches on guard within its territory.

all of its materials for reuse with the minimum of waste, as occurred after the fox killed the hare.

To date, 17 major ecosystems have been recognized in Canada, including those of 3 oceans and of the nation's main freshwater reservoirs. Dividing the ecosystems are areas known as *transition zones*, where one ecosystem merges into another.

When I decided to leave Europe and come to Canada 33 years ago, the main reason for doing so was my desire to study the nation's wild environment, a task that in my naïveté I thought would take 3 or 4 years. Then I planned to go to Australia and study the nature of *that* land!

Soon after my arrival in Ontario, I received my first surprise: I discovered that Canada encompasses 9 203 054 km² (3 553 300 sq. mi.) of land, most of which is composed of wilderness and practically devoid of human settlement. Extending north into the Arctic Ocean to within 660 km (410 mi.) of the Pole at that part of Ellesmere Island that reaches the 83° north latitude, well within the Arctic Circle, Canada sprawls southward to the border of the United States, eastward to the Atlantic, and westward to the Pacific.

Within the nation's boundaries grow 171 main species of trees, among which are to be found 286 subspecies, and many hundreds of species of other plants, including fungi and slime moulds. Canada is home to 163 different kinds of mammals, from the mighty grizzly, the enormous shaggy bison, and the bulbous-nosed moose to such pygmies as the short-tailed shrew (*Blarina brevicauda*), which carries cobra-like venom in its salivary glands and becomes senile before it is one year old.

Between spring and the autumnal migration time, 518 species of birds breed and raise their young on the tundra, in the forests, along the coasts, and on the prairies. From late autumn to the following spring, hardy birds — such as big, ebon ravens; gray jays; chickadees; and nuthatches — continue to inhabit the northern latitudes. A variety of migratory species visit more southerly regions and the coastlines, especially in British Columbia, depending on the severity of winter.

Canada is also home to 42 species of reptiles and 41 species of amphibians, most of which feed on the literally thousands of species of insects that during the frost-free seasons swarm over the land. Into the phylum Arthropoda have been lumped all those land and marine animals that have certain features in common: their legs are jointed, their bodies are segmented, they most typically have compound eyes, and their blood flows freely within the body cavities and tissues. Some fly, some crawl, some, such as cicadas (family Cicadidae) and June beetles (*Polyphylla crinita*), spend considerable time under the soil during their larval development, keeping company with earthworms, hosts of nematodes (such as the round and wire worms), teeming soil bacteria, and many other microscopic organisms. Other insects are only found in the sea or in fresh water, but the overwhelming majority are land denizens.

Arthropods have been divided into two major sub-phylums: Chelicerata — animals without jaws or antennae — and Mandibulata — animals with both jaws and antennae. The Chelicerata have been divided into three classes: the Xiphosura, or horseshoe crabs (5 species); the Pycnogonida, or sea spiders (500 species), and the Arachnida, which includes scorpions, terrestrial spiders, ticks, and mites (35 000 species). The Mandibulata have been divided into four main classes: Crustacea, including lobsters and crabs (30 000 species); Chilopoda, or centipedes (3000 species); Diplopoda, or millipedes (10 000 species), and Hexapoda, or insects (one million species).

Collectively, the Arthropods are more numerous than all other animal species combined. Within the phylum, the insects are by far the most numerous and the most successful. It has been estimated that there are at least two million species of insects in the world that are still waiting to be discovered, studied, and named — at least one estimate suggests that ten million species of insects may exist on earth. Whatever the accuracy of the estimates, it is a fact that some 7000 new species are being discovered every year. The beetle order, for instance, contains more than 300 000 species; and it is almost a foregone conclusion that more will have been added to the list before these words are typeset!

Fossil evidence tells us that sea spiders and primitive terrestrial insects first emerged during the Silurian period of the Paleozoic era, some 360 million years ago, while the more modern ancestors of today's species were already common during the Pennsylvanian period 275 million years ago. It is indeed fortunate that the majority of insect species are beneficial and that only a fraction of the total are harmful. In undisturbed natural environments, however, the terms "good" and "bad" are not applicable. The so-called pest species act as population checks on other species, in some instances being able to bring about the demise of animals and plants unaided, at other times being just one of a series of reactions that combine to keep certain populations in check. In any event, for every pest insect, there is a control insect, and, of course, birds and some specialized mammals that prey upon them.

▲ **Short-tailed shrew**

OVERLEAF   **Canada geese** rest after feeding during a summer afternoon. ▶

▲ **This dung beetle**, labouring over a perfectly round ball of cattle manure, will eventually convert the waste into usable organic matter. Dung beetles are members of a large family, the Scarabaeidae, that contains more than 30 000 known species world-wide.

When I had made a partial inventory of the land animals and plants of Canada I turned my attention to the plants and animals that inhabit the nation's fresh and salt waters — the fish and crustaceans; the worms, insects, and bacteria; and the lilies, algae, and many other kinds of visible and microscopic lifeforms.

Canada has more coastline than any other nation in the world, with a total of 58 509 km (36 357 mi.), excluding islands. In the off-shore waters, the marine lifeforms are uncountable! Whales, porpoises, dolphins, seals, sharks, cod-fish, tuna, and salmon are among the better known and most spectacular, but thousands of species of fish, crustaceans (such as lobsters, shrimps, and crabs), molluscs (such as clams and oysters), sea worms, marine plants, microscopic and macroscopic planktonic organisms, and a host of other strange creatures defy inventory. Because of the ocean's inaccessibility, despite modern submarine exploration techniques, there is much life in the seas about which scientists know only a very little. And certainly there are many animals below the surface of the water that have yet to be discovered.

Before I could even begin to study the nation's plants and animals, the great majority of which were new to me, I had to make myself at least passably familiar with their scientific names. Common names are useful identifiers in many instances but they can also be misleading, especially when regional "nicknames" are employed. For instance, ruffed grouse are frequently called partridges in some parts of Canada. The scientific system used today throughout the world for naming plants and animals has been in use for over 250 years. Earlier, the international nomenclature for plants and animals had been in a chaotic state until a Swedish physician and scientist took it upon himself to sort out the mess during the eighteenth century. His name was Carl von Linné (1707–1778). He was to become known as Linnaeus. This indefatigable researcher, who was in effect the father of modern biology, decided that the study of life would bog down unless an international system of classification was devised. This he did. He eventually completed and published his famous work, *Systema Naturae*, in 1735 at the age of 28.

Systema Naturae set out the principles for defining the taxonomy (also called systematics) or hierarchy of living things. The categories are kingdom, phylum, class, order, family, genus, species and subspecies. For practical purposes, scientific names are usually given in three parts: genus, species and name, often abbreviated, of the scientist who first described and named the plant or animal. In this book, the names of the discoverers have not been given. Adding the discoverers' names is a practice generally used only by those who write formal texts and scientific papers.

It took years before I was able to compile a modest assessment of Canada's wild environment. Long before I had done so, I realized that I had set for myself an impossible task. No one person can ever hope to become intimate with the biology of all of the known plants and animals that inhabit Canada. And the knowledge that there are so many lifeforms that are as yet virtually unknown, especially among the insects, bacteria, and oceanic animals, almost caused me to abandon my project in favour of specializing in just one or two species. Nevertheless, because I feel that the sciences have become top-heavy with specialists and short on generalists, I persevered. Today, after more than three decades of field and academic study, I consider that I am still only about half-way to my goal. But living full time in the wilderness as I do, it is a rare day that passes without yielding a new bit of the gigantic jig-saw puzzle, a little piece that on some future occasion *may* be fitted into the ecological picture.

Without the green plants, life as we know it would not exist on earth. It is for this reason that terrestrial and aquatic plants are called *primary producers* (of food). Through photosynthesis, a complex process that uses the sun's energy in order to manufacture organic compounds from water and carbon dioxide, green plants produce their own nourishment. They, in turn, serve as food for the herbivores, or *primary consumers*, which are then eaten by the *secondary consumers*, or carnivores.

It is therefore not surprising that plant communities dictate the shape, size, and climate of all land ecosystems as well as the number, size, and nature of the animals that live in them. Each ecosystem contains a variety of communities of plants in addition to animals (the term "animal" refers to all living things capable of independent movement). The major vegetation zones found on the planet are classified as *biomes*. These include, for example, the great boreal forests that dominate Canada's northland and encircle the northern hemisphere; the tundra; the prairies; the deserts; and, indeed, all regions of the planet where climate and plants combine to produce a particular kind of habitat, or home, for the animals found in each ecosystem. In Canada, there are 11 major terrestrial plant habitats south of 75° north latitude (see map, page 12).

TUNDRA: This biome is characterized by shrubby plants, lichens, mosses, grasses, a few stunted evergreens in sheltered locations, small willows, and many varieties of small flowering plants. Extending irregularly from the Atlantic Ocean, on the north-east coast of Labrador, the Canadian tundra dips southwards into Hudson Bay, then extends

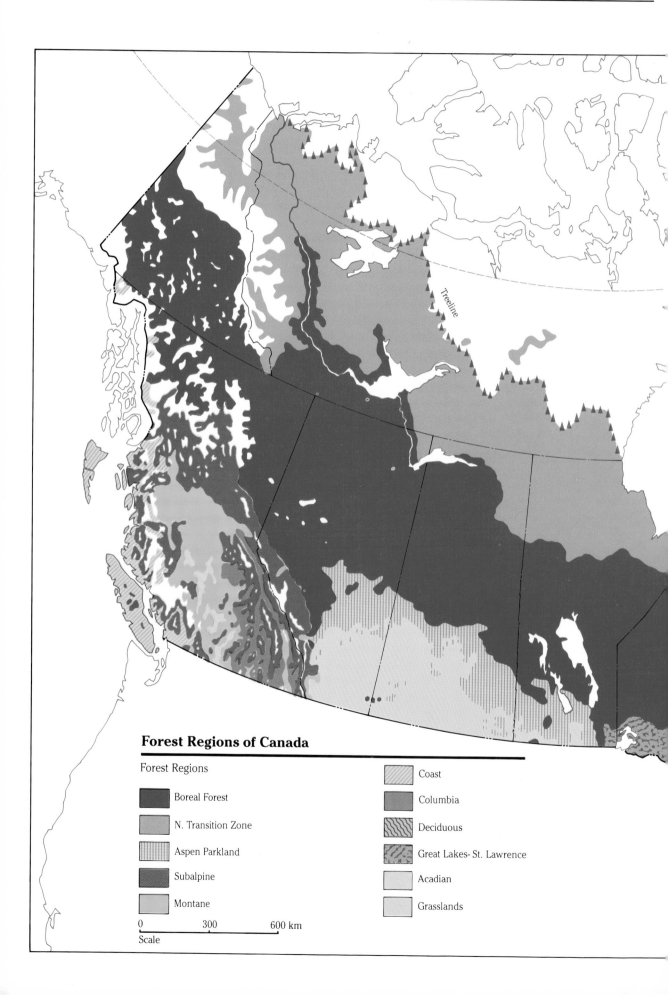

Forest Regions of Canada

Forest Regions

- ■ Boreal Forest
- ▨ N. Transition Zone
- ▥ Aspen Parkland
- ▨ Subalpine
- ▨ Montane

- ▨ Coast
- ▨ Columbia
- ▨ Deciduous
- ▨ Great Lakes- St. Lawrence
- ▨ Acadian
- ▨ Grasslands

Treeline

0   300   600 km
Scale

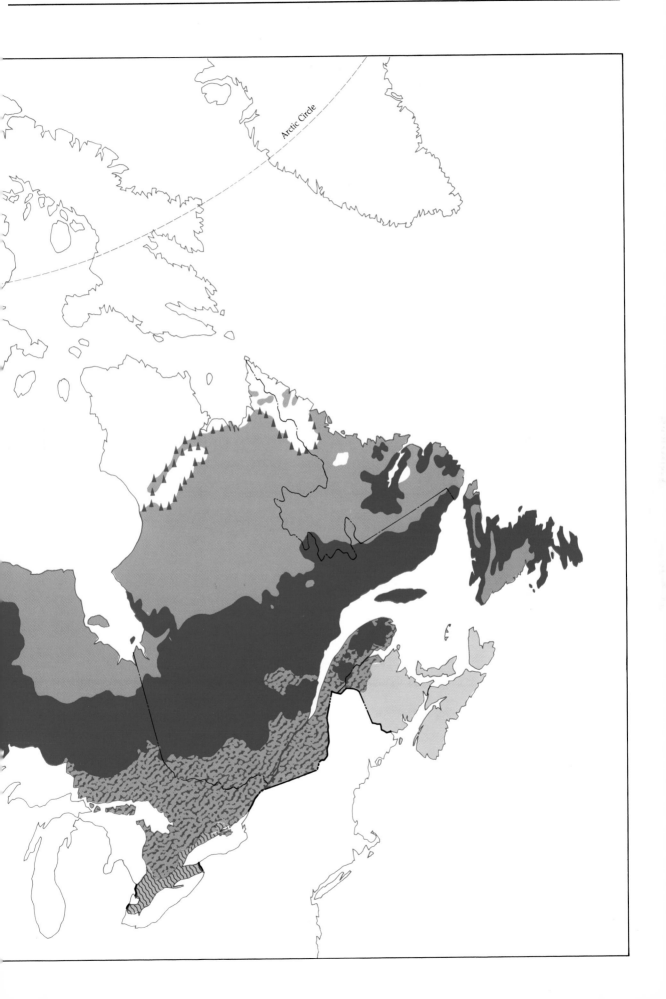

Arctic Circle

north, east, and west above the sixtieth parallel of latitude, and continues above the Arctic Circle until it eventually encounters the polar ice. Winters are long, with extremely low temperatures; summers are short, but the growth rate of plants is rapid because of the almost continual sunlight in this, the "Land of the Midnight Sun", which in winter becomes the "Land of Perpetual Night". Major tundra animals include: muskoxen, Arctic caribou, wolves, polar bears, wolverines, Arctic hares, foxes, and lemmings. Snowy owls are present year round and, from spring to autumn, uncountable other birds live here. For those humans who explore the tundra during the warm season, the blackflies and mosquitoes are the greatest hardship. They swarm in their millions!

ALPINE: The alpine biome is almost identical to the tundra because it shares the same climate. It is encountered above the tree-line in the mountains of Alberta and British Columbia at high altitudes in areas that are often dominated by glaciers, or by peaks that are covered in snow year round. Growing seasons are usually longer in more southerly alpine habitats because the sun continues to shine during winter daylight hours in the absence of cloud cover. Vegetation is similar to that found in the tundra. Mountain goats, bighorn sheep, Dall's sheep in northern British Columbia and the Yukon Territory, a few woodland caribou in the Selkirk Mountains of Alberta–British Columbia, grizzly and black bears, cougars, wolverine, lynx, pikas, bald eagles, hawks, and rock, willow, and white-tailed ptarmigans are some of the typical alpine wildlife.

BOREAL FOREST: Called "taiga" (pronounced *tie-gah*) by some authorities, this is Canada's largest and most dominant biome and one that is shared by the United States and Eurasia. It is characterized by white and black spruce, balsam fir, jack pine, white birch, trembling aspen, balsam poplar, willows, and alders. Interspersed among these dominant species are to be found a variety of grasses, small plants, shrubs, mosses, and lichens. The taiga extends from Newfoundland through Quebec and Ontario all the way west and north to the Northwest and the Yukon territories. Typical mammals include the black bear, moose, wolf, coyote, lynx, wolverine, mule deer, and, in the west, elk. Among the birds that are permanent residents of this biome are the ruffed and spruce grouse, owls, and the usual hardy northerners, such as woodpeckers, gray jays, chickadees, and nuthatches.

In many parts of the boreal, the forest floor is often composed of muskeg that in places is 3 to 4 m (10 to 13 ft.) deep. This soupy, dark-brown layer of decomposing vegetation is most often covered by thick

moss, a treacherous carpet that when stepped on can cause travellers to fall into the organic gruel and sink up to the waist, or even to be sucked down and drowned in the quicksand-like material. In such places, from spring to the autumnal freeze-up, travelling is confined to ancient trails beaten into areas of firm ground by generations of large animals. After the surface is frozen, however, human or moose or bear can travel anywhere in safety.

Taiga country is peppered by lakes and criss-crossed by rivers and streams, and where many of these are encountered, the thick forests thin out. In such localities, ancient Pre-Cambrian granite outcrops of the Canadian Shield are dominated by pure stands of white birch, or trembling aspen, trees that allow sunlight to reach the understory of small plants and shrubs. These more open sections of the biome are the home of otters, beavers, and muskrats as well as of migratory birds such as coots, ducks, grebes and, in some locations, white pelicans. In northern Alberta and the southern Northwest Territories, the taiga includes Wood Buffalo National Park, where roam thousands of plains

▲ **This view of the Mount Hector region**, Banff National Park, shows Hector Lake in the background and Margaret Lake in the foreground. The difference in the colours of the waters stems from the amount and kind of glacial silt in each lake.

bison and a good number of wood bison. The park is also the only natural nesting place of North America's tallest bird, the whooping crane, which flies 4000 km (2500 mi.) from its wintering grounds in the southern United States to Wood Buffalo's marshlands. The whooper is today perilously near extinction, although biologists in Canada and the United States are gradually increasing its numbers through captive breeding programs.

COAST: Canada's largest trees grow in this temperate rain-forest habitat. Running north from the Washington border, the coast forests are found along the western quarter of British Columbia and throughout Vancouver Island, the Queen Charlotte Islands, and on the many islands that dot the Inside Passage, from North Vancouver to the Alaska Panhandle. Enormous Douglas-firs, some of which may reach a height of 90 m (295 ft.) and a diameter of 4.5 m (15 ft.), and western red cedars, which may be 60 m (200 ft.) high and more than 3 m (10 ft.) in girth, are not uncommon in this biome; and almost as spectacular are the hemlocks and Sitka spruces.

SUBALPINE: As its name implies, this biome is found in valleys and along the lower slopes of the western mountains. It is dominated by two major species of evergreens: Engelmann spruce and lodgepole pine. Many of the mammals and birds found in the alpine and boreal milieus are also encountered in this biome. The subalpine runs north from the United States and is found within the Rocky Mountains and Coastal Mountains before it veers north-west and continues through the mountain ranges of British Columbia's interior. In some locations, this habitat merges with the Columbia.

MONTANE: These forests cover the central interior of British Columbia. They enter Canada from the state of Washington and run north in a broad band to end at about 55° north latitude, in the region of Terrace, British Columbia. Dominant trees include ponderosa and lodgepole pines, spruces, and Douglas-fir.

An immature golden eagle perches on the edge of its nest in Grasslands   ▶
National Park, Saskatchewan. The nest is located high above a large coulee,
typical of some of the landforms within the park.

▲ **Plains bison** like this enormous bull once roamed in their millions over the Canadian prairies. Merciless hunting brought them to near extinction by the turn of this century. Bison are now protected in sanctuaries. The largest of these is Wood Buffalo National Park, Alberta/ Northwest Territories.

COLUMBIA: This habitat thrusts north into Canada from the state of Washington and continues in that direction through the eastern interior of British Columbia. It is frequently interrupted by the subalpine system and ends rather abruptly some distance north of the Columbia River's Big Bend country. Dominant trees are Engelmann spruce, Douglas-fir, western red cedar, western hemlock, and larches (tamaracks). The Columbia shares its wildlife species with the subalpine and with the montane.

GRASSLANDS: This biome is divided into two sections: the prairie, and the aspen-grove zone. Beginning in south-eastern Manitoba, aspens dominate the landscape, but in Saskatchewan and Alberta, open country predominates. This entire region was once the range of the plains bison, which migrated north from the United States in their millions, lured by the prairie grasses; these are coarse and unpalatable-looking when compared to cultivated pastures, but they are rich with minerals, ideal fodder for the great, shaggy bovines that fed on them exclusively. Today, however, few areas of the original grassland habitat remain. Wheat farming and cattle ranching have almost entirely altered the natural ecosystem. Some of the historic animals are still to be found on the prairies, such as the pronghorn antelope, mule and white-tailed deer, badger, and black bear, but not in the numbers that were present during the closing decades of the nineteenth century, although bird species, especially waterfowl, abound.

In the extreme southern sections of the grassland biome, where the rolling land is often interrupted by deep coulees (ravines) and sculptured buttes, lush, oasis-like areas of vegetation grow in well-sheltered and naturally irrigated localities. Winters are long and cold in the grassland biome, but summers are hot and dry. Surviving in the coulees, and especially in the rough, rocky country known as "The Badlands", are rattlesnakes, western porcupines, coyotes, and large, fleet-footed jack rabbits, native hares that may weigh as much as 5 kg (11 lb.). Singly or in clumps on the banks of streams and rivers are found tall western cottonwoods, a species of poplar that may grow to a height of 60 m (200 ft.) and have a diameter of 1 m (40 in.). Shrubs and wildflowers, berry bushes (such as saskatoons), reeds and rushes in the low, alkali sloughs, and patches of tumbleweed are characteristic grassland plants.

In the aspen-grove section, the trembling aspen dominates, its pure stands bordering the prairie in a belt that runs from eastern Manitoba to south-central Alberta, where it ends at the foothills of the Rocky Mountains.

GREAT LAKES–ST. LAWRENCE: The most dominant trees in this biome are white pines, spruces, and yellow and white birches. The biome extends from Quebec's Gaspé Peninsula along a corridor within Quebec and Ontario and as far as the south-eastern boundary of Manitoba, thence south into the United States. Wildlife species include white-tailed deer, wolves, coyotes, black bears, moose, raccoons, skunks, and a wide variety of resident and migratory birds.

DECIDUOUS: The deciduous biome is composed largely of winter-tolerant hardwoods such as maples, oaks, beeches, and a variety of other species. The biome extends in Canada along a narrow corridor of irregular shape that borders the northern shores of Lake Ontario and Lake Erie, then continues into the United States. It shares most of the wildlife found in the Great Lakes–St. Lawrence and Acadian habitats.

ACADIAN: Characterized by spruces, balsam fir, yellow birch, and maples, this biome is encountered throughout New Brunswick, Nova Scotia and parts of Newfoundland. Acadian forests were once dominant on Prince Edward Island, but intensive logging and farming eliminated all but a few, isolated examples. This biome extends across the international border to all of those American states that border Canada from New Brunswick to lakes Ontario and Erie. Species of animals encountered in the Acadian biome are much the same as those encountered in the Great Lakes–St. Lawrence biome.

All of Canada's biomes and ecosystems will be discussed in more detail in the following chapters of this book. In this context, it should be noted that the plants and animals named during description of the biomes are not the only ones found in the vegetation habitats. In favoured locations grow other species of plants that may furnish shelter and food for other kinds of animals, just as hardier plants are often found interspersed among dominant species. Similarly, each tree habitat supports considerable numbers of plants such as shrubs, wildflowers, mosses, lichens, and liverworts. Clear-cut divisions between biomes are only rarely encountered because, in the main, one habitat blends into the next at the transition zones, within which occur a mix of species of plants and animals from two or more habitats. Nature has seldom been given to drawing straight lines. This characteristic, in conjunction with such factors as unusual climatic changes, pressure from wildlife populations and from human interference, landslides in mountain country, and other geological changes, continue to alter the boundaries of the habitats and transition zones.

Individual accounts of the biomes, ecosystems, and transition zones of Canada's shoreline and marine environments have been omitted from this introduction because of the complexities of the oceanic systems. The seas and the animals and plants that live in them are simply too *fluid* to permit simple bio-geographical delineation. A brief general description of the marine environment follows.

The shape of an ocean conforms rather loosely to that of an upright basin, a name that has been applied to the saltwater environments. From all of those places where the sea meets the land, oceanic *continental shelves* slope gradually downwards, continuing into deeper water for an average distance of 70 km (43 mi.), although these gradients extend over much longer distances in many parts of the world. The shelves, roughly equivalent to the gently inclined rim of a basin, often end abruptly at given locations. The points at which the bottom drops away mark the upper boundaries of the *continental slopes*, which descend slowly or abruptly, depending on the region, all the way down to the sea bed. The flattest portions of the ocean floor are known as *abyssal plains*. These enormous expanses of relatively flat submarine terrain are not all that dissimilar to the Canadian prairies. In many locations they are interrupted by tall undersea mountains and exceptionally deep canyons.

Two major marine habitats are currently recognized. The first, known as the *pelagic*, is the ocean water itself. The second, known as the *benthic*, is the ocean bottom. These are further divided into various zones. Each oceanic zone contains many different species of animals and plants, a large number of which will not, or cannot, live in any other marine environment. Many species move from zone to zone and some are permanent residents in all of them.

In contrast to land, where lack of water inhibits life in deserts, in permanently frozen regions, and in other habitats during conditions of drought, shortage of moisture is of course never a problem in the oceans and is therefore not a critical factor in the distribution of marine plants and animals. Temperature, however, influences the biology of sea life much as it does that of the terrestrial environments, except that the sea is uniformly cooler than the habitable land in all regions of the world. The temperatures at the surface on the open sea range from $-2°$ C (29° F) to 30° C (86° F). In the deepest parts of the abyss, however, temperatures drop to between 0.5° C (32.9° F) and 2.5° C

◄ **Monarch butterflies** are widespread in North America and remarkable because in autumn they congregate in mass and migrate as far south as Central America. In Canada they feed largely on milkweed plants.

(36.5° F), yet animals live, breed, and multiply in that chill and perpetually dark nether world.

Seemingly, these living things, some of which have been identified and found to be quite bizarre in shape and development, are all carnivores, or carrion feeders, for the presence of plant life in the great deeps has not as yet been confirmed. But in as much as discoveries made during the last two decades have confounded the statements and predictions made during the first quarter of this century, it would appear that almost anything is possible in the oceans. Quite recently, submarine probes off the Galapagos Islands established that volcanic rifts at the bottom of the Pacific produced heat and sulfurous gasses that nurtured some very special kinds of bacteria. These in turn were preyed upon by other organisms, which themselves were consumed by others. Up to the time of that discovery, it was believed that life could only exist in the presence of oxygen and carbon. Now science knows better.

The sunlight that nurtures terrestrial life, and which also gives energy to the majority of the marine plants and animals, penetrates water only to a depth of 76 m (250 ft.); the longer waves of the spectrum, the reds and yellows, disappear first, the shorter waves, the blues and violets, penetrating to the greatest depths.

All of these things have a bearing on the biology of Canada's marine environment in as much as a large proportion of sea animals are, in effect, international in scope and travel. However, the economy of life within the three oceans surrounding Canada is more heavily dependent upon sunlight and upon the host of minute plants and animals that are collectively called *plankton*, a Greek word meaning "that which is made to wander or drift". Planktonic life may be vegetable or animal. The former are called *phytoplankton*, the latter *zooplankton*. Phytos abound in their billions. They are tiny algal plants, some of which cannot be seen individually, such as the microscopic *diatoms*, single-celled algae that are found in fresh water as well as in the sea. The zooplankton are minute animals; most are grazers that feed on the phytoplankton.

Like terrestrial plants, phytoplankton can build starches through photosynthesis by absorbing energy from the sun. As a result, they are the principal foundation of the oceanic food pyramid. Some species of plankton are incapable of voluntary movement and must drift with the surface currents; others can swim but, being so small, are also at the mercy of currents and storm disturbances.

Plankton, and the larvae of crustaceans as well as small fish, are the only prey of the baleen whales, including the blue whale (*Balaenoptera musculus*), the largest animal on earth. Growing to a maximum length of 30 m (98 ft.) and having a mass of up to 131.5 t (145 tons), the blue, like some other baleen whales, swims through the masses of plankton with wide-open mouth, scooping up huge quantities of the tiny animals and plants during each pass. The two largest sharks also feed on plankton in the same way. Neither the great whale shark (*Rhincodon typus*), which can attain a length of at least 15 m (49 ft.) nor the almost as large basking shark (*Cetorhinus maximus*) prey on large animals or on humans.

Phytoplankton, although photosynthetic, nevertheless prefer cool waters and dim light. They migrate downwards during the hours of sunlight and rise closer to the surface at night. These movements affect the distribution of marine life in the ocean zones, because the small fish that also feed on krill (small crustaceans) follow their quarry; and such fish are in turn preyed on by larger fish. As a result of these regular migrations, surface waters contain fewer fish during the day and many fish during the hours of darkness.

The seas are home to at least one-sixth of all the vertebrate animals known to date, these being represented by 12 000 species of fishes and 117 species of mammals. In addition, as noted earlier, the marine world hosts untold numbers of plants and invertebrate animals. All of these living things, regardless of size, shape, and the special adaptations that they have had to acquire in order to survive in the oceans, have the same needs as land animals: they must be able to breathe, eat, find shelter, and reproduce in an environment that, like the terrestrial milieu, comprises mountains, plains, canyons, and valleys. For these reasons, it is difficult to decide whether the sea is an extension of the land, or the land is an extension of the sea. The fact is that the two environments combine to form our planet and are thus not to be divorced from each other. This brings into focus the biology of those locations where salt water and dry land meet, the coastlines of Canada and the rest of the world.

Because of the shape of the land, coastline biomes and ecosystems are difficult to classify. In some areas for example, British Columbia and the Atlantic provinces, the forests end at sheer cliffs. Such boundary zones can rightly be termed coast biomes in British Columbia, or boreal-forest biomes in Newfoundland. In the beach and marsh zones grow plants that have become adapted to salt. In the north, there are areas where tundra vegetation ceases only a few metres from the Arctic

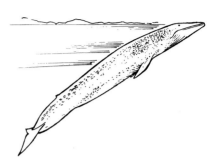

▲ **Blue whale**

OVERLEAF **Atlantic Ocean waves** batter the jagged coastline of Cape Breton ▶
Highlands National Park, Nova Scotia. Here, where water and land are partners, countless numbers of marine birds raise their young each spring.

▲ Gull

▲ Tern

Ocean and other areas where no plant life exists because of ice. And then there are the islands. On Canada's west coast the plant and animal life of the islands are much the same as that found on the mainland. This holds true for much of the east coast as well, with some notable exceptions. One exception is a part of Quebec that borders the Gulf of St. Lawrence. Here, intermittently occupying 82 km (51 mi.) of the gulf where salt and fresh water mingle to form what is in effect an inland sea, lie the 43 islands that make up the Mingan Archipelago. All are unique in that they offer landscapes and some biological forms found nowhere else in Canada. In 1983, with the agreement of the province of Quebec, 40 of the islands were purchased by Parks Canada and have been set aside as the Mingan Archipelago National Park Reserve.

Compared to such islands as Newfoundland, Victoria, Ellesmere, and Prince Edward, the Mingans are tiny. Battered by the Atlantic and composed of sandstone, eroded by quite literally thousands of years of sea and weather, these Quebec islets have a unique bio-geology that cannot be fitted into any of the other natural systems to be found in the nation.

For years I had heard of the Mingan Islands and was curious about them, but it was not until I happened to discover the poetry of Roland Jomphe, Quebec's justly famed fisherman-poet, that I dropped all other projects in favour of doing some Mingan field research. Jomphe, born in the community of Havre St. Pierre, on the St. Lawrence River's North Shore and facing the unusual archipelago, has written many verses and was awarded the Order of Canada in 1981. He is a man committed to the conservation of the islands, having long ago recognized their uniqueness.

Eroded into a variety of shapes, the rocks found on each island of the archipelago might have been fashioned by a master sculptor. There is an enormous boot, upside down, its heel and sole facing the heavens; there is a giant sandstone duck squatting on the shingle of one isle, and an eagle staring majestically from the height of another. Each of the 43 islands has its own unique natural sculptures.

Impressive as these may be, however, what is even more fascinating is the biology of the Mingans. Birds are everywhere in all seasons, even during the tough gales of winter. Trees are limited to a few stunted, wind-shaped spruces; plants are salt- and weather-resistant on shore, seaweeds in the water. Surrounding the islands in season, majestic marine mammals sail by: the huge blue whale; the humpback whale (*Megaptera novaeangliae*), of lesser mass and length, but a giant none the less compared to land mammals; the killer whale (*Urcinus orca*), a black-and-white, sleek animal that, like the wolf, has been wrongly accused of attacking humans. These, and eight other species of whales, dolphins, and porpoises are frequent visitors to the deep waters surrounding the Mingan Islands.

Common eider ducks, cormorants, murres, puffins, razor-bills, guillemots, red-throated and common loons, and gulls belonging to a variety of species live on the islands and feed on the fish that abound in the waters.

The most intriguing of the plants that grow in the thin soil covering the Mingans is a thistle found only on five of the islands and nowhere else in the world. This plant, of the genus *Cirsium*, has so far remained unclassified as a species because botanists are still debating its origins, despite the fact that it was first discovered in 1924 by Frère Marie-Victorian, an avid Quebec naturalist. One of the characteristics that makes the thorny plant unique is the ability of its seeds to lie dormant, but fertile, in the ground for several years if weather conditions are unfavourable.

In addition to Quebec's Mingan Islands, there are other ecosystems on islands scattered along Canada's coasts that cannot be neatly classified, a circumstance that graphically illustrates the difficulties facing those scientists and naturalists who have for many years sought to identify all of this enormous country's biological assets.

In the majority, if not actually all, of the different coastal habitats, terrestrial animals are to be found within a wide variety of what might be termed mini-ecosystems or mini-biomes. Naturalists have thus had to decide whether coastlines should be considered part of the marine world or of the terrestrial environment. Arbitrarily perhaps, but for the sake of clarity, *The Natural History of Canada* will describe the coast regions according to the degree of influence exerted upon them by the land, or by the sea.

It is clear that no single book can possibly deal with all of the natural subjects that are to be found in a country the size of Canada. Indeed, although the federal government has for years been discussing the need for a national biological survey, all that has emerged to date is a partial review of the terrestrial Arthropods (insects, spiders and relatives) that are found in our land. Only about half of these have so far been classified. This means that if the entomological evidence is accurate, of the 66 000 species of Arthropods estimated to exist in Canada, more than 30 000 remain to be studied!

▲ **The small pickerel frog** is widely distributed across eastern North America. It is often found in moist, grassy meadows.

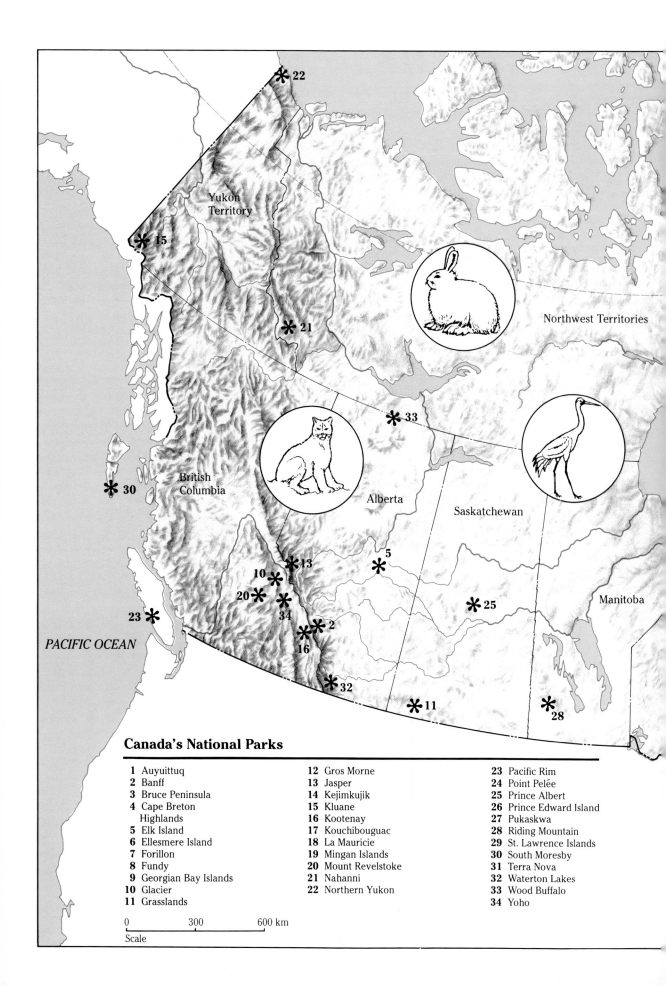

Canada's National Parks

1 Auyuittuq	**12** Gros Morne	**23** Pacific Rim
2 Banff	**13** Jasper	**24** Point Pelée
3 Bruce Peninsula	**14** Kejimkujik	**25** Prince Albert
4 Cape Breton	**15** Kluane	**26** Prince Edward Island
Highlands	**16** Kootenay	**27** Pukaskwa
5 Elk Island	**17** Kouchibouguac	**28** Riding Mountain
6 Ellesmere Island	**18** La Mauricie	**29** St. Lawrence Islands
7 Forillon	**19** Mingan Islands	**30** South Moresby
8 Fundy	**20** Mount Revelstoke	**31** Terra Nova
9 Georgian Bay Islands	**21** Nahanni	**32** Waterton Lakes
10 Glacier	**22** Northern Yukon	**33** Wood Buffalo
11 Grasslands		**34** Yoho

0   300   600 km

Scale

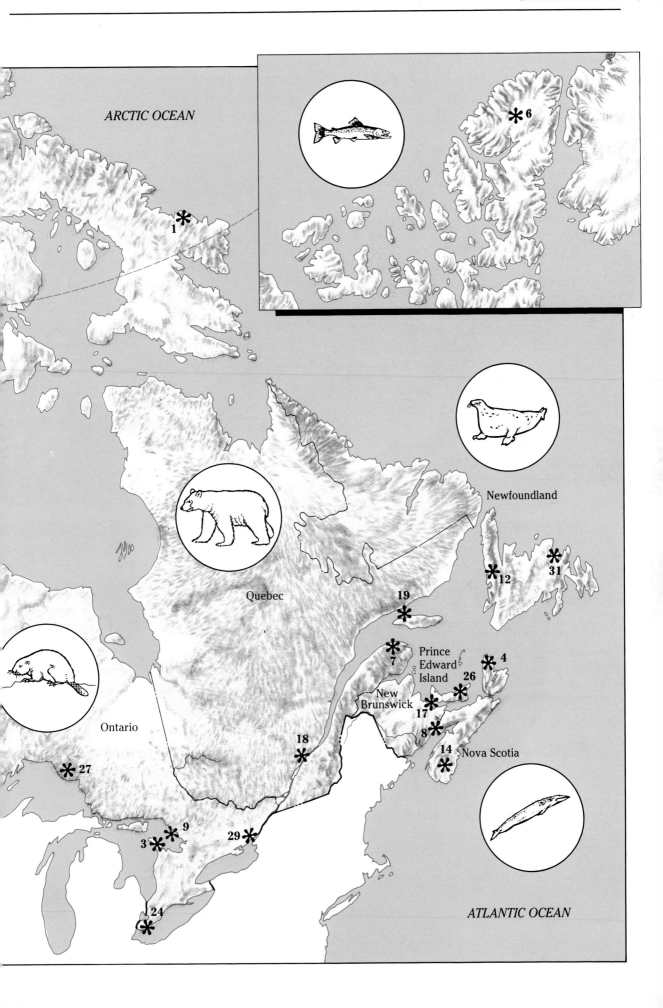

IN THE BEGINNING

1

IN THE LATE 1950s A MINING ENGINEER IN THE Yukon Territory found the nest of a lemming buried 6 m (20 ft.) deep in permafrost — a layer of moisture-filled, permanently frozen soil of which only 1 m (40 in.), at most, of the uppermost surface thaws during the short northern summers. The grass nest, shaped somewhat like a small melon and in perfect condition, contained the well-preserved skeleton of the rodent and a quantity of seeds that it had gathered and stored.

The finds were sent to the National Museum in Ottawa, where they were examined by scientists who became puzzled by the depth at which the discovery had been made, for the lemmings, relatives of the hamsters and gerbils, dig short, underground burrows in summer, but in winter nest on the surface, under the snow.

After many painstaking tests were performed, it was eventually established that the lemming had been buried under the permafrost for *10 000 years*, a fact that caused considerable surprise and cast doubt upon the theory that postulates that the last Ice Age had already ended by then in that region. But there was more to come! While some scientists were wrestling with the first puzzle, others identified the seeds that the prehistoric lemming had gathered. They were lupines (*Lupinus* sp.), a species still growing in the north. Some of the seeds were planted. Not only did they germinate, developing stems and leaves, but they actually blossomed, becoming the oldest-known seeds to have bloomed, beating by 8000 years the record previously set by lotus seeds found in Asia. Now came a second puzzle. How had the seeds remained fertile for ten millennia?

In defiance of scientific logic, the seeds had evidently not absorbed moisture during the time that must have elapsed after the lemming had died; yet, flash-freezing is not known to occur in nature. Instead, the land remains moist during the transition from autumn to winter, the frost gradually penetrating more deeply over a period of days.

During the interval between autumn and winter, the lupine seeds *should* have become swollen by moisture and *should* have become infertile after they were frozen. Then, too, in as much as the nest was so well preserved, it had evidently been constructed underground during summer and so had been protected from the pressure exerted by the weight of snow and ice, and especially by the tonnes of soil, which

◀ **The awesome beauty** of an ice-sculptured landscape is graphically demonstrated in this scene, photographed in Auyuittuq National Park, Baffin Island. The large boulder, forced by pressure to the surface of the Caribou Glacier, points the way to Mount Asgard in the background.

▲ Lemming

would have crushed a winter nest built on the surface. Theories were advanced, but provable answers have not been offered to date. Logic, however, suggests that the lemming had been alive during a time of moderate climate, which endured between the end of one glacial period and the sudden beginning of another. Since the animal's skeleton was found to be approximately 10 000 years old, it would appear that the fourth and last Ice Age did not *end* ten millennia ago, but rather *began* about that time — at least in that region.

In any event, the fourth period of glaciation is not over yet. Ice sheets still cover the north and south poles; Greenland is almost entirely covered by a great ice cap; and Canada's northernmost territory, Ellesmere Island, boasts some respectable ice caps, as do the mountains of Alberta, British Columbia, and the Yukon Territory.

Currently, geologists theorize that the climate of the northern hemisphere, including that of the whole of Canada and the more northerly regions of the United States, gradually started to get colder, a progressive chilling that was accompanied by ever-increasing amounts of snow, longer and longer winters, and shorter and shorter frost-free seasons. Eventually, the temperature did not rise above the freezing point and the snow remained on the ground, becoming thousands of metres thick. The enormous mass of the upper strata of snow compacted the bottom layers, turning them into ice that was squeezed by the pressure until it became semi-plastic. Glaciers began to flow from the heights, travelling slowly, but inexorably, across the land until they covered almost two-thirds of the North American continent.

Why did the temperature drop so radically? No one really knows. There are a number of theories. Some suggest that the sun's radiant heat may have been deflected away from the earth causing the planet's surface temperature to fall; or, perhaps atmospheric carbon dioxide increased to a point where it filtered out a portion of the sun's energy; or, volcanic activity may have poured dust into the atmosphere and prevented sunlight from reaching the earth.

Regardless of the *why*, there is no doubt that the great cold did occur and that Canada was intermittently influenced by it for many thousands of years. But, considering that scientists believe that the earth is about five *billion* years old, the interval between the first glacial period and the last (or present, as the case may be), is equivalent to a few seconds on the evolutionary time-clock. As the mass of ice advanced over the land, it bulldozed all before it, at the same time picking up soil, gravel, trees, and enormous blocks of rock. These abrasive materials scoured the earth further, carving lines and patterns over great areas of bare granite, tearing at the foundations of some mountains, and digging basins where none had been before. Wherever the advancing ice met

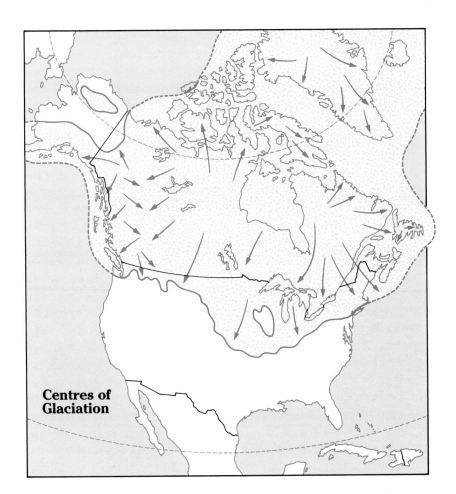

Centres of Glaciation

obstructions, it cleared them away, in many regions actually polishing the surface of rock after the debris that had gouged the stone had moved on and was followed by a layer of smooth ice. Ancient river valleys were deepened and widened; the tops of low mountains were sheared off, leaving hills with rounded edges, or with flat crowns, like the buttes found in Saskatchewan.

Between each of the four glacial periods, the debris carried by the melting ice was deposited helter-skelter, creating what at first must have looked something like the moonscape, with piles of gravel, strewn boulders, and mounds of topsoil. And no living thing was to be noted for millions of square kilometres, for when each icing took place, those animals and plants that survived the deep freeze did so by moving south — the animals, of course, under their own power, the plants carried by animals and birds, or travelling as seeds in high winds.

At its height, the fourth Ice Age blanketed most of Canada and Alaska, and a good part of the northern United States. There were at first four different icings during the last period of glaciation: one in Greenland, another in the western mountains, a third west of Hudson Bay, and the fourth in Quebec's Ungava Peninsula. From these centres, icefields flowed outwards and in time joined their neighbours, becoming one gigantic mass. Meeting the Atlantic and Pacific oceans, the ice "paved" their waters for some distance before it succumbed to the influence of the sea salts and broke away, the huge pieces becoming ice islands, which eventually melted. It is estimated that ice at one time covered more than 6.5 million km^2 (2.5 million sq. mi.) of North America (see map, page 33) and that during each ice age, the amount of water absorbed from the world's oceans and locked up as ice must have lowered sea levels by between 60 and 90 m (200 and 295 ft.).

As the climate slowly became more temperate, geologists conclude, the ice began its retreat at the southern edges of the field, melting northwards. In time, the waters that were released flooded valleys and lowlands and formed many large lakes such as the Champlain Sea in Quebec. The largest of these prehistoric bodies of water has been named Lake Agassiz. It was greater in extent than the area presently covered by all of the Great Lakes, occupying almost the entire portion of southern Manitoba, northwestern Ontario, eastern Saskatchewan, and northwestern Minnesota.

Another glacial lake, which has been named Algonquin, was formed in the regions now occupied by lakes Superior, Michigan, and Huron. Remnants of its beaches are still to be seen in parts of Ontario. Some of Algonquin's waters flowed south to the Mississippi, but a large portion drained into the St. Lawrence Valley via the route that is roughly occupied today by Ontario's Trent River system. Occasionally, the ice and debris blocked the drainage channels, but the pressure of water made new outlets into the St. Clair River and Lake Erie and then into the area currently occupied by Lake Ontario, forming a glacial body of water that geologists have named Lake Iroquois.

These events took place not once, but four times, the first beginning between 100 million and 60 million years ago, according to current estimates. In between the periods of glaciation, climates warmed up and the land recovered and was recolonized by plants and animals that were the ancestors of today's species. It is also probable that the ancient lakes altered their boundaries and depths during and after each ice age, especially so because the enormous pressure exerted by the volumes of snow and ice actually pushed the earth's crust downwards in some of the areas occupied by the prehistoric basins and by those bodies of fresh water that exist today.

◀ **The last ice age** still retains its grip in Kluane National Park in the Yukon Territory, where vast areas are dominated by glaciers. A section of the St. Elias Mountains icefields is shown in this aerial photograph.

OVERLEAF **The first hardwood forests** appeared in what is now Canada during the late Cretaceous period. ▶

The ice ages were the most recent of a series of prehistoric cata-
clysms, the cumulative effects of which combined to create the
topography and bio-geography of Canada and, indeed, of the entire
world. To describe in detail all of the geologic changes that have affected
the North American continent during the past is beyond the scope of
a single book. But in order to provide a better understanding of the
nature of our country as it exists today, a brief description of the early
geologic timetable is necessary, although it should be noted that the
date estimates have been modified during the last two decades and
that they are likely to change again in the future as more discoveries
are made (see geologic table, page 41).

Before quite recent times, estimates of the age of our planet and of
the events that have shaped its surface and influenced its lifeforms
were based more on educated guesses than on scientific evidence.
During the late 1940s, radio-carbon dating was introduced, a method
that relies on the fact that certain radioactive elements are slowly transformed into other elements at rates basically unaffected by temperature
and pressure. The time taken for the breakdown, or decay, of half the
radioactive material in a given sample is known as the element's *half-
life*. Thus, for instance, the half-life of carbon 14 is 5568 years. This
technique was used largely to date fossils and organic materials, but
its disadvantage was that the age of anything that was *really* old could
not be dated.

A more accurate dating system that allowed measurements of time
to be made for very old rocks was later devised. It works on the same
principle as the carbon-14 test, but relies on the rate of decay of radioactive uranium, which breaks down into lead. Unlike carbon 14, however, the rate of uranium decay is *slow*. It will take *billions* of years to
convert half of the uranium into lead. By measuring the amount of
uranium and lead found in a sample of rock, its age can be deduced.
Employing the uranium method, it has been estimated that the rocks
of the earliest geologic period are over 3.8 billion years old and that
younger rocks, like those of the Cambrian period, are more than 500
million years old.

Yet another method of measuring was introduced in 1959. Known
as potassium-argon dating, this technique was first developed in Italy

Klutlan Glacier, creeping down the St. Elias Mountains in Kluane National ▶
Park, is Canada's largest valley glacier. A virtual river of ice, Klutlan from a
distance looks somewhat like a strange, white-topped highway that at its
widest location is 8 km (5 mi.) wide.

to establish the age of lava and volcanic ash near Rome. Like the two methods mentioned above, it also hinges on the half-life of an element, this time of radioactive potassium, which breaks down into argon. By the early 1960s, uranium and potassium-argon methods were in general use by scientists investigating the world's past. Using these means, it is now possible to get more accurate dates for materials that are millions of year old — even for fossils and other organic remains, because if a fossil is found surrounded by a stratum of ancient sedimentary materials that dates back, for example, one million years, it must have been deposited in that location at the same time as the minerals and soil. Thus, aided by modern methods as well as by the findings of early scientists, who despite technologic limitations were yet able to make some remarkably accurate deductions, the palaeo-geologic and palaeo-geographic antecedents of the planet are better known today than ever before.

Historically, the geologic timetable of *eras*, *periods*, and *epochs* has been based upon the recognition world-wide of five major rock formations, each of which has been divided into secondary formations.

Representing the primary formations and the evidence of life found in each, five eras have been named. The first and second, the *Archeozoic* and the *Proterozoic*, have not been divided into periods; the next two, the *Paleozoic* and the *Mesozoic* have been divided into periods, but not into epochs; and the last era, the *Cenozoic*, has been divided into periods and epochs.

The Archeozoic is estimated to have begun some four billion years ago and to have lasted about two billion years. The Proterozoic began perhaps two billion years ago and lasted about one billion years. Both eras were characterized by great volcanic activity.

Evidence of life during the Archeozoic is limited to the discovery of organic materials in rock. Proterozoic evidence reveals that primitive marine plants (algae and fungi) had developed during the early part of the era and that, towards its end, such animals as molluscs, worms, and a number of other marine invertebrates had also emerged.

◀ **Thousands of years** of erosion by wind, ice and rain have created some of the unusual formations found in Alberta's Dinosaur Provincial Park. The park is famous for its fossil record of dinosaurs and their contemporaries.

THE GEOLOGICAL CALENDAR

ERA	Period	How Long Since it Began in Millions of Years
CENOZOIC	Quaternary Pleistocene	1
CENOZOIC	Tertiary Pliocene Miocene Oligocene Eocene Paleocene	70
MESOZOIC	Cretaceous	125
MESOZOIC	Jurassic	165
MESOZOIC	Triassic	200
PALEOZOIC	Permian	230
PALEOZOIC	Pennsylvanian	260
PALEOZOIC	Mississippian	290
PALEOZOIC	Devonian	330
PALEOZOIC	Silurian	360
PALEOZOIC	Ordovician	420
PALEOZOIC	Cambrian	500
PROTEROZOIC		2000 ±
ARCHEOZOIC		4000 ±

OVERLEAF **The Pre-Cambrian** rocks of the Canadian Shield have been ▶ scoured by glaciation. This example of Shield country is in Ontario's Quetico Provincial Park.

The Paleozoic era (the age of ancient life) has been divided into seven periods: *Cambrian, Ordovician, Silurian, Devonian, Mississippian, Pennsylvanian*, and *Permian*. From its start at the Cambrian period 500 million years ago, to its end in the Permian period 230 million years ago, this era experienced a gamut of upheavals, including flooding, warm conditions even in the Arctic, and mountain-building eruptions during which the Appalachian Range arose. Land plants and the first fishes and corals are thought to have appeared during this era. By the end of the Paleozoic era, many archaic animals had become extinct, replaced by mammal-like reptiles and the first modern insects, such as houseflies and ants.

The Mesozoic era began 200 million years ago and has been dubbed the "Age of Reptiles". It is divided into three periods: *Triassic, Jurassic,* and *Cretaceous.*

During the Triassic period the land became divided into continents. Desert conditions existed in many parts of the world, but in other regions evergreen trees became dominant and ancient seed ferns became extinct. The first dinosaurs appeared. They were joined towards the end of this period by pterosaurs or strange flying reptiles, fossils of which are usually associated with marine deposits. The skeletons of these fliers suggest that they could not stand upright on land, prompting the view that, somewhat like bats, they swooped and skimmed through the air, taking their food from the seas while on the wing. Egg-laying mammals also emerged during the Triassic, and primitive amphibians became extinct.

The Jurassic period began 165 million years ago and lasted 40 million years. It saw the spread of some flowering plants and of the cycads. The latter are tropical plants only one of which, the sago palm of Florida, is now native to the North American continent. Coniferous trees were common and the first toothed birds made an appearance. By this time dinosaurs had become larger and specialized, insects were plentiful, and the first marsupials had developed. Marsupials are animals such as the Australian kangaroo and the North American opossum. Their young begin to grow inside the mother's uterus, but are born in an undeveloped state. Essentially embryonic in appearance, they are nurtured inside the female's specialized pouch.

After earlier inland seas and swamps had retreated, the Rocky Mountains arose during the late Cretaceous period. This period began 125 million years ago. The first oak and maple forests appeared in the lands now occupied by Canada and the United States while one class of flowering plants declined and another took its place. During the Cretaceous the dinosaurs and toothed birds became extinct, replaced by modern birds and the first archaic mammals.

◄ **Two horned dinosaurs** (*Tricera-
tops*) graze among gum trees and
bald cypresses in the Wood Mountain region of Saskatchewan during
the Jurassic Period some 150 million
years ago.

The Cenozoic era (the Age of Mammals) has been divided into two
periods — Tertiary and Quarternary — and seven epochs.

The Tertiary period has been divided into five epochs: *Paleocene,
Eocene, Oligocene, Miocene,* and *Pliocene.* This period began 70 million years ago and ended about 1 million years ago, a time more or
less coincidental with the first Ice Age. Archaic mammals were then
common, including carnivorous creodonts. They looked something
like large mink with long tails and big heads and they preyed on grass
eaters, such as a tiny ancestral species of horse that was about the size
of a new-born calf. These mammals changed gradually, becoming specialized and eventually dominating the land environment.

At the time of the Oligocene and Miocene epochs the Cascade Mountains arose in the west, accompanied by much volcanic activity. Mastodons and mammoths (ancestors of modern elephants), huge Dire
wolves, camels, horses, sabre-toothed cats, and many early birds, reptiles, fish, invertebrates, and mammals that are now extinct lived in
Canada by the end of the Pliocene and during the early part of the
Pleistocene epoch, the first epoch of the Quarternary period.

The Holocene epoch, dubbed the "Age of Man", followed. It began
25 thousand years ago and continues as the twenty-first century
approaches.

THE TROPICAL ARCTIC

WAS CANADA THE BIRTHPLACE OF *TROPICAL* life? The scientific jury is still out on this question, but discoveries made in Ellesmere Island and its adjacent neighbour, Axel Heiberg Island, have led some paleontologists to conclude that the answer is yes.

The search for evidence of prehistoric life in the permafrost of the two northernmost Canadian islands in the Arctic Archipelago by Dr. Mary Dawson, curator of vertebrate fossils at the Carnegie Museum of Natural History in Pittsburgh, Pennsylvania, and Dr. Robert M. West, also with the museum, began in 1973. With the blessings of the Geological Survey of Canada, a division of the federal Ministry of Energy, Mines and Resources, and the advice of Dr. Ray Thorsteinsson, a Survey geologist based in Calgary, Alberta, the U.S. scientists explored the terrain during the short Arctic summer, but failed to find any terrestrial animal fossils.

Returning to Ellesmere Island in 1975, Dawson and West started again. Success came soon during this field expedition when they began to uncover the teeth and bones of ancient tapirs, rhinoceroses, horses, alligators, and tortoises. Apart from the fact that the fossils were the first of their kind to be found anywhere within the Arctic Circle, the presence of alligators and tortoises in that latitude came as a surprise to their discoverers and to the scientific community at large. Such reptiles are at present confined to habitats that are frost-free and where the day and night divisions occur on a 24-hour basis the year round.

At face value, the finds contradicted current views accounting for the distribution of life on the planet, theories that have themselves been modified during the last five decades. The first scientifically backed hypothesis, proclaimed in the mid-1920s, contended that because the fossils discovered in North America up to that date were similar to those found in an area of northern France termed "the Paris Basin", animal life must have colonized the continents of North and South America via the land bridge that existed across the Bering Strait (connecting what is now the Soviet Union to Alaska) during the Eocene epoch of the Cenozoic era. The Eocene, which evidently ushered in warmer climates throughout the world, is believed to have begun about 65 million years ago and to have lasted some 20 million years.

The Bering hypothesis lost support when it was discovered that a

◀ **The Hazen Plateau** has one of the driest climates in the northern hemisphere. Recent evidence found elsewhere on Ellesmere Island suggests that this region of the Arctic may have been the birthplace of tropical plants and animals.

vast arm of sea water cut across Russia, interrupting the route to the land bridge. During the early 1960s, another hypothesis was presented. It postulates that a second prehistoric land bridge may have developed from northern Europe to the Canadian Arctic, allowing migration from a point near Svalbard (Spitsbergen), Norway, and along a corridor that traversed the Atlantic Ocean to the Faerøe Islands, thence over Iceland to Greenland and eventually to the Canadian Arctic. This theory is the more prevalent today.

During the Eocene, Ellesmere Island may have been a few degrees farther south than what it is now, but it was still widely separated from the world's present-day tropical zones. In view of this fact, how had alligators and tortoises arrived in the Arctic region? And, having done so, how had they survived the continuously dark winters, which have evidently occurred in the far north ever since the earth began to orbit the sun?

As work continued on Ellesmere, more discoveries were made, each strengthening the possibility that modern animals and plants may have developed in the Canadian Arctic and spread from there to other parts of the world. Two of the most extraordinary finds were the complete skull of an ancient flying lemur, which did not actually fly but glided from tree to tree, much as the flying squirrel does, and the stumps of a species of early redwood tree.

Today's lemurs (genus *Lemur*) are found only on the island of Madagascar (located in the Indian Ocean off the south-east coast of Africa), in the jungles of south-east Asia, and in the Philippines, although they were evidently distributed all over the world until the late Oligocene epoch, when they began to disappear from Europe and the Americas. A number of species are recognized, and except for one ground-foraging lemur that moves about in daylight, all the others are arboreal animals that forage at night. Did this nocturnal trait develop in the Canadian Arctic during winters that are dark 24 hours a day for some four and a half months? The question may never be definitely answered.

Similarly, the presence that far north of what are scientifically referred to as *dawn* redwoods is difficult to explain by means of the

An Arctic boulder is colourfully decorated with lichens, plants that result ▶
from a partnership between various species of fungi and various kinds of
algae. Lichens come in a variety of colours, according to the species of the
partners; resistant to drought, heat and cold, they grow in practically
every environment.

land-bridge theory. The species, *Metasequoia*, which on Ellesmere grew to a height of 49 m (161 ft.) is now only found in one isolated area of China. In addition, a number of deciduous trees, such as sycamores and elms, developed enormous leaves.

Dr. Leo Hickey, a specialist in prehistoric plants and director of the Peabody Museum, New Haven, Connecticut, was invited in 1979 to join the field expedition. He was astonished when he found sycamore leaves that were more than 0.5 m (1.6 ft.) wide. He was also surprised to discover that the fossil trees showed annual growth rings, a normal condition in lower latitudes, where perennial plants respond to seasonal changes of cold or drought by shedding their leaves, storing their sap in the root systems, and ceasing to grow until the next favourable season, when latent buds develop and produce the leaves.

Hickey reasoned that the enormous size of the leaves came as a result of the 24-hour periods of daylight that dominate the Arctic environment during the growing season, when the sun does not set at all. Experiments have demonstrated that plants exposed to continuous light develop larger leaves than those that are exposed to regular cycles of light and dark. In the Arctic, no large deciduous trees exist today, but during the Eocene, with warm, swampy conditions and exposure to 24 hours of daylight for many weeks of the year, the trees grew huge leaves. These were used to trap large supplies of energy to store in the trees' root systems, food reserves for the long and continuously dark winters.

In a paper published by *Science*, Dawson and Hickey postulated that a number of plants were growing in the Canadian Arctic about 18 million years *before* they were to take root in lower latitudes. They also hypothesized that some mammals, particularly ancestral species of camels, rhinoceroses, and horses, emerged in the far north between two million and four million years before they did so in other latitudes. Reaction from the scientific community to the Dawson-Hickey paper was swift and critical, a not unexpected reception from a fraternity that must always treat with suspicion claims that are not backed up with irrefutable proof. Nevertheless, although Dawson, West, and Hickey cannot as yet prove conclusively that their theories are valid, no other scientist has been able to prove that their theories are *not* valid. Meanwhile, work continues on Ellesmere, the northern 35 500 km² (13 700 sq. mi.) of which has now been declared a national park.

Ellesmere Island, almost 800 km (500 mi.) in length by about 500 km (300 mi.) in width at its longest and widest points, represents an ecological area termed the Eastern High Arctic Natural Region. It is considered to be one of Canada's most outstanding landscapes, a fact that quickly becomes evident to a visitor from "the outside". The third

largest island within the Canadian Arctic Archipelago, Ellesmere is rich in animal and plant life despite its harsh climate.

A mixture of ancient rock, tundra vegetation, and ice caps, the island's northern exposure faces the almost always ice-bound Arctic Ocean. Within contemporary human history, Ellesmere has been the jumping-off point for a number of polar expeditions, including the one led by the American explorer Robert E. Peary, who, after a number of tries, reached the North Pole on April 6, 1909. Among the island's unusual characteristics are the only ice shelves to be found in the northern hemisphere, distinctive aprons of ice that have clung to the shore for thousands of years, "paving" the sea just as their companions must have done during the height of the ice ages. One of these, the Ward Hunt Ice Shelf, covers hundreds of square kilometres of ocean

▲ **Resplendent in its winter coat**, a weasel seems to be posing for a photograph. In reality, it is merely pausing to identify the intruder. Weasels are common throughout Canada; agile and daringly defensive, they show little fear of humans.

and in places is as much as 80 m (260 ft.) thick. As occurred during the periods of widespread glaciation, part of the ice shelves break off now and then and become floating glacial islands, which drift in the Arctic Ocean. These stable platforms last for decades and today often serve as floating laboratory stations from which Canadian, U.S., and Soviet scientists work on high-latitude research.

The Grant Land Mountains extending across the northern part of the island are covered by icefields. Some are nearly 2000 m (6560 ft.) thick and produce massive glaciers which flow towards a relatively flat region known as the Hazen Plateau as well as into the deeply cut fjords that abound on the north coast. It has been estimated that the Ellesmere icefields contain ice that is at least 100 000 years old.

Within this region of prehistoric ice, it comes as something of a shock to realize that mountains are almost entirely buried under it, only their tops being visible. A number of peaks reach heights of 2500 m (8200 ft.) above sea level; the tallest, Barbeau Peak, reaches an altitude of 2616 m (8583 ft.). It is the highest mountain in eastern North America. The Inuit people christened the peaks "nunataks".

At the south end of the Grant Land Mountains the terrain drops suddenly to the Hazen Plateau and Lake Hazen, a body of glacial meltwater 70 km (43 mi.) long and 260 m (850 ft.) deep, the bottom of which is actually 100 m (320 ft.) below sea level. Here is encountered one of the driest climates in the northern hemisphere. It is, in fact, a polar desert; yet it contains areas of lush sedges, grasses, and Arctic willows, the food resources of small numbers of muskox and caribou. Wolves, Arctic foxes, weasels, Arctic hares, and lemmings are other inhabitants of the Hazen Plateau, especially in river-valley habitats along the northern side of the plateau, for Lake Hazen and the surrounding basin trap solar energy that radiates downwards from the Grant Land Mountains. As a result, the summers are long and warm and there is an abundance of vegetation. This region, located less than 800 km (500 mi.) from the North Pole, is referred to as a *thermal oasis* by those scientists who study the climate.

Marine mammals occasionally enter arms of the Arctic Ocean that cut into the land on all of those sections of Ellesmere's coasts that are open during the short, frost-free season. But away from the Hazen Plateau, the climate is too harsh even for the tough polar bear and the walrus, only a few of which enter the northern channels.

During the time of seasonal migration, birds abound on Ellesmere Island. Marine species are the most common, but populations of snow geese, oldsquaw and king eider ducks, red-throated loons, and snow buntings are large, particularly below 81° north latitude in regions

where open water and tundra vegetation are plentiful. Among the salt-water species, gull-like long-tailed jaegers (*Stercorarius longicaudus*), predatory birds with webbed feet and powerful hooked beaks, harass other birds until they disgorge the food just taken from the sea, then snap it up in mid-air when the rightful owners escape. At times, jaegers kill other birds for food. The jaegers and Arctic terns (*Sterna paradisaea*) are long-distance migrants, some of them flying as far as the Antarctic and Africa.

The fossil finds, the ice and the water, the land itself, and the animals and plants now living on Ellesmere Island form a mosaic that tangibly demonstrates the stages of physical development that have taken place during the last 50 million years. On Ellesmere, these bio-geographic changes are chronicled to show the continuity of time, rather than a

▲ **A horned lark** fledgling crouches immobile in its ground nest, relying on camouflage for protection. Adult females of the species usually lay four eggs that hatch at intervals of from ten to fourteen days. Horned larks inhabit open areas over much of Canada.

▲ Long-tailed jaeger

reversal of it. On the North Pole, on the other hand, it *does* seem as if one has entered a backward time warp. This becomes quickly evident to a visitor who arrives there in summer and walks away from his or her companions and from the aircraft that carried the party to the top of the world.

Out of sight and out of hearing of any living thing, a Polar visitor is transported back to the ice ages during the height of their tenure. The sun, low on the horizon as it circles the earth, has a strange yellow colour, turning to a light saffron shade the jagged, hard-frozen snow. In the shadows of the wind-sculpted crags the ice is blue. From the height of a snowy tor, hard as rock even though it is entirely composed of water that has been frozen for millennia, the awesome vista stretches into the infinite blue of an Arctic summer sky, the ice-scape corrugated in some locations, mounded up untidily in others, or swept smooth by glacial winds in low places. Early July on the North Pole: solitude, eternal ice, a weak sun, and a compass that is useless, for here, at 90° north latitude, all directions point south. A sense of panic can easily grip a lone explorer. Will he be able to return to the aircraft and to his companions? If not, will he be rescued before becoming a frozen lump of organic matter that in time will be absorbed by the solid water?

Scraps of thoughts and visions flutter through the mind like moths whirling around a light. The Canadian flag, back there near the aircraft, waving feebly, held fast to a twisted metal pole and lashed with sea-farer's knots, its edges tattered already, although it has not been in place long. A little farther from the red maple leaf, an American flag, its stars and stripes faded, the fluttering edges torn almost to ribbons. Images of companions, all swathed in parkas, near-strangers, met for the first time during the flight but now loved ones whose presence means security. The last glimpse of bare soil, as the aircraft dipped down over Alert, a whistle-stop on the north-east coast of Ellesmere. Even a mosquito would be a welcome sight; the tiny *living*, flying thing would be invited to take a sip or two of blood, not cursed as it and its milliard companions are cursed "down south" on the tundra. It is with relief that the outward-bound footprints are noticed on the sprinkling of early snow that covers the hard-pack; they are a clear trail back to the flags and to the people and to the gasoline-smelling contrivance that has flown north like some giant mechanical pterosaur that might once have flapped its leathery wings over this same place at a time when the world was young. And as the path is retraced, the mind "sees" into the ice mass, where deeply entombed lie uncountable animals, gaunt mummies of incongruous size and shape; mastodons with long,

curving ivory tusks; gigantic bison; enormous ground sloths; short-faced bears, animals more powerful than the grizzly that weighed almost 1000 kg (2200 lb.); and many others, including birds and insects and plants. All dead for thousands of years, but preserved. Unreachable.

▲ **The tundra swan** nests in the low Arctic. Like all birds that nest on the ground, its eggs are vulnerable to predation.

NORTHERN IMAGES

◄ **Immature great horned owls** crowd a stump, awaiting food from their parents. These large birds of prey occur over most of Canada, from the northern tree limit south-wards. Like all owls, the margins of the feathers are very soft, allowing for almost silent flight.

Barren-ground caribou bucks ▶ interrupt their summer browsing to stare at the photographer. In the autumn, such bucks form huge "bachelor" herds and migrate south to join similarly large concentrations of does in winter ranges in the Yukon and Northwest Territories.

Lichens and bilberry leaves ▶ splash colour over a boreal forest opening.

▲ **The tundra** in autumn can be as colourful as any section of the eastern hardwood forest.

▲ **Three young red foxes** play in a section of tundra, Yukon Territory. Play is serious exercise among young wild predators: it develops their future hunting techniques.

The bearberry dwarf willow ▶ (*Salix uva-ursi*), here shown in its fall colours, should not be confused with the evergreen bearberry (*Arctostaphylos uva-ursi*). The former is a true willow commonly found in the tundra; the latter, a member of the heather family, is a trailing shrub known in the West as kinnickinnick.

◄ **In winter**, a cluster of rather spindly black spruce trees forms a virtual island of greenery on an otherwise flat and open tundra landscape.

▼ **Polar bears** are often followed by Arctic foxes. The small predators, relying on their speed and agility to escape the jaws of the giant carnivores, feed on leftovers and even dart in to steal morsels of meat while a bear is feeding on a kill.

The red-throated loon, the ► smallest of Canada's loons, mostly favours northern breeding grounds along the shores of ponds and lakes in the tundra, but also occurs in some areas of the southern mainland and along the Pacific and Atlantic shorelines.

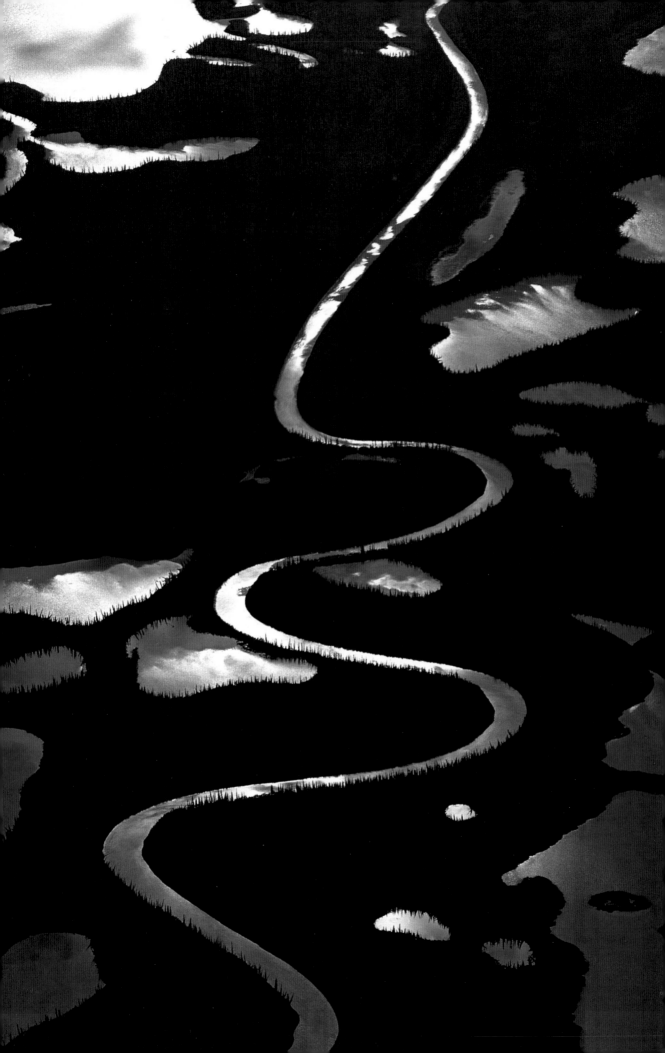

▲ **In summer**, young grizzly bear siblings enjoy playing in water and often engage in wrestling bouts. Slow to develop, cubs den with their mother during their first winter and remain with her until she chases them away the following summer, when she is usually ready to mate again.

◀ **The Mackenzie River** delta seen from the air resembles a gigantic snake winding its way through the flatlands that flank its banks. This mighty waterway, once the lifeline of northern transportation, flows for more than 4000 km (2400 mi.) to empty into the Beaufort Sea.

▲ **White whales** are usually found in sociable groups. Their second common name, *beluga*, is Russian in origin and means "whitish". These small toothed whales feed on a variety of fish as well as on octopus, squid and shrimps.

◀ **The Arctic dwarf willow**, shown in full blossom, is one of the most colourful of the shrubby willows. A total of some 75 willows grow in North America, the majority being found in Canada.

▼ **Sabine's gulls** are among the most distinctively patterned members of the Laridae family, which includes gulls and terns. These strong-flying sea-birds breed along the mainland and island shores of the Canadian Arctic.

◀ **Folded and scalloped** by wind and weather, the treeless Richardson Mountains in the northern Yukon Territory are an example of an unglaciated landscape.

SOUTH TO THE TUNDRA

3

 STARTING ABOVE 60° NORTH LATITUDE AND stretching from the Atlantic to the Pacific oceans, then north into the High Arctic, lies a gigantic land that has been divided into two national regions, the Northwest Territories and the Yukon Territory. The NWT occupies a total area of 3 379 684 km² (1 305 024 sq. mi.); it is equal in size to India, larger than Texas, Alaska, California, and New Mexico combined, and contains one-third of Canada's total area. The Yukon, much smaller, but yet impressive, occupies 482 515 km² (186 317 sq. mi.). Together, the two territories total almost 4 million km² (1.5 million sq. mi.) that consist mostly of wilderness and in which only about 70 000 people reside.

Between the permanently frozen High Arctic wastes and the extreme northern boundaries of the evergreen forests lies the tundra. But, popular misconceptions notwithstanding, this fascinating habitat does not cover all of the land between the ice and the trees. Rather, it can be likened in summer to a series of patches sewed at random into an enormous, predominantly white, quilt, the southern boundaries of which are haphazardly edged in green. In some areas the tundra may stretch for hundreds of kilometres in all directions; in others it may be encountered as relatively small oases of life surrounded by ice; in yet others, it interacts with small trees that have followed sheltered lowlands and managed to retain a fragile hold on the land.

The tundra began as a vast, desolate region littered with boulders and gravel left behind by the glaciers, which tortured the land. Gradually, plants colonized the uppermost surface of this debris during the short, frost-free seasons that occur in those latitudes, the richest growth being found in valleys, ravines, and locations sheltered by high land.

In the NWT, only the western and extreme northern parts of which are mountainous, tundra habitats are spread along a vast, semi-desert plain, which is frozen for about seven months of the year on average. Spring and autumn in that region are at best brief intervals between the end of one winter and the start of the next. Summers are short, but warm (up to a record 39.4° C [103° F] noted in July 1941, at Fort Smith, a community in the extreme south-central part of the Territories, on the border of Alberta). Nevertheless, refrigerated year round as it is by the underlying permafrost, only one metre or less of soil thaws each year to become the rather soggy nursery for some 2000 different species of small plants, many of which bear tiny, but beautiful flowers.

◀ **Oxbow streams**, ponds and late summer vegetation form a scenic aerial landscape in the lowlands below the north slopes of the Ogilvie Mountains, Yukon Territory.

THE TUNDRA

1 Cotton grass
2 Common raven
3 Snowy owl
4 Wolves
5 Wolverine
6 Arctic tern
7 Tundra swans
8 Caribou
9 Lemming
10 Blackfly
11 Mosquito
12 Horsefly
13 Lapland longspur
14 Arctic poppies
15 Snow bunting

NOT TO SCALE

▲ **Arctic poppy**

▲ **Purple saxifrage**

In some locations grow gnarled evergreen trees that may be hundreds of years old, but are not much more than a metre in height and are only a few centimetres in diameter at the bases of their trunks. Deciduous willows (*Salix* spp.) are found in many locations. They have adapted to the harsh environment by growing outwards instead of upwards, forming dense mats that may not be taller than 0.5 m (1.6 ft.) and which bear delicate, yellow-blossomed catkins.

From the air, the tundra's summer landscape is seen as a flat expanse composed of polygonal shapes and broken up by thousands of small-to-large, shallow lagoons, a landscape created by the freeze-thaw cycles. The polygons occur when the soil freezes and contracts and then thaws and expands, the larger particles and rocks being pushed to the outside and the finer soils being concentrated in the centre of each patch. As a result, the landscape is laid out rather like a checker-board composed not of squares, but of geometric shapes, in the centre of which grow such plants as wildflowers, sedges, and grasses surrounded by gravel and rock margins of varying width on which only lichens can grow.

Experienced on the ground, the tundra looks quite different. The geometric shapes are not apparent. Instead, uncountable tussocks of plants rise like green molehills, offering themselves as stepping stones to those who would walk dry-shod through such regions, for between each stand of green run channels of slurry composed of plant detritus, fine gravel, and small stones. The meltwater component of this mixture is unable to sink into the ground because of the frozen barrier that everywhere lies close to the surface.

The vivid pink flowers of bog rosemary (*Audromeda glaucophylla*) in some places contrast dramatically with the white of cottongrass (*Erio-phorum* sp.), while in other locations the scarlet blossoms of Sudetan lousewort (*Pedicularis sudetica*) paint brilliant swaths over the tundra. These and many other small plants hurry their growth and bloom cycles so dramatically that from day to day the colours of the landscape are changed, each of the many species emerging successively from the ground, raising stems, growing leaves, and producing flowers at pre-cisely the right times. The perennials add to their growth and store energy in readiness for next year's season; the annuals form their seeds after insect pollination has taken place, but while there is still enough warmth to dry the tiny grains in readiness for their dispersal by the wind, by mammals, and by birds. Many of the seeds produced in the tundra each year are the source of life for numerous animals; however, there are always more than enough left over to produce new growth the following summer.

In the Mackenzie Delta and other locations, underground water has

▲ **Backdropped** by a clear, intensely blue sky, snow geese in spring wing
their way north to ancestral breeding grounds.

▲ **Willow ptarmigan** in winter plumage. These birds, and the related rock and white-tailed ptarmigans, are grouse found in northern, open regions and in the western mountains.

been concentrated during successive thaws and then forced upwards by the permafrost, gradually creating ice hills, called pingos, shaped rather like small volcanos. Some pingos may be only a few metres in diameter and height, others may be 40 or 50 m (131 or 164 ft.) high and 70 or 80 m (230 or 260 ft.) in diameter. Inside each of these upthrusts is blue ice. The Inuit people, and early European explorers, used the pingos as summer refrigerators, digging an entrance, then scooping out an interior chamber in which they kept their perishable foods. The doorway was closed with ice blocks so as to keep out wolves, barren-ground grizzly bears, polar bears in coastal areas, and the ever-present and ever-hungry Arctic foxes.

The summer tundra is a land in a hurry. And, like the landscape and the plants that grow in it, the animals that live there are also frantically active. Even as the first patches of plants emerge, the hordes of insects come, the mosquitoes (family Culicidae) so thick that they literally coat the bodies of caribou and other animals and, of course, of those humans who venture or live in the north at that time of year. The droning of these bloodsuckers is loud and continuous, almost damping the more robust buzzing of bot and warble flies (*Hypoderma tarandi*), parasitic insects that at times seriously incapacitate many mammals, especially the caribou. The nose bot fly (*Cephenemyia jellisoni*) lays its eggs in the nostrils of the deer. On hatching the larvae enter the nasal passages and clog the sinus cavities. Warble flies lay their eggs on the bodies of their hosts. When the minute larvae emerge, they immediately tunnel under the skin, migrating eventually to the back on either side of the spine, where they grow into maggoty worms 2.5 cm (1 in.) long. The worms have a pair of hooks at the end of their bodies with which they hang on to the host's tissues. After cutting a small breathing hole in the animal's hide, they live warmly through the winter, feeding on the animal's living flesh.

▲ Swan

Another bot fly, the robust bot (*Cuterebra approximata*), so named because it is larger than the nose bot, parasitizes small mammals, such as ground squirrels and lemmings, causing huge swellings on the back, stomach, or groin. Most mammals survive these tortures if food is abundant and competition from their own kind or from other species is not severe. When conditions are poor in any area of the tundra, however, animals infested by parasites are among the first to die off.

▲ Goose

Of the 518 species of birds found in Canada, about half are found in the tundra during the summer. Some of the more spectacular include yellow-billed, Pacific, and red-throated loons; tundra swans; snow geese; Canada geese; jaegers; gyrfalcons; ravens, and a large number of songbirds of various species. The latter raise their young on top of the world each year while devouring millions of insects. The whistle of wings is commonly heard as large birds fly low overhead and the voices of songsters like the white-crowned sparrow, the Lapland longspur, and the snow bunting fill the long days.

▲ Loon

During the frost-free seasons, the tundra is home to 280 species of birds, 80 species of mammals, and a large number of insect species, many of which have not yet been definitely identified. But in winter only a few hardy birds remain, such as the two species of ptarmigan that winter in the north, the common raven, and the snowy owl.

All three species of ptarmigan rely on the camouflage that is provided by the change in their plumage colour twice a year. In summer, the bird is woodsy brown on the head, sides, and upper body, the edges of the feathers highlighted by narrow white bands; the wing primaries and their coverts are white, as is the underside of the body. The tail feathers of the rock (*Lagopus mutus*) and willow (*Lagopus lagopus*) ptarmigan are black, but the upper tail coverts are white. The three species have black beaks, but the rock ptarmigan has a narrow black

▲ Merganser

▲ Grebe

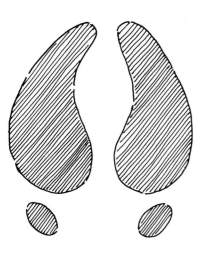

▲ Caribou hoofprint

▲ Caribou tracks

band that starts just behind each eye and extends to the base of the beak. These details are hardly noticeable until a bird angles upwards in flight, when the tail is spread like a fan. The contrast between the twin black bands and the arrowhead of white is then startling. The swiftly moving, dazzling pattern momentarily distracts a predatory bird or mammal, giving the ptarmigan a few extra seconds in which to try and make good its escape. In winter, rock and willow ptarmigans keep their black tail feathers, but the white-tailed species (*Lagopus leucurus*) is snowy-white all over the year around.

The three mammals that are most characteristic of the tundra are the caribou, the wolf and the Arctic fox, each species being dependent upon the food resources that are available and jointly contributing to the ecology of the habitat.

The caribou (*Rangifer tarandus*) of North America and the reindeer of Eurasia are now believed to belong to the same species and are one of the most numerous and widely ranging animals of the Northern Hemisphere. Probably the major difference between the North American caribou and their Old World relatives lies in the fact that reindeer have been domesticated for many centuries, even to the point where they are used as mounts by the Laplanders of Scandinavia and the north-west area of the Soviet Union, hence the name *rein*deer.

Ungainly when compared to the more svelte white-tailed deer, caribou nevertheless belong to the same family, together with the moose, elk, and other members of the Cervidae family, composed of those animals that grow and shed antlers each year. (Only one Asian deer doesn't have antlers.) But, unlike their relatives, these deer are given to long-range seasonal migrations and have developed a number of special characteristics that allow them to survive the harsh conditions encountered in the north. They are further distinguished by the fact that both the males and the females grow antlers.

Five subspecies of caribou inhabit Canada today, including a herd of reindeer that were imported from Europe and now survive in the Mackenzie Delta of the Northwest Territories. The others are: the typical barren-ground caribou (*Rangifer tarandus groenlandicus*) of the tundra; the woodland caribou (*R.t. caribou*), which at one time was common in more southern regions across Canada but which has now been drastically reduced in numbers through hunting and the destruction of habitat by logging and farming; the caribou of the Yukon Territory (*R.t. granti*); and a smaller subspecies (*R.t. pearyi*) found in the

This barren-ground caribou buck is in prime condition after a summer of ▶ lush grazing. Because of a special arrangement of the bones and tendons in their ankles, caribou make a clear, clicking sound when on the move.

▲ **Many thousands** of barren-ground caribou massed during spring migration cover the land in an area of the Yukon Territory north of Old Crow Flats. At this time of year, the sexes separate. Bucks travel to distant grazing ranges; does to traditional calving grounds.

Arctic Islands. A sixth subspecies was once a resident of Graham Island, of the Queen Charlotte Islands group, but it is now extinct.

Several physical factors help the caribou survive. Chief among them is a large, blunt muzzle that is well furred, allowing the animal to nuzzle imperviously into the snow in search of the lichens that are its main source of food — the so-called reindeer mosses, *Cladonia rangiferina* and *Cladonia alpestris*.

In winter, the caribou's coat is composed of warm, woolly underfur and long, hollow guard-hairs. These hairs offer superb insulation and act rather like a life-jacket, keeping the animal afloat in the water at those frequent times when it must swim across rivers and lakes.

The caribou's hooves are also unusual and designed for its habitat. In summer, the pads of the feet become enlarged and quite soft while the edges of each hoof are worn flat, allowing the pads to act as cushions on the spongy ground; in winter, the hooves grow long, the pads shrink and become hardened, and insulating hair grows between the toes. Such hooves serve two purposes: they allow the animal to dig down in the snow to find its food, and they help protect the pads from the cold. The feet are large and allow the animal to walk or run through deep snow in winter and spongy ground in summer. Unusual bone and tendon construction causes the ankles to produce a rather strange clicking sound as the animals move. When several thousand caribou are migrating, the sound of their clicking carries for quite a distance.

Although both sexes are able to grow antlers, about 30 per cent of females do not. Why this is so has not been established, although it may be that some females are weakened by the process of bearing young; or they may not be able to find sufficient food, and so cannot spare the energy needed to grow antlers. Bucks grow the larger racks, in some cases sporting spectacular crowns, the lowest of which, called the brow tines, point forward and downward and act as shields for the eyes, protecting them during those times when bucks in the breeding season engage in antler-rattling dominance contests.

Antlers of males begin to grow in March, at first showing as bumps, then developing fairly quickly. Each antler is protected by a velvety sheath composed of skin and blood vessels that nourish growth. By early September the sheath becomes dry and starts to peel away, giving the animal an untidy appearance. By October, all the velvet has gone and the antlers are shiny and regal. But not for long. By early November, after the breeding season, the antlers of the older bucks are shed. (The difference between antlers and true horns is that the former are solid branching structures and are shed annually, while the latter consist of a hard sheath over an unbranching bony core and are retained permanently.)

Caribou like the company of their own kind. At times they gather in small bands of 15 or 20 individuals, but during migration they congregate in huge herds that may number as many as 100 000 animals. Such herds gather three times each year: in late winter, just before the spring migration; immediately after the fawning time; and just before the autumn migration.

With so many caribou shedding their antlers each autumn, it might be expected that these discards would litter the tundra. A herd of 100 000 animals, in which about 30 per cent are females (on average) that do not grow racks, would yet carry 70 000 *pairs* of antlers, or a total of 140 000 individual horns. In fact, although in some areas

▲ **Wolves** are family-oriented predators whose complex, highly social relationships are not yet fully understood. They live in packs of from two to perhaps a dozen animals.

SWALLOWS AND LICE

All birds are hosts to chewing and/or biting lice of the suborder Mallophaga, of which some 2500 distinct species are known worldwide. Most are minute, measuring between 0.8 and 1 mm (0.03 and 0.04 in.), and host-specific; i.e., they parasitize only one species of bird and will not attack any others. This means that bird lice, although they do crawl over people who handle birds as well as on animals, such as cats that hunt birds, will not seek to feed on humans or other mammals.

Swallows (family Hirundinidae, of which seven species inhabit Canada during the breeding season) have long been notorious for the numbers of lice that they harbour, a fact that has caused investigators to believe that the insects exert only harmful effects on their hosts. Recently, however, close studies of two fledgling barn swallows (*Hirundo rustica*) that had fallen out of the nest and were settled on a dwelling's window-sill so that the parent birds might care for them, revealed that at such times when the adults were unable to feed the young for relatively long periods (from 30 to 60 minutes) because of a shortage of flying insects, the fledglings preened their wings and bodies and ingested the lice that they harboured. These "emergency rations" sustained their rapid metabolism until such time as the parent birds could return with more substantial food supplies. Thus, based upon this one study, which lasted for a period of eight days (until the young swallows took to the wing), it appears that the relationship between lice and at least one

▲ Barn swallow

species of bird is at times beneficial to both host and parasite. Young birds are fed by their parents at frequent intervals (usually about every 10 or 15 minutes during the daylight hours) and consume large amounts of food. If, however, weather conditions such as high winds, heavy rain, or drought cause feeding delays, it is biologically useful for the fledglings to have on their own bodies a ready supply of lice to sustain at least minimally their protein needs (unpublished findings: Sharon and R.D. Lawrence, 1987).

discarded antlers are present in large numbers for a time, they are consumed by many animals for the calcium that they contain. Caribou themselves gnaw the discarded antlers, as do mice, voles, lemmings, foxes, wolves and, indeed, all other mammals. The leftovers eventually break down and become organic matter in the soil.

Male caribou are approximately 25 per cent bigger and heavier than females. There is also a marked difference in the size and weight noted among the various subspecies. The barren-ground caribou bucks are between 160 and 210 cm (5 and 7 ft.) long; they weigh between 81 and 153 kg (179 and 337 lb.). Females of this species average 137 cm (4.5 ft.) in length and weigh 63 to 94 kg (139 to 207 lb.). The woodland subspecies is larger and heavier, males weighing as much as 280 kg (617 lb.); females, about 200 kg (440 lb.).

Mating occurs between early October and early November. The males are polygamous. Females that have not become pregnant during their first annual oestrus, or heat, become receptive again later on, hence the rather long breeding season. Gestation times vary between seven-and-a-half and eight months, and calving occurs from mid-May to early July, depending on when the females have become inseminated.

In the absence of interference by human activity, caribou numbers are controlled today, as they have been for many thousands of years, by a variety of influences that take effect singly or collectively. The most radical control is overpopulation, although its effects are at first gradual. As competition increases, more and more caribou die, until eventually the population crashes. At the same time, predation increases. Wolves and other hunters have an easy time securing food, often not even having to resort to a chase in order to finish off starving or sick animals, or those that are weakened by a combination of hunger and infestation by parasites. Eventually, the fittest are left, usually at a time when there is more than enough food to keep them well nourished. Now the survivors thrive. The cows give birth to strong, healthy calves, the food plants recover from heavy overbrowsing, and the herd starts to build up again.

Although wolves (*Canis lupus*) play a major role in such ecological "numbers games", they are themselves affected by the cycles of feast and famine, for when prey animals are plentiful, predators increase their own numbers to keep up with the increase. But after the prey reaches the low point, wolf populations begin to go into decline and in about two years their numbers become greatly reduced. Food is, after all, as Charles Elton, an eminent British ecologist, said 60 years ago: "the burning question in animal society, and the whole structure and activities of the community are dependent on questions of food supply."

Wolves are pre-eminent hunters that obey a natural dictum, which states that animals must be opportunists and wherever possible take those foods that are easiest to procure; they therefore prey most heavily on the old, the unfit, and the young, although they do take prime animals on occasion.

Biologists love to discover animal subspecies, even if at times the differences between one "sub" and another are so slight that they can only be determined by dissecting a dead specimen. As a result, some 27 subspecies of wolves have been classified in North America. Slightly more conservative estimates list 17 subspecies in Canada of which four inhabit the tundra and two, smaller and predominantly white in colour, are found on the Arctic Islands.

Size and weight vary considerably among all wolves, no matter their species or subspecies. The largest are found in the western region of the NWT, the Yukon, northern British Columbia and Alberta, where some exceptional individuals may weigh as much as 73 kg (161 lb.). Generally, the smallest wolves are found on the Arctic Islands and in

OVERLEAF   **Grizzly bears** once roamed Canada as far south as the prairies and ▶ as far east as Manitoba's Red River valley.

southern parts of Canada; they may weigh between 26 and 45 kg (57 and 99 lb.). Colour is also variable. Black, white, grey, or brindled coats can occur anywhere. Thus, not all the so-called grey wolves are grey, and not all Arctic wolves are white.

The major prey of tundra wolves are caribou, which the hunters kill after having first isolated a deer from the herd during migration times; when the caribou are more sedentary and dispersed, the wolves may choose a target animal that is careless, or weaker than its neighbours. Calves are taken whenever opportunity presents itself, but, by and large, a pack seeks out adult prey, which furnishes considerably more food.

A large wolf on its own can pursue and kill a white-tailed deer under ideal conditions, but big animals like caribou, muskox, bison, moose, and elk require the concerted efforts of at least three wolves. The packs follow the caribou during migration times, picking off the stragglers, but rarely venturing into the thick of the herd.

Caribou can run for short distances at speeds up to 76 km (47 mi.) an hour, which tops the wolf's maximum speed of about 48 km (30 mi.) an hour, a rate that can only be maintained during a relatively brief chase. Despite their speed advantage, caribou do not run far when pursued, being in the habit of stopping at intervals to look back at the cause of alarm. This trait has caused some observers to believe that caribou are insatiably curious, but it is more probable that the animals feel secure when in a compact herd and so pause to allow scattered laggards to catch up. In any event, most wild animals can be said to be curious at all times, although a better word would be *vigilant*; but prey and predator alike display such "curiosity" from a safe distance.

The barren-ground grizzly (*Ursus arctos*) also preys on caribou, mostly on the calves. This predator has adapted to tundra living during the warm seasons. It is a formidable hunter, but because of its bulk, it is not agile enough to chase and catch adult caribou, although it has been known to kill old and diseased adults.

A much smaller predator, but one to be reckoned with, is the wolverine (*Gulo gulo*). This, one of the largest members of the weasel family, is extremely agile and strong. It will take calves and drag them away with seeming ease and, if the terrain is appropriate, it may also kill adult caribou after lying in ambush on a height of land and springing on the prey's back.

The most extraordinary animal to inhabit the tundra is the great, shaggy muskox (*Ovibos moschatus*). This bovine-looking mammal is a true prehistoric relic, having browsed the vegetation of Canada and Eurasia since before the last Ice Age in the company of mastodons and sabre-toothed cats. Although it is somewhat similar in appearance to the bison, certain anatomical characteristics suggest that it is a distant relative of the goat, despite the fact that it looks nothing like its much smaller kin.

As far as can be determined, muskoxen populations have always been sparse in the Arctic, but their numbers were greatly reduced during the nineteenth century, when they were hunted with rifles for meat and hides. Today, only about 12 000 muskoxen are found in Canada, the majority inhabiting the mainland tundra zones and some of the Arctic Islands. A small population survives in the south-eastern part of the NWT, in the Thelon Game Sanctuary of the Keewatin District, a sheltered region through which flows the peaceful Thelon River. This lush habitat provides abundant food in all seasons for the muskoxen as well as for caribou, moose, and many other animals.

Muskoxen are occasionally killed by wolves and grizzlies, which prey mostly on lone, old bulls, or sick animals. However, these predators do not pose a serious threat to the muskoxen's survival, for the shaggy animals have developed a remarkable defensive technique. When threatened, they form a tightly packed circle, adults on the outside, heads down and lethal horns at the ready to repel attack, while the young are safely ensconced in the centre of the ring. This impregnable formation discourages most wolves and bears, especially when one of the adults charges out of the defensive ring to drive away any predator that ventures too close, then wheels around swiftly and returns to take its place in the circle. But whereas the defence is excellent when the animals are threatened by natural predators, it became a death trap when firearms were introduced.

Continuing to employ a defensive tactic that had served them well since prehistoric times, the muskoxen stood their ground when attacked by man and so could be shot at leisure from a safe distance. Between 1864 and 1916 records show that 15 000 muskox hides were shipped from Canada to overseas buyers. Then too, Arctic explorers at one time hunted the animals for their meat, killing about 1000 of them on Ellesmere Island and about 500 on Melville Island. They are still being hunted under licence, for the muskoxen have been given only limited protection.

Because cows give birth to a single calf, the rate of increase barely keeps pace with the rate of natural mortality. Bulls of this species are about 2.5 m (8 ft.) long and may weigh up to 600 kg (1320 lb.). Cows measure about 2 m (6.5 ft.) and weigh 270 kg (595 lb.) or more. Both sexes have horns, which grow out of massive bosses, rather like those of South Africa's Cape buffalo. The horns project downwards, but their sharp tips turn upwards and outwards.

Mating takes place during the first two or three weeks of August after

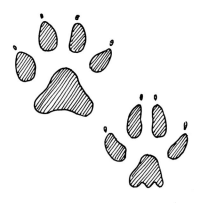

▲ **Wolf pawprints**

▲ **Wolf tracks**

▲   **To protect their young** from such predators as wolves and bears, muskoxen herd the calves into the centre of a defensive circle of outward-facing adults. Bulls will often dart out to charge persistent attackers.

Dew-laden soapberries brighten the northern landscape. ▶

▲ Buteo

▲ Falcon

▲ Accipiter

the polygamous bulls have driven away their challengers, in many cases engaging in a series of ground-shaking, fur-flying fights, when a loser may be badly gored. Calves are born 8 months after mating and the newborns are able to nurse within about 15 minutes of birth. At first the young are dressed in a coat of short, chocolate-brown hair, but by September they acquire a longer, thicker coat. By their third winter they are protected by a dense, woollen undergarment and an overcoat of guard hairs, which in the older animals are nearly 0.5 m (1.6 ft.) long on their forequarters. Muskox feed on a wide variety of plants. In winter they browse Labrador tea, bilberries, crowberries, ground birch, and willows. Their summer diet includes grasses, sedges, willows, rushes, horsetails, and other plants.

As has been noted, the "balance of nature" is never entirely stable, but it appears to have been designed to favour the long-term continuity of life.

Wolves and other predators of the tundra are controllers of prey populations, just as they are in other ecosystems. The main difference between the animals and plants of the tundra and those of the same, or even different species that live in less harsh environments is to be found in the special adaptations that have developed through natural selection. Plants alter their habits in accordance with the amount of light that reaches them, the soil in which they grow, and the climate to which they are exposed. Animals are also affected by environmental conditions, but they are additionally gifted with intelligence that allows individuals to learn from experience and to improvise new survival tactics. Predators seek to hunt, and prey animals seek to escape in different ways in accordance with the bio-geography and climate in which they live. Wolves, for instance, employ different tactics when hunting white-tailed deer or other large prey than when hunting barren-ground caribou.

Woodland caribou are less gregarious than their tundra relatives, gathering in small bands during the frost-free seasons and congregating in smaller numbers during seasonal migrations. Wolves hunt these animals much as they do the moose and the deer, for the woodland herds, prevented by the trees or alpine terrain from bunching in large groups as barren-ground caribou do, are more likely to disperse when attacked, each animal depending on its own alertness and speed in order to escape.

The behaviour of animals of the same species appears to alter radically between widely separated ecosystems, but at those locations where one habitat blends into another, behavioural adaptations can actually be observed in those animals that move back and forth across two ecological thresholds. Such changes are particularly evident in the transition zone that separates the tundra from the boreal forests.

NORTHERN TRANSITION ZONE

This biome stretches in a semicircular direction from the Atlantic coast to the Yukon, running for some 5000 km (3100 mi.) along a corridor of variable width that is bounded in the north by the tundra and in the south by the boreal forests. Its deepest region lies in the Quebec-Labrador area, occupying about 450 000 km² (173 762 sq. mi.), but interrupted on the east coast of James Bay by a spur of the boreal biome.

Like all terrestrial areas where one kind of habitat meets another, the plants and animals of two biomes are intermingled here. The northern transition zone, also known as the boreal barren, is thus part forest and part tundra. Its northernmost extremities mark the *tree-line*, a term that is rather misleading because it suggests that at a given northern latitude trees suddenly cease to exist along a tidy and well-defined boundary. In fact, the tree-line is more like an untidy squiggle, almost as though it had resulted from a graph traced by the stylus of an electroencephalograph (see map, page 12).

The trees of this zone are of the same species that grow in the boreal biome, which will be described in the next chapter. On the whole evergreens predominate, but they are of lesser diameter and are considerably shorter in height than those encountered farther south because of the more severe weather and the greatly reduced daylight hours experienced in winter. White birch and aspens often mix with the spruces and balsam firs in lowland areas as well as on the banks of lakes and streams, where also grow willows, a variety of shrubs, such as Labrador tea, bearberry, small cranberries, and wild red raspberries (*Rubus idaeus*) — as opposed to black raspberries (*Rubus occidentalis*).

Most of the mammals found in the boreal biome also inhabit the transition zone, including moose, wolves, black bears, wolverine, lynx, red foxes, beaver, snowshoe hares, the ubiquitous mice and voles, and a variety of other small animals. Barren-ground caribou are encountered within the northern edges of the habitat; woodland caribou at

OVERLEAF **A pingo** seen from the air in Canada's tundra. These ice-cored hills ▶
range from 2 to 50 m (7 to 164 ft.) in height.

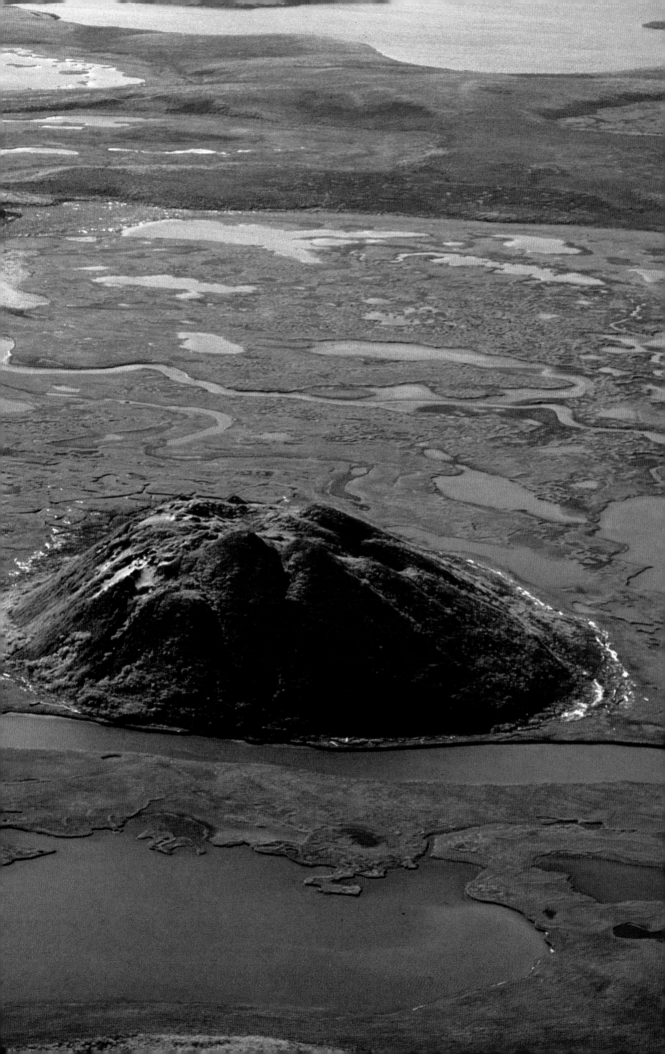

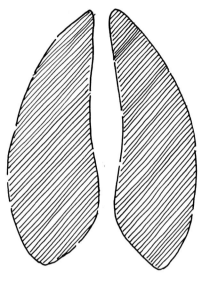

▲ Moose hoofprint

▲ Moose tracks

times wander into the southern part of the transition zone, especially in western regions.

Migrant species of birds are plentiful in the zone from spring to autumn and include Canada geese; a variety of ducks; red-breasted mergansers; common, red-throated, and Pacific loons; horned grebes; merlins; some bald eagles and ospreys; short-eared owls; and a large number of songbirds, such as horned larks, tree swallows, flycatchers, gray-cheeked thrushes, ruby-crowned kinglets, several species of warblers, and many more that are annually drawn there by an abundance of insects and a large variety of seed plants.

Year-round resident birds include ravens, gray jays, snowy owls, great gray owls, boreal owls, great horned owls, and hawk-owls, as well as willow ptarmigan (in some areas rock ptarmigan, particularly in winter), boreal chickadees, and several species of woodpeckers.

Within the northerly regions of the transition zone it is possible to note the different hunting tactics employed by those wolves that commonly cross into the habitat from the open tundra. Barren-ground caribou, the principal prey of wolves in the tundra, almost invariably run when threatened by a hunting pack, but the moose (*Alces alces*) is not usually that obliging. It often stands its ground and by posture and other signals announces that it will attack any wolf that comes near. An adult moose, whether it is a huge bull or a somewhat smaller cow, is a formidable opponent, an animal that most often attacks with its large, sharply pointed front hooves and is capable of stabbing a wolf to death with one swift, powerful thrust; or, if approached from behind while it is engaging a frontal opponent, it will kick like a horse with enough force to crush a wolf's ribs and to send it flying for several metres.

All animals are inherently cautious, especially when confronted by new or unusual events; additionally, and contrary to some opinion, they are well able to rationalize and to learn from experience. Wolves encountering an animal that they have never before hunted and that demonstrates untypical behaviour, do not brashly rush at it; they study it instead, seeking to determine its motives and intentions while at the same time considering the tactics that they may best employ in order to kill it.

Faced by a belligerent moose that refuses to run and weighs between 375 and 540 kg (825 and 1190 lb.) — 10 to 14 times heavier than an average-sized wolf — a pack stops 8 to 10 m (26 to 33 ft.) from it and watches the quarry intently before spreading out to encircle it and then to slowly move around it. Now and then, one of the dominant wolves will make a feint charge, dodging out of harm's way agilely when the moose rears, front hooves flailing in the air. After perhaps ten minutes of such behaviour, the wolves lie down around the moose, which quite

often begins to feed when browse or grass are within its reach. If the quarry continues to stand its ground, the pack will usually give up after about twenty minutes, leaving the area to look for a less dangerous source of food. But if a moose panics and runs — regardless of whether it does so upon first scenting, hearing, or seeing the predators, or whether it is provoked into doing so while it is standing at bay — the wolves immediately give chase and will probably kill it after a short time.

A number of long-term, predator-prey behaviour studies in the field show that wolves must test between 10 and 13 moose before they are able to kill one healthy adult, whereas the success rate when hunting caribou on the open tundra is much higher, not only because the prey numbers are so much greater, but also because few caribou will stand their ground. A large animal on the run is much more vulnerable to attack than a similar quarry that is determined to stand at bay.

However such things may be, it has been amply demonstrated that wild animals are capable of altering their behaviour through rational assessment of their environment, a factor clearly reflected in all transition zones by the behaviour of the predators and their prey.

▲ **A bull moose**, shown in top breeding condition, browses during early autumn in Alberta's foothills country.

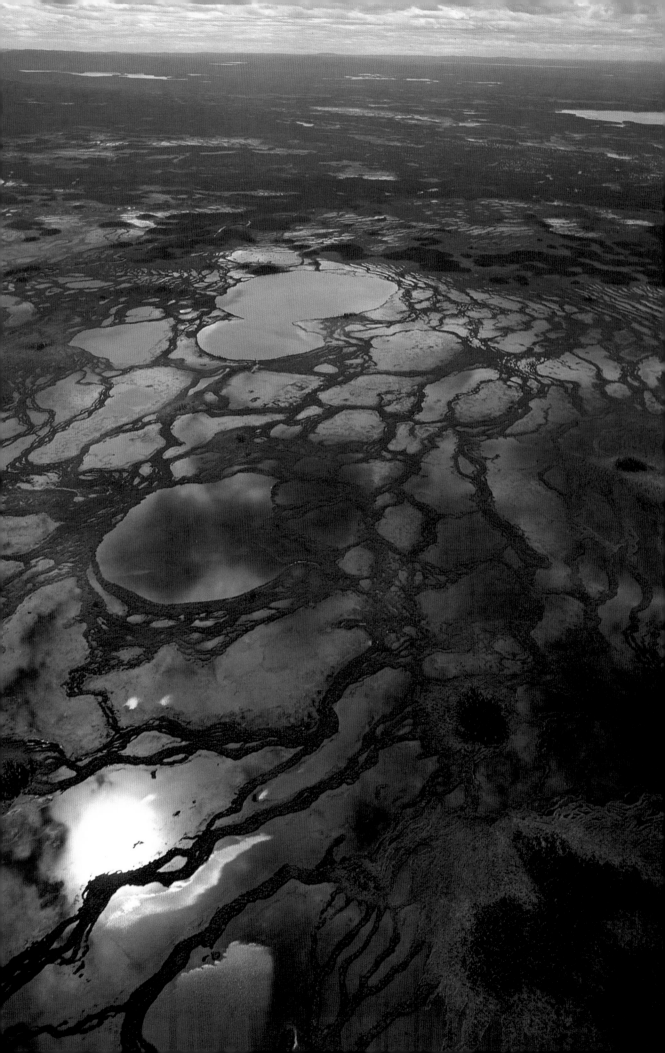

THE BOREAL FOREST

4

SPRUCE TREES ARE THE MOST NUMEROUS AND distinctive plants of the boreal biome, that great belt of forest that encircles the entire northern hemisphere from where it blends with the tundra in the northern transition zone to the more southerly temperate biome. Often referred to as the "taiga", the Canadian section of the boreal forest ranges in a north-westerly direction from the Atlantic coast right across the nation to northern British Columbia and the Yukon Territory, in places being some 2000 km (1200 mi.) wide.

The heart of the boreal forest is composed of black spruce *(Picea mariana)*, trees that grow at a slow rate, are usually between 16 and 26 cm (6 and 10 in.) in diameter, and attain heights of between 9 and 15 m (30 and 49 ft.). Running for seemingly endless kilometres and packed in serried ranks, these trees cast a continuous gloom over a land carpeted by thick layers of old and slowly decaying needles, which are often covered by sphagnum moss and lichens; otherwise the forest floor is devoid of plants that require sunlight.

In regions where the ground is well drained, it offers good footing, but travel is frequently impeded by the closely packed trees, the lower branches of which are dead and brittle. Reaching outwards, the limbs interlace with those of their neighbours to form an entanglement that hinders the progress of humans, even if they are walking on one of the many well-defined trails left by animals, which — with the exception of the tall moose — are all built closer to the ground than people and can easily glide through the tunnels that generations of their kind have made through the branchy barriers.

Traversing black-spruce habitat is never easy, but conditions become worse in low-lying, poorly drained areas, of which there are many in the taiga. These vast tracts of land have remained wet for centuries and have given rise to deep muskeg bogs, which are composed of a kind of organic gruel formed by the decomposing bodies of long-fallen spruces and by an incessant rain of dead needles. Here, hindered also by the dry limbs, human progress during the frost-free seasons is slow, devious, and actually dangerous, for in places the muskeg may be 5 m (16 ft.) deep, a bog that can suck down an animal or a person and which has even been known to swallow a bulldozer irretrievably.

In the James Bay region of Ontario, for instance, the muskeg stretches for many thousands of square kilometres over an area that has been dubbed "The Great Swamp". Travelling through this kind of

◀ **Typical of some regions** of the boreal biome, water-divided areas of muskeg, known as string bogs, lead to open woodlands in northern Quebec.

▲ Red squirrel pawprints

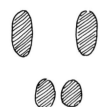

▲ Red squirrel tracks

▲ Mouse pawprints

▲ Mouse tracks

country in winter is fairly easy because the upper surface of the muskeg is frozen and covered in snow; but from break-up to freeze-up it is necessary to walk along the animal trails that, while leading over the most solid sections of the understory, meander incessantly. This means that in order to reach a destination that is, say, one kilometre away from the starting point, a traveller may have to walk four or five times that distance. Where trails have not been made, the thick cover of moss conceals the soupy bog, tempting the inexperienced traveller to walk on the misleading green cover.

The really dense forests of black spruce are not used as permanent habitats by most large mammals. The grazers and browsers, such as deer and moose, can find little to eat within the penumbral taiga and because they only move through it while travelling from one feeding range to another, their predators, the wolves, bears, coyotes, and cougars, use the trails only occasionally, perhaps when chasing prey, or when they are themselves moving to a new territory.

By and large, only small mammals are permanent residents of the deep black-spruce taiga: red squirrels and several kinds of mice, voles, and shrews are relatively abundant. The first three eat the buds and seeds of the spruces, various species of fungi, insects in season, and carrion when they can get it. The tiny, carnivorous shrew (Family Soricidae) preys on insects, mice and voles; it also eats seeds and almost any kind of edible thing that it comes across, for its metabolic rate is so high that it needs to eat at least its own weight in food — preferably meat of some kind — every 12 hours (pregnant shrews have been known to consume three times their own weight of meat in that time).

A number of insect-eating species of birds arrive in the deep forests to breed in the spring and then migrate south in the fall. Year-round residents, however, are few; they include the spruce grouse, woodpeckers, boreal chickadees, and some red-breasted nuthatches.

Insects abound in the taiga during the frost-free time. Some, like the spruce budworm — the larva of a species of Tortricid moth whose caterpillars feed on the spruce needles — can be particularly destructive to the trees when present in large numbers. Then there are the biting insects — the mosquitoes and the tiny, pestiferous blackflies; and the wood ticks (*Dermacentor* spp.). These relatively sedentary, slow-moving kin of the spider can survive without food for several years if no " host " is available; but, sooner or later, an unsuspecting mammal, bird, reptile or human will brush past their hiding places. Then the scale-like creatures, which at this stage only measure 4 mm (0.2 in.) in length, will climb nimbly on their victims and soon thereafter will begin to suck blood, inserting their syphon tubes through the skin so stealthily that they are rarely noticed. Not long afterwards, they become

THE BOREAL FOREST

1 Black spruce
2 Boreal chickadee
3 Spruce budworm
4 Black spruce cones
5 Great gray owl
6 Wood tick
7 Spruce grouse
8 Red squirrel
9 Northern three-toed woodpecker
10 Red-breasted nuthatch
11 Spruce forest

NOT TO SCALE

gorged and swollen to the size of a black grape. At this stage, mature females measure almost 2 cm (0.8 in.) long and about 1 cm (0.4 in.) wide, and are ready to drop off in order to lay their eggs on grass stems, bushes, or rotting logs. Their normally reddish-brown bodies have turned bluish-black, the hue imparted by the engorged blood, which shows through the thinly stretched body covering. Wood ticks are found in other forested areas of Canada, of course, but they seem to be particularly abundant in the black-spruce forests, remaining active from spring to late summer. Such ticks and their kin are responsible for tick paralysis and the spread among man and animals of diseases such as Rocky Mountain spotted fever.

Outside these gloomy forests, the boreal biome is more hospitable. The contours of the land may be rolling, or mountainous; rivers and lakes abound; forest-fire burns and areas where the soil is rocky and not able to sustain large trees contain openings where grow fruit bushes, ferns, young saplings, and many other plants that are utilized as food by birds and herbivores. In other regions white spruce *(Picea glauca)* are common. This tree, which can attain a height of 37 m (120 ft.) and a diameter of 1.25 m (4 ft.), is considered an important tree by the lumber industry. In some areas it forms pure stands, in others it mixes with black spruce, balsam fir, white birch, and trembling aspen and, in the Rocky Mountains region, with Engelmann spruce *(Picea engelmannii)*.

Trees and other plants, like most animal species, undergo periodic cycles of decline and abundance. During what may be termed *normal* years, seed production is adequate for natural reforestation and as food for animals. During peaks of production, populations of seed eaters are able to increase and their surplus numbers then become food for other animals. In years of abundance the white spruce, for example, can produce many thousands of cones, the seeds of which are eaten by squirrels, chipmunks, and a number of birds. Jack pine *(Pinus banksiana)* is another important boreal species of dry, well-drained areas. They are found from Nova Scotia to northern British Columbia and the Mackenzie River valley in the Northwest Territories growing in pure stands, or as rather stunted lone trees in poor locations, or mixed with spruce, aspen, and birch. An unusual characteristic of this species is that its cones stay closed on the tree for many years, often remaining in that condition until a forest fire sets the parent pine alight, possibly destroying it; however, the heat causes the cones to open and to propagate the seeds. Dead and fallen jack pines may lie on the ground for

A sheer canyon in Ontario's Canadian Shield country. At the bottom of the ▶ gulch grow thick stands of trembling aspen.

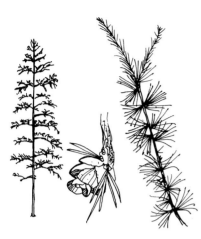

▲ **Tamarack**

many years before their seeds germinate through fire, or after the body of the tree has rotted. In the latter situation, the cones are harvested by squirrels and mice, but at least some of the seeds are returned to the soil to produce new trees.

Another abundant and distinctive boreal tree is the tamarack (*Larix laricina*), a species of larch. Larches are the only northern conifers (cone-bearing trees) that shed their needles in the autumn and grow them again in the spring. Tamaracks extend from the Atlantic coast to British Columbia, the Yukon Territory, and the more southerly and sheltered areas of the Northwest Territories. These trees are found most often mixed with other species, such as spruces, balsam firs, aspens, and birches; in the south, they favour wet ground, and in northern areas they grow on better-drained land. In the autumn, stands of tamarack glow a rich, butter yellow just before their needles begin to fall. In the spring, the tiny distinctive clusters of developing needles are light green, while the previous year's cones, each opened after having released its seeds and about 1 cm (0.4 in.) in diameter, look like small, reddish-brown roses.

Modern conifers belong to one of the oldest and largest groups of seed plants, their history dating back for millions of years. World-wide, 400 different kinds of conifers have been identified. Thirty-one species grow in Canada, of which all but the larches are evergreens (plants that maintain their leaves, or needles, all the year around and thus can grow even in winter, although at a greatly reduced rate).

All *tracheophytic* plants (a botanical division consisting of plants that have vascular, or tube-like, tissues through which nutrients and water are transported to all parts of the plant body) have evolved adaptations that allow them to grow successfully in a wide variety of terrains and climates. Based upon such adaptations botanists have recognized three distinct groups: perennials, biennials, and annuals. The first group embraces plants that normally live for more than two seasons — in some cases for many hundreds of years — and that after maturity usually produce flowers every year. All trees are perennials. The second group consists of plants that live for two years by storing food in their root systems during the first year for use during growth and seed production in the second year. The third group is composed of plants that grow from seed, produce flowers, cast their seeds, and then die. Their species continuity depends on the germination of at least some seeds during the following year unless, as in some species, the seed can remain dormant for more than a year.

Perennials and biennials can survive the cold because at the approach of winter they are able to convert the interior of their cells into a gel condition, an anti-freeze that contains very little water and is technically known as a *colloidal material*. This conversion is never described in household cookbooks, yet it applies to the manufacture or preparation of such things as butter, whipped cream, mayonnaise, jelly, and soap, to name but a few colloidal substances. There are many different kinds of colloids. All are unique in that they are able to change from a liquid to a solid or semi-solid condition. Some colloids cannot return to their liquid state after becoming solid (for example, an egg-white that has been boiled), but others are able to return to a liquid state after they have gelled, such as plant cells and warmed-up jelly.

At the approach of winter, tracheophytic plants manufacture large quantities of colloidal materials, the change from liquid to gel being triggered by temperature. The contents of cells are liquid during temperate, or warm weather, and semi-solid, or gelatine-like, during cold temperatures. The result is that little water remains inside the cells in the latter condition.

During winter, colloids in the cells of deciduous perennials and biennials cannot protect their leaves, and this is why these are shed each autumn. But the colloids *do* keep the rest of the plant from freezing, and since nutrients have previously been stored in stems and roots, growth continues at the advent of spring. This adaptation is known as *winter hardening*.

Evergreen leaves survive intense cold because they can retain enough colloidal gel to prevent them from freezing. In winter, this allows the trees to continue to produce energy through photosynthesis and so to grow at a slow rate.

Several species of lichens grow well in the boreal forests — as, indeed, they grow everywhere in the world where life can be even marginally supported. They are humble plants; and they may go entirely unnoticed by the uninitiated, or they may be mistaken for mosses. Yet they are an extremely important part of any ecosystem.

It is possible that lichens actually paved the way for other terrestrial plants and can be credited with the creation of the boreal biome, for it is believed that they — and other ancestral plants such as mosses, liverworts, and hornworts — developed from marine algae and were the first living things to become established on land after they emerged from the ancient seas millions of years ago.

Lichens are not a single plant, but an irrevocable partnership between thread-like fungi and green, photosynthetic algae (a natural combination known as *mutualism*). The fungi construct networks of

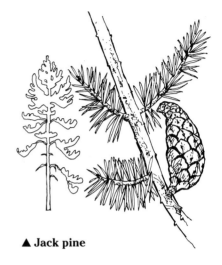

▲ **Jack pine**

▲ **Black spruce**

OVERLEAF **Alpine larches** in late autumn form a golden screen in front of ▶ early snow and mountain granite in Kootenay National Park, British Columbia.

 Mule deer inhabit the mountains and foothill country of western Canada. More sociable than the white-tailed deer, these cervids are also larger and heavier, some bucks of the species attaining a weight of 215 kg (474 lb.).

threads that cling to rocks or to the wood of trees; these interwoven filaments support the algae while soaking up rain water. Additionally, the fungi produce nitrogen-rich wastes (fertilizers) and carbon dioxide, substances that enable the algae to produce food for both partners by means of photosynthesis, even during periods of intense drought, cold, or heat. Because of these characteristics, lichens play an important role in soil making — they are, in fact, believed to have been among the first producers of soil — because they slowly dissolve and crumble the surface of the rocks upon which they cling tenaciously.

During changes in temperature, lichen contract or expand, moving the rock dust that they have produced and mixing it with their own wastes to make a thin soil, which is slowly enriched as the lichen partners continue to grow. Eventually, the depth and quality of the soil will sustain mosses, which will release their own organic wastes, further enriching the growing environment. As the build-up continues, conventional fungi colonize the fertile wild gardens provided by the lichens, and small plants and tree seedlings take root, all of which produce wastes that add to the content of the natural compost. Slowly, the soil area grows wider and deeper; larger plants take root. Finally trees are able to stand and grow in the good earth that has covered the barren rock.

Eighteen thousand species of lichens are known world-wide, each kind distinguished by different species of fungi and algae. An as-yet-undetermined number of these plants grow in Canada, the most common varieties being a leafy type growing on trees, an encrusting kind that grows on rocks and often looks more like a green-grey stain than a living thing, and the best-known but misnamed *reindeer mosses,* two kinds of lichens that are found throughout the Canadian wilderness: *Cladonia rangiferina* and *Cladonia alpestris.* The foliage of the former has an open and thready appearance; that of the latter is more compact and generally somewhat larger. Both are eaten by caribou and other animals. Additionally, *Cladonia* can be gathered, washed and dried, then ground up as flour. This was once a staple of a number of North American aboriginal people and later of European wilderness explorers, for the bread made of this flour is rich and nourishing.

Various colour pigments released by lichens were at one time used to dye wool, one of which, litmus, is still widely used as an acid-base indicator. In fact, because many lichens are exceptionally sensitive to atmospheric acidic contamination, they have often been used as pollution indicators.

The majority of animals that inhabit the more hospitable regions of the boreal biome are described earlier in the section on the northern transition zone. Additionally, in the western mountain regions live grizzly bears, mountain lions (cougars), and elk in scattered locations of mountain country in Alberta and British Columbia. Small populations of elk are also found in various parks in Saskatchewan and Manitoba, and in the southern area of Wood Buffalo National Park (where they were re-introduced some years ago). Mule deer, coyotes, river otters, striped skunks, fishers, and martens also live within the boreal habitat.

In heavily forested areas there are fewer birds than in the transition zone, but many species nest in the more open regions, especially in the vicinity of lakes and rivers.

Insects abound in the boreal biome during the frost-free seasons and include a great majority of the species that are found elsewhere in Canada. In most regions, members of the Hymenoptera order — which includes wasps, ants, bees, and a number of related species — are forever busy plying their various "trades". The most conspicuous (and usually the most feared by humans) are the stinging wasps and hornets,

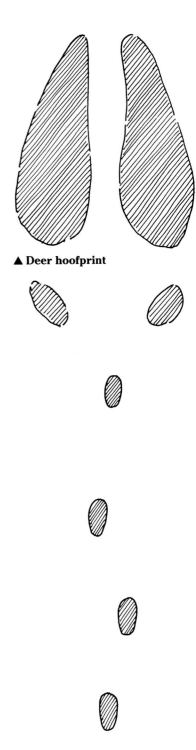

▲ **Deer hoofprint**

▲ **Deer tracks**

▲ Eastern cottontail rabbit

HARES AND RABBITS
Everybody knows the difference between a hare and a rabbit . . . or *do* they? In fact, hares, although larger and quite different from smaller relatives, are most often referred to as rabbits. The snowshoe hare (*Lepus americanus*), for instance, which is widely distributed across the North American continent and found over most of Canada's forested areas, is frequently called the snowshoe "rabbit", even in some biological reference books, despite the fact that the only true rabbit native to Canada is the cottontail (*Sylvilagus* spp.). The eastern cottontail (*Sylvilagus floridanus*) has a small range in this country consisting of the extreme southern region of Quebec and Ontario and a small section of prairie in south-western Manitoba and south-eastern Saskatchewan.

Apart from being considerably larger than rabbits, Canadian hares have longer ears, change their coats from brown or grey to white in winter, and bear their offspring in above-ground nests. New-born hares, or leverets, enter the world with their eyes open, are dressed in warm fur coats and are able to eat tender green plants within a week of birth. Young rabbits are born almost naked, blind, and helpless in a below-ground burrow dug by the female; such nurseries may be located a metre or more under the surface, or only a few centimetres down. In any event, the young rabbits do not leave the nest until two weeks after they are born and continue to be tended by the mother for about two more weeks, after which they are on their own. Young rabbits are able to breed during the first year of their lives, whereas hares do not reach sexual maturity until the start of their second year.

The snowshoe hare's common name is derived from the fact that it has large, back feet with webbed toes that, when spread, keep the animal on the surface of the snow. Cottontails owe their name to their short, fluffy, pure white tails. Both species are active all year around.

but there are a large number of species belonging to this important order that, though present in large numbers, are so small that they are hardly ever noticed. Then, too, others do not at all resemble wasps, ants, or bees.

More than 90 000 species of Hymenoptera have so far been identified, one of the smallest and least likely to be noticed being a minute wasp named *Trichogramma minutum*, a grand name for an insect that barely reaches 1 mm (0.04 in.) in length! Yet members of this family are mighty parasites, their larvae attacking the larvae of 15 families of butterflies and moths, 4 families of wasps, 2 of dobsonflies and alderflies, 2 of flies, and others as well. Like so many other insects, the *Trichogrammatids* exert control over a very large number of species that, should they overpopulate, would seriously damage the natural environment. For this reason, humans class this strange little wasp as beneficial, especially when it is present in agricultural areas.

The *Trichogrammatid* is perhaps the most unlikely looking of all wasps. It comes in three colours, black, brown, or yellow; its head is wider than its body; it has large eyes; two pairs of wings, the rearmost being narrow, the foremost shaped somewhat like table-tennis bats edged with fine hairs (*tricho* is a Greek word meaning "hair"). Females lay from one to five eggs on a larva of a host species. When the eggs hatch, the wasps eat the insect larvae.

The majority of wasps are also predatory on a large number of other insects, that without such control would harm their environment. Hornets and yellow jackets prey on many species of flies, hunting them in flight and eating all but the wings, legs, and heads. There is no doubt that these Hymenopterons can inflict painful stings when they are disturbed, in some instances causing death if the person stung is allergic to the venom, but most attacks on humans by wasps and hornets result only when the insects feel themselves to be threatened. Nests built in the vicinity of human dwellings in locations that are bound to be disturbed as the occupants enter or leave the home should, of course, be removed as should paper wasp nests in garden shrubbery or underground on a domestic lawn. Otherwise, all the members of this order should not be persecuted, for they are valuable to the environment. Often, yellow jackets will buzz around a person's head or body. In such situations if the individual merely stands still, the wasp will soon leave. It has most probably been attracted by some mark on the person's clothing or body that resembles a fly: a small mole, a fleck of black on the clothing, etc. Wasps invariably check such blemishes, just in case they are flies. It is not unusual to see a yellow jacket checking every nailhead in a board, for, seemingly, unless a fly is actually moving, the wasp must get close to it before it is sure of its identity. Persons so buzzed by a wasp are asking to be stung if they flap their arms or jump about; the insect interprets such actions as threatening.

Normally, wasps and hornets are not aggressive. In fact, they can even become quite tame, recognizing individual humans and, at least in one case, joining them for a snack when the food was being regularly eaten out of doors during summer. The yellow jacket in question came daily during a period that began in late June and ended in late July 1979. Every noon, when the people set the food out on the outdoor table and sat down to lunch, the wasp would appear. It would take minute bits of ham from the fingers, lick butter from a digit if this was offered, and would allow itself to be moved (gently) from places where its presence was not desired. Never once did it attack the two humans during the course of five weeks, despite almost daily contact.

Ichneumon, *chalcid*, and *braconid* wasps also parasitize a variety of flies and beetles. Others, like *pelecinid* wasps, lay their eggs on the root-feeding larvae of beetles. *Pelecinids* are conspicuous; the females measure almost 5 cm (2 in.) in length and are extremely slender, the last five segments of their bodies having become thin and elongated. These wasps are not abundant, but any long, shiny-black, wasp-like

▲ **Snowshoe hare**

OVERLEAF **The wooded craggy cliffs** of Western Brook Pond in Gros Morne ▶
National Park, Newfoundland.

▲ **Yellow jacket wasp**

insect seen in North America is likely to be a member of this family.

The Apidae is a large family that incorporates all the bees. These insects have always been highly prized by humans as purveyors of honey and wax and, most important, as pollinators of plants. The honey bee *(Apis mellifera)* is present in the wild state in Canada, but is an import to our continent, one of the few cases where an introduced animal has proven beneficial rather than destructive. There are four native bees. Hairy flower bees *(Anthophora occidentalis)* resemble honey bees, but are somewhat larger — they are valuable pollinators inhabiting the prairie regions; carpenter bees *(Xylocopa virginica)* are large pollinators that have yellow on the back and chest and black on the head and abdomen; bumble bees *(Bombus americanorum)* are well-known and extremely active pollinators; sweat bees, members of the family Halictidae, are small, useful pollinators that can be a nuisance at times because they seem forever anxious to obtain salt from human sweat. Peaceful when undisturbed, sweat bees will sting if brushed away, although they can be gently moved with a finger. The sting is not nearly as painful as that inflicted by wasps and other bees, neither does the discomfort endure for more than a few minutes in the absence of allergic reaction to the venom.

Ants are related to bees and wasps, but have been classified in the family Formicidae. All known species are highly social, existing in colonies that are first established by a single female. During a short-lived winged stage, the prospective queen ant mates with a male, who is also winged and destined for death after the act of procreation. After shedding her wings, the mated female selects the site for the new colony: this may be in tunnels under the soil, under rocks, within dead wood, or in living, but ailing trees, and in human dwellings. The queen lays her fertile eggs and personally raises a brood of workers, which, when mature, will take over the nursery and tend the royal female, who can continue laying fertilized eggs for the remainder of her life, which may last 10 to 15 years.

Ant colonies may contain from several dozen individuals to half a million or more, depending on the species. These insects are, in fact, the most dominant of all lifeforms on earth in terms of numbers of individuals. Of the species in Canada, none is a serious pest to humans, although some, like the large carpenter ant and the tiny, so-called sugar ant, at times create problems — the former by boring tunnels in wooden beams (carpenter ants don't *eat* wood, they chew it so as to make room in their expanding colony), and the latter by invading food cupboards.

Ants are herbivorous, carnivorous, or omnivorous, depending on the species. Most of them are valuable from a purely human standpoint as controls of harmful species of insects and plants and as food for a large number of birds, of mammals such as bears and raccoons, and even of other insects. On the debit side — again from a human standpoint — some ants are "dairy farmers", caring for and "milking" aphids, those minute insects that can cause a great deal of damage to agricultural crops and home garden plants.

Aphids, feeding as they do on plant sap, excrete a liquid high in sugar. The ants assiduously lap up this honey-dew, often stroking with their forelegs an aphid's abdomen to stimulate excretion. At the same time they actually clean the aphid, removing from it minute bits of detritus picked up while the insect is feeding, tiny particles of dust, or dried bits of plant that are made sticky by honey-dew and become "glued" to the aphid. The ants also protect the aphids from predators.

Some small species of ants are slave-makers, raiding the nests of larger ants and stealing larvae from them. These captives are nurtured alongside the raiders' young and, as adults, work as slaves, performing tasks that their small masters are too weak to manage without such labourers. Strangely, the small ants seem to be impervious to the defences of the large ants, the soldiers of which appear to become disoriented when invaded. Instead of attacking the intruders, the husky defenders mill about in a disorganized way, molesting the attackers not at all and allowing them to form long lines that enter the brooding chambers of the colony, where each raider seizes a larva in its jaws before retracing the journey back to its own colony.

Other ants make large hills on top of which they "farm" grass. Such hills are easily recognized. They are somewhat conical in shape and, in old, established colonies, are up to 1 m (40 in.) high and 1.5 m (5 ft.) in diameter at the base. The outside of these hills are "weeded" by the female workers, a circumstance that may cause an observer to wonder why only short, fresh, green grass stems are growing on the mound, each stem emerging at a given distance from its neighbour instead of growing in a mass, as is the case on lawns or other grassland areas. But if a person takes the time to study such a mound, it will be noticed that while some workers are "weeding", others are harvesting, snipping off grass stems and carrying a load down into the colony to serve as food.

Ant larvae are white, somewhat curved in shape, eyeless, and small-headed. As they near maturity, the typical ant shape can be discerned, including legs, a larger head, and minute bulges where the eyes will eventually develop. When the newly emerged ant is first exposed to daylight, it must spend up to several hours turning itself round and around, orienting a built-in "compass" system, a biological clock that must be programmed by the sun. Without it, an ant cannot find its way

▲ **Honey bee**

▲ **Crow**

about the land when scouting for food. When a supply has been located the ants leak minute amounts of a powerful scent as they return to the colony; other scouts are then guided to a good source of nourishment, be this a kitchen food cupboard, a dead animal, or a plant covered in honey-dew–producing aphids. Nevertheless, since ants apparently do not discharge their scent as they travel in search of food, those that have not oriented their sun compasses will get lost. When alarmed, ants also produce a scent that serves to alert all the colony's defenders, who, in face of the alarm, come boiling out of their fortress-like domain.

World-wide, more than 8000 species of ants have so far been classified. It has been estimated that at least a further 4000 species are waiting to be discovered.

BOREAL PLAINS

Bison, North America's largest terrestrial mammals, are the dominant species found in that part of the boreal biome that is encountered in Wood Buffalo National Park, a reserve that encompasses 44 807 km² (17 300 sq. mi.) and contains outstanding examples of a particular kind of wilderness that, although lumped into the boreal system, deserves special mention.

This national park, Canada's largest, straddles the sixtieth parallel of latitude. Approximately one-quarter of the reserve is located in the Northwest Territories about 32 km (20 mi.) south of Great Slave Lake; the remainder lies in northern Alberta and extends south to the Birch Mountains. Within this section, the park runs east to the south-western shore of Lake Athabasca and the Athabasca River and west to the Whitesand River.

The majestic Peace River, which begins in the Rocky Mountains of eastern British Columbia and courses for 1923 km (1195 mi.), meanders through the southern portion of Wood Buffalo Park for about 200 km (124 mi.) before it reaches the delta of the Athabasca River, gathers the latter's waters and continues north, where it becomes the Slave River. Thereafter, the combined waters of the Peace, Athabasca, and Slave run north along the eastern boundary of the reserve until they are discharged into Great Slave Lake, from where they will eventually join the Mackenzie River, which flows into the Beaufort Sea.

In natural terms, the Peace and Slave rivers are one and the same stream, given two names during the early days of European exploration of the region. The latter can be distinguished at a glance because of its brown waters, which collect soil eroded from a maze of rocky hills and from lake waters that discharge from Pre-Cambrian Shield regions immediately east of the park as well as from run-off issuing from a series of flatlands known as the Interior Plains.

From an aircraft flying over the eastern boundaries of the park, three topographical regions are immediately noticeable, each having a different elevation and leading downwards, like giant steps, from west to east.

The Caribou and Birch uplands are large, circular plateaus located on the western and southern boundaries of the park, which rise for more than 400 m (1300 ft.) above the surrounding plains. These mesas are the remains of vast, sedimentary rock elevations that date back to the Cretaceous period of 125 million years ago, a time when the Rocky Mountains were formed and during which ancient inland seas and swamps gradually drained, leaving deposits of chalk and shale that are still to be seen in the region. These uplands are difficult to reach; as a consequence, their biology and geology are not well known, a fact that impresses those few who gain access to their flat tops by laborious climbing (and often slipping). To stand within a rugged wilderness

▲ **The tremulous but musical call** of tundra swans is always a welcome sound each spring as these great white birds beat their way to Canadian Arctic breeding grounds from their winter range along the Pacific and Atlantic coasts of the United States.

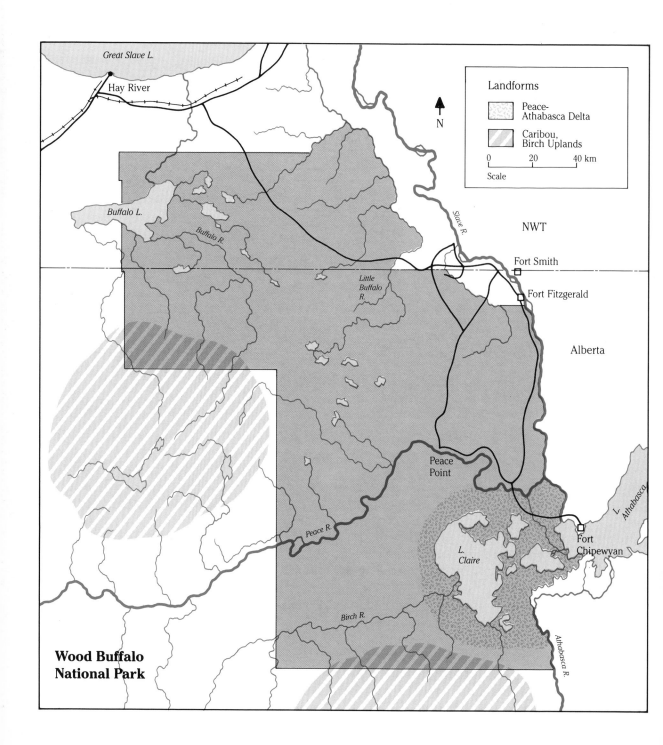

Great Slave L.

Hay River

Buffalo L.

Buffalo R.

Little
Buffalo
R.

Slave R.

Landforms

Peace-
Athabasca Delta

Caribou,
Birch Uplands

0   20   40 km

Scale

NWT

Fort Smith

Fort Fitzgerald

Alberta

Peace
Point

Peace R.

L. Athabasca

Fort
Chipewyan

L.
Claire

Birch R.

Athabasca R.

**Wood Buffalo
National Park**

A small herd of plains bison photographed from the air as the animals ▶
moved over a lush grazing area in Wood Buffalo National Park.

where few other humans have been, and to know that one is completely cut off from contact with one's own kind, is at once daunting and exhilarating! Fear must be sternly put down, but its conquest is greatly aided by the environment and its wild occupants, the mammals and birds that have rarely known the presence of man and thus exhibit neither fear nor aggression.

Below the uplands lies the vast Alberta Plateau. An enormous, poorly drained plain, it is criss-crossed by small, meandering streams, contains many shallow lakes, and is dotted by muskeg bogs. This biogeographic region covers a major portion of the park.

East of the plateau, the landscape is dominated by large deposits of gypsum, a chalk-like mineral used, among other purposes, to make plaster of Paris. Because this soft rock has for many thousands of years been continuously dissolved by surface waters and by underground rivers and streams, numerous caves and sinkholes have been created.

The underground rivers and caves are not readily apparent, but sinkholes are the most obvious features in some areas of the plateau. These depressions were once underground caves scooped out of the gypsum by water action. Slowly, the water enlarged the subsurface caverns, eroding their roofs to the point of collapse. The resulting craters are filled with rock and earth debris and crowded by bushes and small trees. As the gypsum underlayers continue to wear away, the sinkholes deepen and the debris and vegetation slide downwards. New holes appear periodically as other underground caves collapse. In some parts of the plateau the surface of the ground is virtually pitted with the sinks, making travel difficult for animals and humans.

In the south-eastern section of the park, the Slave River Lowlands contain an area known as the Salt Plains. Here, salty water rises and flows across open lands from springs located at the foot of a low escarpment. This phenomenon has considerable influence on animal and plant life. Bison and, in fact, all mammals that inhabit the region, frequently visit the many salt licks, but only salt-resistant plants can grow in the saline lowlands, which in places contain salt deposits that are metres deep and mound upwards on the surface.

The spectacular Peace-Athabasca Delta, located between the park's Lake Claire and the western shore of Lake Athabasca, is a unique feature of this section of the boreal biome and is one of the largest inland deltas of the world. A series of mineral-rich lakes, marshes, sedge meadows, and meandering, narrow water channels offer abundant food for mammals, birds, fishes, and insects.

Dominant trees in the forested regions of the reserve are the same as those encountered in other parts of the boreal biome. In some locations evergreens such as white and black spruce form dense stands; in others a more open landscape produces mixed groups of poplars, birches, jack pine, and spruces; while in some parts of the open plains trembling aspen and birches are scattered among the lowland plants and often serve as scratching posts for the shaggy bison that graze the region.

That part of the boreal biome found in Wood Buffalo National Park by its uniqueness illustrates the difficulties that are always encountered by biologists when they seek to chart the geographic boundaries of natural regions. The practice is necessary and useful, but it must often resort to generalization for the sake of clarity and order. It cannot, therefore, take into account the many differences that exist within each designated region, for in nature, it seems, rules and exceptions are constant companions. Try as we may to blueprint the precise boundaries and workings of any biome or ecosystem, some part of it is going to be missing from the plan, despite the undeniable fact that during the last 100 years scientific knowledge has increased dramatically.

A major problem facing biologists is that nature has always been in a state of flux, even without the rapid changes that humans have effected, and continue to effect, on the environment. All those who study the workings of life sooner or later become aware that no matter how much they know, there is always so much more that they *don't* know! It is as Ralph Waldo Emerson noted: "But in the mud and scum of things / There always, always something sings."

Discovery of those "singing somethings" often comes late, perhaps when an animal, or a plant, or even an entire ecosystem is damaged to the point of no return. During the nineteenth century literally *billions* of passenger pigeons lived in Canada and the United States, but, in 1914, the last member of this species died in captivity. Similarly, but with a somewhat happier ending, the plains bison *(Bison bison bison)*, more than 30 million of which once ranged from Florida to Canada's three prairie provinces (see map, page 116), were brought to near extinction by the turn of this century. With only a few hundred wild bison remaining at that time, a small number of farsighted conservationists banded together and managed to save the species.

The story of the bison — like those of the passenger pigeon, the whooping crane, and the many other species that have been made extinct, or endangered through human ignorance — clearly demonstrates the importance of careful and long-term biological investigation. Between 1850 and 1900, an estimated total of 20 million bison were slaughtered for their hides and for sport, the great majority of their carcasses being left to rot. Wolves and a host of other predators could not consume the mountains of meat that day after day and year after year were left scattered over the plains of the United States and Canada,

▲ Swift

Swallow ▶

Distribution of Bison

Legend

- Prehistoric range of wood bison
- Historic range of wood bison
- Historic range of plains bison

0   400   800 km

Scale

the stench of the rotting carcasses drifting over the prairies for long distances.

In 1893, the Canadian government passed a law for the protection of wood bison *(Bison bison athabascae)*, a close relative of the plains species. Their historical distribution in Canada included most of the boreal biome of north-eastern British Columbia, northern Alberta, north-western Saskatchewan, and the south-western forested area of the Northwest Territories (see map, page 116). The prehistoric range of the wood bison extended north to include the northern interior of British Columbia, the Yukon Territory, and the Alaskan interior up to the Bering Sea.

Protection for the wood bison came only just in time, when their numbers had been reduced to some 300 animals. Living in the region that was to become Wood Buffalo Park, the bison prospered, by 1914 increasing to about 500.

The Canadian government established the park in 1922, a time when the herd was estimated to have increased to between 1500 and 2000 wood bison. It seemed that the subspecies had been saved. But, as noted in 1986 by Canadian Wildlife Service biologist H.W. Reynolds in an unpublished cws report, wood bison were once more to be threatened:

> . . . [t]heir seemingly secure survival was again set back in 1925 when the Canadian government decided to move excess plains bison from Wainwright Buffalo Park [a reserve that no longer exists], located in Central Alberta, to Wood Buffalo National Park — a mistake that nearly caused extinction of the wood bison. Between 1925 and 1928, 6673 plains bison were transferred north and released into the park, where they subsequently mixed and hybridized with the resident wood [bison]. Herd size increased and, by 1940, it was generally believed that pure wood bison had become extinct despite speculation that small, isolated herds still existed in the northwestern region of the park.
>
> It was this speculation that led Dr. N.I. Novakowski, cws [Canadian Wildlife Service], to the discovery of an isolated population of bison in the Nyarling River area in northwestern Wood Buffalo National Park during an aerial survey in 1957. Investigation on the ground in 1959 resulted in collection of five specimens for study at the National Museum of Canada, results of which confirmed that these animals were wood bison.

Following this discovery, Canadian Wildlife Service officials began the Save the Wood Bison Program, which continues today. In the early 1960s, however, the bison were threatened again. This time by anthrax, a disease that was unintentionally imported from Europe during the early days of North American settlement and that is fatal to domestic and wild cattle. Biologists worked hard to save the herd, transferring 18 healthy bison to a new territory on the north-west shores of Great Slave Lake, which has since been designated as the Mackenzie

▲ **Whooping crane**

Bison Sanctuary. The small herd prospered. By 1985, more than 1500 wood bison lived in the sanctuary. In addition, another 23 animals were transferred to Alberta's Elk Island National Park in 1965, there to increase to about 200 at the present time and to serve as seed stock for transfer of wood bison to other sanctuaries in the western provinces and to various zoos.

At this writing, an estimated 2000 wood bison live in Canada, the majority, about 1700, in the Mackenzie Sanctuary, the remaining in various other locations, including Elk Island National Park, Nahanni National Park, and in the provinces of Manitoba and Alberta. In addition to the wood bison, between 4000 and 5000 plains bison live in Wood Buffalo National Park. The combined total of between 6000 and 7000 animals means that Canada hosts the largest remaining bison herds to be found anywhere.

The story of the whooping crane (*Grus americana*) is similar to that of the wood bison, but its ending is not yet as clear or positive. Although this bird, North America's tallest at 1.5 m (5 ft.) from feet to top of head, was never really abundant in Canada and the United States, relatively large numbers ranged from northern and central Canada, where the majority nested, all the way south to wintering grounds in Texas and other regions in the southern United States.

The destruction of their habitat through farming and swamp draining, and the hunting of the birds for their meat and plumage brought the spectacular whoopers to near extinction by 1941, when only 21 birds were then known to exist in the wild state.

The cranes had been protected by law in both countries for some years, but their numbers had nevertheless been steadily declining. It was only when they were brought to the very edge of extinction that authorities in Canada and the United States recognized the severity of the problem and instructed their respective wildlife departments to take a hand in the matter.

Given the go-ahead by their governments, the Canadian Wildlife Service and the U.S. Fish and Wildlife Service joined forces to try and save the whooping cranes. In 1941, however, no one knew where the birds were nesting in Canada, despite the fact that biologists had been trying to discover the breeding grounds for some years. Then, in the spring of 1955, Canadian biologists, surveying by air damage done by a large forest fire that had broken out the previous summer in the northern part of Wood Buffalo National Park, discovered the whoopers' nesting grounds in a large area of marshland in which sphagnum bogs and stunted spruce trees formed a mosaic.

Two years later, Fred G. Bard, of the Saskatchewan Museum of Natural History, proposed that eggs should be taken from whooper nests and given to brooding greater sandhill cranes (*Grus canadensis tabida*) to incubate in captive conditions, thus ensuring that at least a number of hatchlings would survive to preserve the species. This practice was put into effect in 1964, when Canadian Wildlife Service biologist Ernie Kuyt gathered one egg from each of six crane nests (the birds lay only two eggs each season) and flew them, carefully packed in insulated cases, to the Patuxent Wildlife Research Center in Laurel, Maryland, an establishment operated by the U.S. Fish and Wildlife Service.

Initially, the "save the whooper" program was not free of some risk, for no one knew for sure whether or not the birds would abandon their nests if they were disturbed, although Dr. Ray Erickson, of Patuxent, believed that the cranes would not abandon their nests if only one egg was taken from each. He proved to be right.

Today, about 120 whooping cranes live in the wild and an additional 40 live in captivity. The bird is still on the endangered-species list, of course, and many questions about its ultimate fate are still being asked. One of the major ones is: Will sandhill-crane–hatched whoopers mate with their own kind, or will they try to mate with sandhill cranes? Chicks take between five and six years to reach breeding maturity, and because of the difficulty of observing the released birds, this vital question has not yet been answered.

With a wingspan that varies between 213 and 228 cm (7 and 7.5 ft.), the regal whoopers fly at altitudes that may reach 4 km (2.5 mi.) while averaging speeds of about 26 km (16 mi.) per hour during favourable wind conditions. They migrate in stages, touching down in a variety of places along their flyway route in order to rest, or to avoid bad weather. In spring, they head north from Aransas National Wildlife Refuge in south-eastern Texas on their way to their Wood Buffalo National Park nesting grounds. In late summer they leave Canada and return to the southern United States, covering about 8000 km (4970 mi.) in the course of the two-way journey.

The fact that whooping cranes had probably been breeding since prehistoric times in the region now known as Wood Buffalo National Park, yet were not seen there until 1955, dramatically illustrates the size and complexity of the boreal biome. No other terrestrial life zone encountered in Canada offers so many challenges to those who continue to investigate the nation's biology.

OVERLEAF **This aerial photograph** of the Peace-Athabasca Delta shows the ▶ enormous extent of this almost totally flat alluvial plain in Wood Buffalo National Park.

THE COAST BIOME

 THE COAST BIOME IS PROBABLY THE MOST spectacular of all of Canada's fascinating plant zones. It ranges from a point at about 55° north latitude southward to the border of the United States, a serried belt of tall evergreens that clings to the slopes of the Coast Mountains of mainland British Columbia and then crosses the Inside Passage of the Pacific Ocean to continue on the Queen Charlotte Islands and on Vancouver Island.

Although this plant biome is dominated by high-peak glaciers, it is nevertheless a temperate rain forest because of the influence of the Japan current, which brings warm oceanic water to the Pacific coast and creates a mild climate at lower elevations. In those regions where the temperate air rises and meets the cold air that descends from the mountains, above-average precipitation occurs during all seasons. From spring to autumn, the rains are heavy; in winter, some regions of the biome receive Canada's greatest snowfalls, especially in northern areas like Kitimat, located on the 96 km (60 mi.) long Douglas Channel, and Stewart, at the end of the Portland Canal and on the border of Alaska. Total winter accumulations of snow of 15 m (49 ft.) in the former and 25 m (82 ft.) in the latter were recorded in 1970, laying down almost unbelievably deep, soft blankets that by mid-winter filled most of the mountain passes and caused the moose and mule deer (*Odocoileus hemionus*) to shelter in heavily forested valleys. During these conditions, the deer must keep their trails open by continuous passage, but they are virtual prisoners within their *yards*, as such sheltering locations are known, until the thaw; nevertheless they usually find sufficient food in a land where abundant winter fodder exists. Although other large animals are equally handicapped, the small mammals (other than predators), such as mice, shrews, and voles, spend the winter deep under the snow cover scurrying along a veritable maze of tunnels and feeding on ground vegetation and seeds gathered in autumn and stored in grassy nests. Weasels, shrews and other small predators follow their prey as easily in winter as they do in the frost-free seasons.

The most distinctive topographic features of the coast biome are its mountains, especially Mount Waddington. This, the highest peak in British Columbia's Coast Mountains, rises to 3994 m (13 104 ft.) and is located approximately 300 km (186 mi.) north of Vancouver overlooking Bute Inlet. In spring and summer, it feeds this arm of the Pacific

◄ **The peregrine falcon**, one of Canada's most spectacular birds of prey, is slowly becoming reestablished in regions where it was once made extinct by the use of pesticides. Peregrines are vigorously protected.

▲ **Lush vegetation** in Naikoon Provincial Park, Queen Charlotte Islands. This kind of temperate rain forest occurs in British Columbia along the coastal mainland and on the islands.

with glacial meltwaters via the Homathko River and a multitude of streams. Nearby are other impressive summits: Mount Tiedemann: 3827 m (12 556 ft.); Mount Queen Bess: 3048 m (10 000 ft.); and, just south of the latter, Mount Munday: 3505 m (11 500 ft.). This mountain was named for Don and Phyllis Munday, who, with Don Munday's brother Bert, were the first to reach the north-west summit of Waddington in 1928. Officials wanted to name Mount Waddington after the trio, but Don Munday thought it would be more fitting to name it after Alfred Waddington, one of the principals involved in the promotion of the Canadian Pacific Railway.

The Coast Mountains in British Columbia run for 1600 km (994 mi.) from the Yukon Territory to the Fraser River lowlands near Vancouver. Near the Yukon, they are 56 km (35 mi.) wide; in the south-central portion of their range, 161 km (100 mi.) in width.

Douglas-firs (*Pseudotsuga menziesii*) are the most impressive of all the tall trees that grow in this biome. On the Queen Charlotte Islands, the coastal variety (var. *menziesii*) have attained heights of 100 m (328 ft.) and diameters of more than 5 m (16 ft.). Some specimens living today on Moresby and Lyell islands were already growing when Columbus made his first landfall in the Americas (growth-ring records for felled trees have established that the firs can live at least 1200 years). Douglas-firs grow straight and their trunks are clear of branches up to 20 m (66 ft.)

Coastal-growing cedars are usually taller and have greater diameters than those that are found inland. Growth rings show that they are also long-lived: up to 800 years have been recorded.

Yellow cedar (*Chamaecyparis nootkatensis*), like the *Arbor vitae*, is not actually a cedar, but a species of cypress that is known variously as yellow cypress, Alaska cypress, and Alaska cedar. Six species of *Chamaecyparis* are recognized, three growing in Asia and three in North America. The one that grows in Canada, *nootkatensis*, is found only in the coastal regions of British Columbia. This tree reaches a height of 24 m (80 ft.) and a diameter of 1 m (40 in.). Cedar-like in appearance, but having greyish-brown, striated bark, the cypress is rarely found at heights below 600 m (1969 ft.) in the south, its range extending to heights of about 1500 m (4920 ft.) along a relatively narrow coastal band that includes Vancouver Island and the Queen Charlotte and other islands. It seldom occurs in pure stands; on high, exposed ridges, it becomes a sprawling shrub.

Another tree found in this biome and nowhere else in Canada is the arbutus (*Arbutus menziesii*). It is a broad-leaved evergreen with egg-shaped, shiny, dark green leaves. In spring (April–May) the arbutus produces clusters of small white flowers that by August become bunches of bright red berries. It is a low, somewhat branchy tree attaining a maximum height of about 12 m (40 ft.) and a diameter of 60 cm (2 ft.). Its range extends as far as Bute Inlet on the mainland and up to Seymour Narrows on Vancouver Island, although it is limited to a narrow coastal strip at altitudes of below 300 m (984 ft.). The arbutus, or madroña, as it is variously called, has a somewhat larger range than the third unusual species found in the coast biome, the Garry oak (*Quercus garryana*), an attractive tree that reaches 23 m (75 ft.) in height and has a diameter of 1.5 m (5 ft.). This too is branchy; it has a round, wide crown of gnarled and rather heavy branches. The Garry oak is found only on the east coast of Vancouver Island, on other islands in the Strait of Georgia, and on the mainland as far as Sumas in the Fraser Valley.

OVERLEAF **A section of the peaks** of the Coast Mountains graphically ▶ demonstrates the lifeless, polar-like conditions that exist at high altitudes in Canada's West.

THE COAST BIOME

1 Gray jay
2 Chestnut-backed chickadee
3 Mule deer
4 Douglas-fir cones
5 White-breasted nuthatch
6 Vole
7 Mouse
8 Shrew
9 Ruffed grouse

NOT TO SCALE

Large hemlocks and Sitka spruce also grow in this biome; so do other species found in the montane zone. Additionally, transition zones occur where the coast biome blends with the subalpine and montane.

▲ **A dogwood tree** in full blossom. Ten species of dogwoods are native to Canada, most of them being shrubs.

The majority of mammals in the habitat are those that range elsewhere in the west and in many other parts of Canada. Lynx are absent, and bobcats live only in the southern extremes of the range; moose inhabit the central and eastern regions and are absent along a relatively wide belt in the western area, from the border of the state of Washington to southern Alaska.

Inhabiting the extreme, south-western corner of the mainland part of the biome, is the western spotted skunk (*Spilogale gracilis*), a smaller and far more agile relative of the striped skunk (*Mephitis mephitis*). It weighs between 800 and 900 g (28 and 31 oz.), while the weight of the striped skunk ranges between 1.25 and 2.5 kg (2.8 and 5.5 lb.). This species is common in Central America and the western half of the United States, but, although it is only known to occur in Canada in this one location, it is possible that in time it may cross the Canadian border in the region of southern Ontario and Manitoba, for it is reported to have extended its range northward into the Dakotas and Minnesota.

Spotted skunks are rather attractively marked. Superimposed on a black background are swirls of milk-white on the sides, which encircle each ear, reach the rump, and form an S-bend that curls downwards towards the stomach. A white blaze decorates the forehead. The plume-like tail is jet black with a large white tip and has a white, more-or-less oval patch on each side near the body. When alarmed, this skunk arches its tail so that the white plume rests on its back. If an enemy continues to approach despite the warning, the spotted skunk does a hand-stand, pirouetting like a ballerina on its forefeet, but keeping its scent glands aimed at the target by arching its back forward. In this stance, the skunk may dance a little, or it may even advance towards the intruder, its hind feet dangling over its raised head, but spread apart so as not to disturb the trajectory of the twin streams of odorous, acrid musk that are forcefully emitted from anal musk glands. At a range of about 2 m (6.5 ft.), the skunk shoots, sure then of hitting its target. Most animals are incapacitated temporarily by the eye-stinging, powerful discharge.

OVERLEAF   **Giant western cedars** stand arrow-straight on Meares Island, ▶ Clayoquot Sound, British Columbia. The island was named in 1809 after Commander John Meares, Royal Navy, who in 1783 sailed a small vessel from Calcutta, India, to the coast of British Columbia.

**▲ Spotted skunk
in spraying position**

These little skunks are able to climb to the top of trees to escape their enemies and can travel at a rate of about 7 km (4 mi.) per hour when going all out. Unlike the striped skunk, which will eat almost anything, the spotted skunk is largely carnivorous, actively hunting mammals, birds and their eggs, and beetles and their larvae. It also eats berries and in summer consumes a large amount of succulent vegetation. In the north, four to five young are born in a snug den during early summer after a gestation time of 121 days. This lengthy pregnancy period for such a small mammal suggests delayed embryonic growth over the winter; such a development has not yet been confirmed, however.

Young spotted skunks are born almost naked, at best having a thin sprinkling of short, fine hair. Their skins are smooth and black with the white markings that will later distinguish their fur; their ears and eyes are closed for the first 32 days of life. When about four months old, the young skunks are fully grown and venture away from the den on their own, although many of them den with the mother the following winter.

The Virginia opossum (*Didelphis virginiana*), an animal found in Canada only within the coast biome and in extreme southern Ontario, is fairly common in the Fraser Valley region of British Columbia.

Opossums are marsupials, members of an ancient order that consists of about 250 living species and a great number of extinct forms. Living relatives of the opossum are kangaroos, wombats, bandicoots, and phallangers, among others.

Marsupials and placental mammals are believed to have evolved side by side from a common ancestor during the Cretaceous period, which began 135 million years ago and lasted for 60 million years. During this prehistoric time, the Rocky Mountains were formed; dinosaurs reached their peak and became extinct; toothed birds died out and were replaced by modern birds; and archaic mammals, including marsupials, developed.

Opossums, it thus appears, have been around for a long, long time and are as incongruous today as they evidently have always been. They are mammals in that they suckle their young, but are bird- or reptile-like in that they produce within their bodies eggs protected by shells (a female opossum has no placenta, the organ on the wall of the mammalian uterus to which the embryo is attached by means of the umbilical cord and through which it receives its nourishment).

Opossum young hatch one at a time within the mother only 13 days after the eggs have formed. They break out of the thin shells while still in an embryonic, highly undeveloped condition. Weighing only about 0.5 g (0.01 oz.), they are approximately 14 mm (0.5 in.) long. They are born without visible ears, they have essentially no jaws, and no eyes; the back legs are little stubs, useless for crawling; and an embryo's tail looks somewhat like a tiny piece of cooked spaghetti with a blunt point. That which would be called a mouth in other animals is only a small hole without lips, but within this cavity lies a well-developed tongue. In fact, the only external signs of future development are to be noted in the front legs and paws; these are minute, but sturdy; and the paws have fingers equipped with claws.

Just before the first embryo is about to be born, the mother spring-cleans her pouch, or *marsupium* (a term borrowed from Latin and Greek from which the name, *marsupial*, is derived. Latin: *marsuppium*, meaning "pouch", or "purse"; Greek: *marsypion*, meaning "bag", or "pouch".) Afterwards she carefully licks herself from the edge of the pouch down to the cloaca, or birth passage, making a smooth, damp path along which her embryos will climb.

Inside the marsupium the opossum mother has 13 teats; one is in the upper centre of the far wall of the pouch, the other 12 are arranged in horseshoe-shape above and around the central nipple. When she feels the movement of her first embryo, the mother sits upright, usually leaning her back against some sort of support. From then on, it is up to the little bee-sized embryos. On emerging into the world, each embryo must climb paw over paw up the mother's fur along the designated pathway, and, on reaching the pouch, slide into it, immediately thereafter fastening its "mouth" on a teat. Although an opossum has 13 nipples, she may give birth to as many as 25 young; however, a number of embryos are likely to fall off the mother on their way up to the pouch. These are left to die. Then too, when the first 13 young have each claimed a teat, the remainder are also left to die. Mortality continues inside the pouch. Some young are weak and cannot suck enough milk, others may absorb the larvae of parasites inside the pouch. In any event, it has been estimated that out of a nursing litter of 13 opossums, only 8 or 9 will survive.

The opossum's pouch makes an excellent nursery. Its interior is centrally heated by the mother's body warmth, the teats are more like buttons than conventional mammae and allow the developing embryos to cling tightly to them, and the entrance of the marsupium is equipped with a muscle that acts like a draw-string. This muscle closes the opening tightly enough to keep out water when the mother goes swimming, which is often, for opossums will readily cross rivers,

▲ **Virginia opossum**

lakes, and ponds in search of food or a new range. Also, as opossums are arboreal and frequently hang upside down, the draw-string prevents the infants from falling out.

Embryo opossums remain attached to the mother's teats for the first ten weeks of their lives, emptying their bowels and bladders into the pouch for the mother to lick out on a regular basis. At the end of that time, they take their first look at the world, usually peeking from the edge of the marsupium. Not long afterwards they crawl out and scramble onto the mother's back, there to remain in a bunch for short periods while the female forages or sleeps.

When they are three to four months old, depending on range and individual characteristics (some young animals are more precocious than others of the same species), the young opossums strike out on their own. They are then fully equipped. They have long, scaly, and prehensile tails and back feet that have extra long, thumb-like big toes. Each opposable and clawless toe can meet any one of the other four toes on each foot so as to grasp branches or objects. In addition, the tail acts like a fifth "hand", being able to wind itself firmly around branches and to actually carry objects. When collecting nesting material, for instance, an opossum first gathers the grasses and sedges with its mouth, making a bundle out of them and then, sitting up and leaning downwards, transfers the load to the tail, which curls around the material and carries it to the nest.

Opossums are adaptable and exceptionally hardy. Slowly spreading northward during the first and second half of this century, they have acclimatized to the colder conditions in the northern United States and Canada and remain active throughout the winter, despite the fact that their ears and the tips of their tails are sometimes frozen off. Omnivorous, opossums eat just about all animal and plant food that they can find, including mice, moles, young hares and rabbits, grasshoppers, crickets, moths, butterflies, berries, succulent plants, and grass.

Adult males weigh between 1.5 and 5 kg (3 to 11 lb.); females weigh between 1.5 and 3.5 kg (3 to 8 lb.). The coat is made up of short, but thick grey underfur and long, black- or white-tipped guard hairs. Albinos are not rare; brown opossums are relatively common.

Solitary outside of the mating season and during young-rearing times, opossums are preyed on by many carnivores, but the species continues to survive despite a high mortality rate. Much has been said about this animal's habit of "playing possum" when caught in the open by an enemy. It was at first thought that the behaviour was consciously motivated, but it has since been established that the death-like trance is involuntary, brought about by fear and resulting shock. When an

A LIVING FOSSIL

The muskrat-sized mountain beaver (*Aplodontia rufa*) is quite literally a living fossil. As such, it is probably Canada's most unique animal. The mountain beaver is *not* a beaver! It has no living close relatives, but its anatomy suggests that it is a descendant of the earliest known rodents, identified only by their fossils.

Although it is also muskrat-like in general appearance, this mammal has a somewhat stouter body and a tail so short that it is often entirely hidden by fur. It has flat feet that are more like those of the raccoons and bears, leaving tracks that reveal the outline of the entire foot; the toes are armed with long, rather pale, curved claws. Stripped of its coat, the mountain beaver's body looks more like that of a mole, being well muscled in the front, with heavy forelimbs, and less developed in the rear, its hindquarters and thighs seeming to be too weak for such an otherwise stout animal. Two anal glands produce a strong musky odour when the animal is alarmed, or during the breeding season. *Aplodontia*'s coat is made up of guard hairs that are greyish brown on top and along both flanks and pale grey on the undersides of the body. The thick undercoat is fine and slate grey. The average length of adult males is 35.7 cm (14 in.); females are about 20 per cent smaller. Adult weights vary from 1.0 to 1.5 kg (2.2 to 3.3 lb.).

▲ Mountain beaver

This underground-dwelling animal is found in Canada only in the extreme south-west corner of British Columbia. It is beaver-like to a certain extent in that it will chew down trees that are up to 3 cm (1.2 in.) thick on the stump, afterwards eating the leaves and some of the green bark; but it largely feeds on a wide variety of plants, tender roots, and fruits in season.

Breeding takes place only once a year during a five-week period beginning in February and ending in March. Litters of two to three young are usual after a gestation period of about 30 days. The newborns are born slightly furred, but they are blind and helpless at first. Two months later they emerge from the burrow and take their place in the mountain beaver colony, which is usually located in the moist forests of alpine areas.

opossum enters this tonic spasm condition, it immediately falls over, its eyes become glazed and its mouth gaping; breathing is extremely shallow. If the animal is picked up, its body hangs limply. Yet there must be some awareness in the cortex, for when the cause of the spasm is gone, the opossum immediately returns to normal metabolism.

▲ **Horned puffins** in breeding colours perch on a cliff edge in British Columbia. Distinguished from the Atlantic puffin of the East Coast by a differently coloured and shaped beak, this bird, like other puffins, nests in shallow burrows or on cliff sides.

In the coast biome, as in all other maritime zones, forest and ocean mammals and birds meet at the water's edge. In the south, raccoons, foxes, weasels, and other animals canvass the shore for prey or for the eggs of birds; farther north, grizzly and black bears haunt the shallows and river estuaries, especially during the salmon-spawning time. Offshore, whales and porpoises are often sighted, their tall dorsal fins at times cleaving the water right through flocks of water birds, none of which show concern as the huge mammals sail past.

Apart from the large numbers of inland birds that live in the coastal forests, the shores and the ocean itself are inhabited by many species of waterfowl, some only found in the region during winter, others year-round residents.

Trumpeter swans (*Cygnus buccinator*) with a wingspan of almost 3 m (9 ft.) breed inland on lakes, ponds, and rivers, but can be seen in winter at the mouths of rivers and creeks; Brant geese, Canada geese, snow geese, and white-fronted geese inhabit the region. So do eight species of gulls, including Bonaparte's and glaucous-winged. Guillemots, murrelets, auklets, and tufted puffins, Pacific, red-throated, and common loons, pelagic cormorants, northern fulmars, black-footed albatross, pink-footed shearwaters, and two kinds of petrels are only some of the species that inhabit the coast zone's shorelines and water at various seasons. Some species of albatross and petrels, and the fulmars, spend most of their time far out in the Pacific, but now and then move to off-shore waters.

Bald eagles (*Haliaeetus leucocephalus*) are numerous in this region of Canada. They nest in the coast forests and hunt the Pacific waters, feeding on a variety of live fish as well as dead fish that have drifted ashore. Osprey (*Pandion haliaetus*) are frequently sighted and the rare peregrine falcon (*Falco peregrinus*) is even seen on occasion.

▲ **Mature bald eagles** decorate an evergreen tree in western Canada during spring, when these large raptors tend to congregate before pairing in advance of the breeding season.

WATER IMAGES

◀ **The great blue heron** is the largest of our herons. It is widely distributed in southerly regions from Nova Scotia to British Columbia. It feeds on fish and frogs, spearing them with its long, sharp beak.

▲ **A glaucous-winged gull** sails the skies over Georgia Strait, British Columbia. Gulls are common on all Canadian coasts and are often found inland in great flocks.

▲ **A harp seal** rises to the surface. Adult and juvenile harp seals have long been hunted for their coats. Until recent times, annual kills ran into the hundred thousands. These marine mammals are still hunted today, but kills have been greatly reduced.

Victoria Falls, located below the ▶ Great Divide in Yoho National Park, British Columbia, is among our most spectacular cataracts.

▲ **A double-crested cormorant**
watches a herd of walrus. Ungainly
on land, walrus are agile, powerful
swimmers that use their long tusks
to dig up the molluscs on which they
feed.

▶ **Sandstone** has proven a good
medium for wind, sea and weather
sculpture in eastern Canada. Here,
on the coast of Quebec's Magdalen
Islands in the Gulf of St. Lawrence,
the rock has been carved into sharp
cliffs.

The elements have carved a vari- ▶
ety of "flower pots" on the shoreline
rocks along New Brunswick's Chig-
necto Bay.

▲ **Northern gannets** on Bonaventure Island, Quebec. Located 5 km (3 mi.) off the village of Percé, this island is home to one of the largest colonies of gannets in North America. Each year thousands of bird watchers travel by boat to the island to see the birds.

◀ **Cape St. Mary's, Newfoundland,** showing the rugged cliffs and some of the many gannets that colonize the rocks. Gannets feed on fish, diving on their prey like arrows from heights of up to 30 m (98 ft.).

▲ **The bull-frog** is heard over many of Canada's wetlands from spring to early autumn. Growing up to 20 cm (8 in.) long, this frog feeds on large insects and has been known to capture and eat small birds.

▲ **The purple shore-crab** is one of the most abundant crustaceans found on British Columbia's many rocky beaches. Measuring up to 4.5 cm (1.75 in.), these little crabs can remain out of the sea for long periods.

▲ **Crested rollers** that have travelled thousands of miles across the Pacific Ocean are turned into flying spume by the rocks that stud the coast of western Vancouver Island at Pacific Rim National Park.

▲ **In Burnaby Narrows**, British Columbia, low tide reveals a colourful carpet of salt-grass and seaweeds.

◄ **Starfish** are not fish, but members of the phylum Echinodermata, which among others includes sea-urchins. Most starfish live in shallow water, feeding mainly upon molluscs.

▲ **A bull sea lion** and his harem of cows sun themselves on the rocks of Cape St. James, the southernmost point of Kunghit Island, part of the Queen Charlotte Islands group. Sea lions are one of our largest seals and can be sighted almost anywhere off the coast of British Columbia.

Autumn-hued aspens flank the ▶ North Saskatchewan River in western Alberta.

WATER AND LIFE

6

THE TERRESTRIAL BIOSPHERE IS COMPOSED OF three major divisions: the *lithosphere* makes up the solid portions of the planet — the rocks and the earth; the *atmosphere* is the gassy mantle that surrounds the globe; and the *hydrosphere* contains all the water in the oceans, lakes, rivers, and below-ground reservoirs. Water covers approximately 73 per cent of the earth's surface and is the most abundant of all of those compounds necessary for the production and continuity of life. But less than 3 per cent of terrestrial water is fresh; all the rest is the salty fluid contained within the ocean basins.

In the cycle that distributes oceanic water to the land and returns it again to the sea, much of the precipitation falls back into the oceans and only a small proportion reaches the land. Of the somewhat less than 3 per cent of fresh water to be found on the terrestrial habitat at any one time, almost four-fifths remains largely inaccessible, locked away as ice in the North and South poles and in the many glaciers found in the Northern and Southern hemispheres. A further one-tenth of the land's supply is beyond reach in reservoirs that lie about 1 km (0.62 mi.) below the surface of the earth. On average, therefore, only about 0.33 per cent of the fresh water that reaches the earth is available for use by plants and animals. Nevertheless, this supply is more or less continuous. Oceanic water, freed of salt by evaporation, reaches the earth as rain or snow from the atmosphere and is used and recycled by plants and animals in a variety of ways.

The oceans occupy 71 per cent of the surface of the globe. Three of these vast bodies of salt water exert enormous influence on Canada's environment. The Pacific is the largest, encompassing almost 166 million km² (64 million sq. mi.); the Atlantic is next with almost 82 million km² (32 million sq. mi.); and the Arctic Ocean covers nearly 14 million km² (5.5 million sq. mi.).

In the beginning, millions of years ago, geological upheavals of the land created many vast, cup-like depressions that in time became filled with desalinated water sucked up as vapour from the prehistoric oceans and deposited on the earth as rain or snow. The birth of Canada's mountain ranges also created valleys and spillways along which rain coursed, forming rivers and streams that were — and still are — additionally fed during spring by alpine melt-waters. As a result, the oceans gave to Canada approximately one-third of all the fresh water currently

◄ **The setting sun** burnishes the waters of Lake Huron's Georgian Bay in the region known as Thirty Thousand Islands, one of Ontario's beauty spots.

▲ **Arctic char**

▲ **Atlantic cod**

▲ **Sockeye salmon**

▲ **Largemouth bass**

available in the world and they are at least partly responsible for the nation's climate.

Canada's ten major lakes together encompass a huge area: Lake Superior: 84 500 km^2 (32 629 sq. mi.); Lake Huron: 63 500 km^2 (24 520 sq. mi.); Great Bear Lake: 31 400 km^2 (12 125 sq. mi.); Great Slave Lake: 28 400 km^2 (10 966 sq. mi.); Lake Erie: 25 800 km^2 (9960 sq. mi.); Lake Winnipeg: 24 400 km^2 (9420 sq. mi.); Lake Ontario: 19 300 km^2 (7450 sq. mi.); Lake Athabasca: 7940 km^2 (3066 sq. mi.); Reindeer Lake: 6640 km^2 (2564 sq. mi.), and Lake Winnipegosis: 5530 km^2 (2135 sq. mi.). Besides these major bodies of fresh water, there are practically uncountable numbers of other lakes scattered across Canada as well as numerous rivers, streams, creeks, springs, and ponds.

Despite the fact that humans tend to think of the land as separate from the sea, these two principal ecosystems are indivisible; through the water cycle they combine to nurture all the living things found within the planet's biosphere. More than half of all the known, present-day vertebrate animals live in the oceans, including about 13 000 of the 22 000 species of fishes that inhabit the salt and fresh waters of the world. (There are approximately 190 native freshwater fish species.) Conversely, while in excess of 4500 species of mammals live in the terrestrial environment, only 117 kinds have been able to adapt to life in the seas. Additionally, countless numbers of invertebrates (animals without backbones) inhabit the world's oceanic and fresh waters, including bacteria, molluscs, worms, clams, crabs, shrimp, and crayfish, among many other species found variously in seas, lakes and rivers.

It is safe to say that in the ocean deeps live a great many animals that are still waiting to be identified, just as there are others that have been recognized and even named by science, but about whose biology little, if anything, is known. The mysterious hagfishes (family Myxinidae) clearly illustrate this gap in scientific knowledge. These strange, predatory and scavenging creatures belong to a group of prehistoric, jawless fishes known as *agnathans* (from the Greek *gnathos*: "jaws"), which are believed to have evolved more than 500 million years ago. Of these, only two kinds are known to exist today, the hagfishes and the lampreys (family Petromyzonidae). Both lack bony skeletons, their bodies being supported instead by cartilage — the fibrous, elastic tissue that in the majority of animals turns into bone after birth, except in those parts of the body where a cushioning effect is needed, as between ball-and-socket joints. Cartilaginous skeletons are common to sharks as well as to the agnathans.

In off-shore Canada, hagfishes are found in Pacific and Atlantic waters. They are eel-like in appearance, have naked skin, and are blind — or nearly so; they have four hearts, and can almost instantly fill a pail with slime when disturbed; their mouths are round and toothless, but they have teeth on their tongues; each has a tail fin, but no body fins; and they can actually tie themselves into knots! Additionally, as if these characteristics were not bizarre enough, hagfishes have only one nostril located on the top of the head; and they breathe through a series of hole-like gills, somewhat like sharks. Linnaeus believed that a young hagfish specimen he examined was not a fish at all, but a stomach worm, probably because it was recovered within the intestinal cavity of a conventional fish, for a hagfish fastens its sucker-like mouth on the body of a host, rasps with its tongue until it creates an opening, then slithers inside the unfortunate fish and slowly eats it from the inside out. Little is known about the reproductive habits of hagfish despite the fact that in 1864 the Academy of Science in Copenhagen, Denmark, offered a large reward to anyone able to discover the breeding behaviour of these fish. More than a century later, the prize has not been claimed.

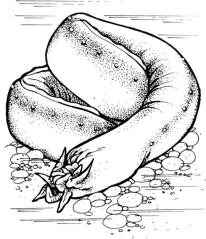

▲ **Pacific hagfish**

The great majority of fishes belong to the superclass of jawed vertebrates, the *gnathostomes*. These fish are found wherever there is water — even in hotsprings such as the Cave and Basin Hot Springs drainage system near Banff, Alberta. Some can sustain a temperature range from −2° to 45° C (28° to 113° F). Their habitats vary from fresh-water and oceanic shallows to the perpetually dark and cold regions of the oceans, submarine chasms such as those found in the Marianas Trench of the south-west Pacific, the deepest of which drops 11 km (6.8 mi.) below sea level.

Among the gnathostomes are the sharks, a number of species of which visit the waters off the coasts of Canada in all three oceans during the warmer seasons. These are the most feared predators, although it has more recently been established that the majority of shark attacks on humans are motivated by invasion of territory and disturbance of the animal itself, rather than a desire to feed on people. Included in Canadian waters are Greenland sharks (*Somniosus microcephalus*), found in the north Atlantic, and basking sharks, off the Pacific coast. The latter can reach a size of about 12 m (40 ft.), but, like the largest of all fish, the whale shark — said to reach 15 m (49 ft.) and found in warm seas — it feeds on planktonic animals. Blue sharks (*Prionace glauca*) frequent the Pacific and Atlantic seaboards and at least one great white shark (*Carcharodon carcharias*) was seen off the coast of Vancouver Island. Other sharks are found in the waters off the Grand Banks of Newfoundland, in the Arctic Ocean during summer, and along the entire British Columbia coast. No shark attacks on humans in Canadian waters have ever been reported.

The best-known group of marine mammals are the cetaceans (Latin: *cetus*, Greek: *ketos*, for "whale"), which incorporate all of the baleen

whales, the toothed whales, active hunters like the sperm whales, and all of the dolphins and porpoises, including the orcas, or so-called killer whales.

The blue whale is now an endangered species. In the past, blue whales attained a maximum length of 30.5 m (100 ft.) and a weight of 131.5 t (145 tons). Such exceptionally large whales are scarce today, or altogether absent due to extremely heavy whaling activities. Between 1920 and 1967, for example, whalers killed a total of more than 300 000 blue whales (an average of 6470 per year) world-wide. At a conservative estimate, the combined weight of all those giant mammals would have been 27 million t (30 million tons). The above figures take into account the unborn young inside harpooned blue whale females which, as newborns, measure 7 m (23 ft.) and weigh 1814 kg (4000 lb.).

As well as blue whales, a variety of other cetaceans live in Canadian waters at various seasons, but although sightings can be frequent at times on both the east and west coasts, the whales, porpoises, and dolphins are not nearly as numerous as they were even a decade ago. Despite the fact that a measure of protection has been extended to these animals by international agreement, whaling still continues, some nations killing as many whales of all species as they can fix in the sights of their harpoon guns, powerful weapons that launch an explosive projectile which bursts within a whale's body.

Eleven species of seals, sea lions, and walrus inhabit the oceans and coasts of Canada at various times. These too have been heavily hunted for many years, although most species of seals in Canada do not appear in danger of extinction. Walrus (family Odobenidae), however, due to active hunting during the fifteenth and sixteenth centuries, are no longer as plentiful as they once were. Tusks that measure between 23 and 66 cm (9 and 26 in.) in length and weigh up to 4 kg (9 lb.) were once eagerly sought for the worth of their ivory. The animal was also hunted for its hide and for the oil content of its fat — a large bull walrus may weigh as much as 1360 kg (2998 lb.).

Sea otters (*Enhydra lutris*), relatives of the river species and of the weasels, were once plentiful along the entire stretch of the British Columbia coast, but were exterminated in Canada by 1910. A few have been re-introduced, but the animal's continued survival is doubtful.

▲ **Wood ducks**, like this drake in full breeding plumage, are among the most beautiful waterfowl. Tree nesters, these ducks spend much time in woodland lakes and streams.

◀ **Steam** envelops evergreens in British Columbia's Liard River Hot Springs Provincial Park, located in the north-central part of the province.

Overleaf **Walruses** often haul out as a group after feeding and lie close-packed ▶ on shoreline rocks or beaches, their reddish coats contrasting with the virtual forest of white tusks.

▲ **River otters** are distributed across Canada, except for the prairies and northeastern regions of the Northwest Territories. Preying mostly on fish, river otters are playful animals that enjoy "tobogganing" down mud and snow slides.

Despite the many differences that are to be encountered within marine and terrestrial animals, there are a great many similarities in both the biology and the topography of the two environments. Could the oceans be emptied, it would be clearly evident that the land and the bottom of the sea are geologically identical. Within the ocean deeps are to be found great plains, canyons, and mountains taller than Everest, the land's highest point. Some of the mountains are concealed beneath the water, others rise thousands of metres above the surface. Mauna Kea, in Hawaii, for example, rises 4202 m (13 786 ft.) above the surface of the Pacific from a base that lies 3658 m (12 000 ft.) below

Virginia Falls, one of the many spectacular sights offered by Nahanni ▶ National Park, Northwest Territories, thunders down-canyon for 96 m (316 ft.), a drop almost twice that of Niagara Falls.

the waters. The Pacific Ocean also contains canyons that are deeper than the mountains are tall.

The most disparate feature of the oceanic world is the quality and chemistry of its water, a medium that as far as can presently be determined has remained unchanged for some two billion years. This is a relatively contemporary discovery that would have confused early geologists, who believed that sea water began as fresh water and slowly accumulated its component salts from minerals washed into the ocean following the erosion of the land. As it now appears, such erosion occurs, but it has little effect on the composition of sea water, which maintains an average of 35 parts of salts per 1000 parts of water, such proportions being more readily encountered in the open seas at a depth of about 300 m (984 ft.) than near the surface. Surface salt levels vary considerably. In the Arctic Ocean, diluted by melting ice water in summer, salinity is low, as it is near the estuaries of large rivers, such as the mouth of the Fraser in British Columbia and the Columbia in Oregon.

Sodium chloride, which we use for cooking, makes up about three-quarters of ocean salt, but there are many other kinds of salts present in sea water. All are absolutely vital to the health of the marine environment, even if some are only present in such minute quantities that they are almost impossible to detect. It is even likely that some salts, present only as merest traces, have not yet been identified, a possibility that may at least partly account for the fact that no matter how hard and long biochemists have worked in order to try and create sea water in the laboratory, all have failed. Humans simply cannot make the stuff! Indeed, if it is kept in test tubes for more than a few hours, it spoils; it putrefies, just like a piece of meat that has been left lying in the sun.

In chemistry, the term *salt* relates to any one of a variety of chemical compounds that result when one or more hydrogen atoms of an acid are replaced by elements or groups of elements that are composed of negative and positive ions and that usually dissolve in water. These reactions occur in the oceans and are responsible for the production of the different salts that give the water its distinctive properties. Such formulas are well understood, but thus far they have not helped to explain why ocean water seems to be actually alive, appearing to be a

◀ **An aerial view of Percé Rock** and its bird colony. Percé Rock is a well-known landmark on the Gaspé Peninsula, Quebec.

OVERLEAF   **The Queen Charlotte Islands**, British Columbia, have long been ▶ famed for their rugged, often eerie landscapes, but although mountain views often dominate, scenes such as this, taken during an overcast day at the Louscome Inlet tidal flats, exhibit a more sombre, yet serene view.

sort of plasma that must be constantly recycled by the plants and animals that live in the medium if it is to remain viable. Significantly, and supporting the theory we are inherently linked to the sea, the blood of humans and other warm-blooded animals contains something in the order of 90 per cent of the same salts that are found in ocean water. We live on land, but wherever we go we carry with us a supply of oceanic chemicals.

The communities of plants and animals found in marine and fresh water are regulated by the same biological interactions as their terres-

trial counterparts, albeit the species, sizes, and adaptations are quite different. Nevertheless, water plants are eaten by herbivorous animals, which are in turn eaten by carnivorous animals, which are themselves the prey of larger carnivores, or the victims of bacterial and viral attacks. The "grasses" of the water world are the algae, which range from microscopic, single-celled forms, to plants that are many metres long. Trees are not represented in the world of water, but seaweeds, waterlilies, and many other forms of leafed plants grow in marine and fresh waters. Insects are found in fresh water, in some instances being

THE OCEAN ENVIRONMENT

1 Cormorant	8 Salmon	15 Bladder wrack
2 Herring gulls	9 Plume worm	16 Dolphin
3 Sanderlings	10 Jellyfish	17 Killer whale
4 Barnacles	11 Sea urchin	18 Squid
5 Anemone	12 Sea cucumber	19 Octopus
6 Phytoplankton	13 Starfish	20 Herring
7 Cod	14 Clams	21 Dogfish

NOT TO SCALE

A FISH THAT WAS ONCE USED AS A CANDLE

The candlefish (*Thaleichthys pacificus*) contains so much body oil that, when dried, it can be lit and will burn like a rather smoky and smelly candle, especially if it has been tightly rolled. Historically it has been, and continues to be, a rich source of fat consumed in quantity by British Columbia natives. Additionally, this fish — its common name, "eulachon" or "oolichan", derives from the Chinook language — was once used extensively as a source of illumination and food by early European explorers.

A sea-dwelling member of the smelt family (the Osmeridae), the candlefish annually spawns in the waters of B.C. rivers from mid-March to mid-May. In countless thousands it migrates in offshore waters along the Pacific Coast from California's Klamath River all the way north to the Bering Sea for the first two or three years of its life and then, in countless thousands, the eulachon migrate towards the land to enter the rivers where, after mating, females lay about 25 000 eggs. Despite being heavily preyed on in the Pacific by seals, salmon,

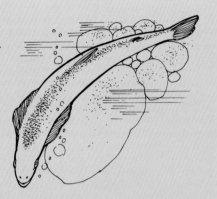

▲ **Candlefish**

and other fishes, and on land by humans and mammals such as bears, otter, and mink, as well as by fresh-water fish, the silvery-grey little eulachons (length: 23 to 30 cm [9 to 12 in.]) continue to prosper, their ability to do so being due to the large number of eggs deposited on sandy or gravelly river bottoms by the females. If every egg laid by 1000 eulachons were to produce one fry, and if every one were to survive, 25 million fish would result. It has been estimated that only about 2 per cent of the total produce fry. Nevertheless, this survival rate will yield 50 000 young fish per 1000 females each year.

the larvae of terrestrial species, in others living their entire lives in lake, pond, or river. In Canada, predators in both mediums include fish, mammals, reptiles such as snakes and turtles, and amphibians such as frogs and salamanders, and there are numerous birds from highly specialized divers such as cormorants and loons, leaf striders, such as coots, to stilt-legged, long-beaked fish eaters such as herons, and sturdy paddlers such as ducks and geese.

Belted kingfishers are widely distributed in Canada. Expert fishers, ▶ they inhabit regions at the edge of fresh or salt water.

THE WESTERN MOUNTAINS

7

THE VAST REGION OCCUPIED BY THE WESTERN mountains also illustrates the problems that face those who seek to establish the boundaries of biomes and ecosystems. Here, field biologists must deal with polar-like conditions at high elevations, tundra-like plants and animals above the tree line, two separate biomes at lower elevations and several transition zones, as illustrated in the life zones chart (page 170). These tiers of life are hardly ever sharply separated in tidy, straight lines. Instead, they are haphazardly influenced by climate, soil, and topography, circumstances that combine to create irregular boundaries and that attract those species of plants and animals best suited to each particular habitat.

In the western mountains, many of the highest peaks remain snow- or ice-covered year round and ice-age glaciers are common. Such regions are lifeless and akin to the polar environment; below them, the alpine biome begins. This natural system is quite similar to the Arctic tundra and blends with the subalpine biome at lower-elevation transition zones. The subalpine is characterized by alpine firs, Engelmann spruce, lodgepole pine, and a variety of other trees, shrubs and plants. At tree-line in the upper transition zones, stunted evergreens blend with tundra-like vegetation at altitudes that vary from about 600 to 2000 m (1969 to 6560 ft.), depending on shelter or exposure.

Trees of the north-western boreal biome include those distributed elsewhere in Canada within this habitat and, additionally, western white spruce (*Picea glauca*), first described in 1927 from specimens found in the Alberta mountains. Before this, the western variety had been considered a local form of the white spruce. This tree reaches a height of 24 m (80 ft.) and a diameter of 120 cm (4 ft.). It has a narrow crown and its branches usually extend almost to the ground.

Dwarf junipers (*Juniperus communis*) are common at almost all life-bearing altitudes in this biome as, indeed, they are in most other locations in Canada, for this shrubby tree has the widest distribution of all plants within the Northern Hemisphere. Its blue-black berries supply feed for a variety of animals and birds and are used as spices in many kitchens of the world.

At elevations that are below approximately 1400 m (4600 ft.) and all the way down to valley bottoms grows devil's club (*Oplopanax horridus*), which, as its second scientific name implies, is indeed "horrid".

◄ **Autumn colour** in the Yukon Territory's Ogilvie Mountains.

OVERLEAF **This part of the Miette Range**, Jasper National Park, Alberta, is ▶ eroded and subject to landslides.

Standing almost 2 m (6.5 ft.) tall and mixing with other shrubs, this plant is plentifully equipped with long, sharp, yellowish spines. Unwary climbers may grasp its stems for an upward assist only to be stabbed by a multitude of thorns. *Oplopanax*, however, has redeeming features: in June it is resplendent with clusters of white flowers, and by August bright red berries decorate the plant and are eaten by birds and small animals, such as mice, that seem to be impervious to the shrub's spiky defences.

Other plants found in these regions include: cotton grass perennials that conceal their tiny flowers under a pure-white head of cottony fibres and which, in such places as Nahanni National Park, in the Northwest Territories, can cover a flat area to such effect that from a distance it appears as if a freak summer snowstorm had blanketed the terrain; long-leaved sundew (*Drosera anglica*), an insectivorous little plant with bristly, light burgundy leaves; several species of sedum (*Sedum acre*) which range from the boreal up to the subalpine system and produce scarlet or yellow flowers; yellow monkey flower (*Mimulus guttatus*), plants that in blossom spread a spectacular, butter-bright carpet in wet locations of the high mountains; and coralroots (*Corallorhiza* spp.), so named because their knobby roots form masses that resemble marine coral. Several kinds of coralroots are found in the boreal and subalpine biomes. They are saprophytic, taking their food from dead plant material, and have small scales instead of leaves; they produce orchid-shaped flowers of various colours. These and many other small plants and shrubs abound in the mountain boreal and the subalpine systems and transition zones.

▲ **Striped coralroot** is one of several varieties of this orchid-like plant found in Canada. It is saprophytic and has small scales instead of leaves.

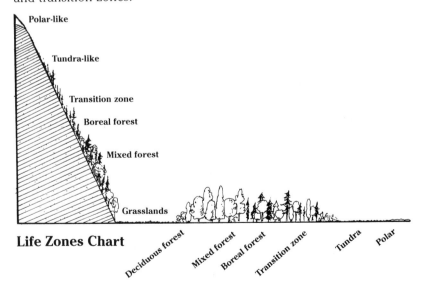

Life Zones Chart

Although many of the major mammals and birds that live in these natural regions are of the same species found elsewhere in Canada, there are a number of purely western species that inhabit the boreal-subalpine biomes and transition zones.

The mountain goat (*Oreamnos americanus*) is a typical boreal mountain species. It is *not* a goat, however, despite its name, but is related to a small group of mountain antelopes, such as the chamois (*Rupicapra rupicapra*) of the European Alps. Helped by hooves the undersides of which are equipped with what amount to suction cups, the mountain goat is perhaps the most adept alpinist of all of Canada's mammals. More agile than a circus high-wire performer, it can scramble up sharp, rocky inclines to the very peaks of some of the steepest mountains.

Sharing the mountain goat's range at somewhat lower elevations is the Dall's sheep (*Ovis dalli*), named after American naturalist William H. Dall (1845–1927). A somewhat smaller and more slender relative of the southern-dwelling bighorn sheep, the Dall's is a close mountain-climbing competitor of the mountain goat. Its eyes have a golden iris and the oval, horizontal pupils common to the sheep family. Rams may attain a weight of about 90 kg (200 lb.).

Pikas (*Ochotona princeps*) are attractive little members of the order Lagomorpha, which includes hares and rabbits, although superficially they do not resemble their larger, long-legged relatives as much as they do guinea pigs. There are ten species found in Canada, two of which live in the subalpine and boreal biomes.

More cougar, or mountain lions (*Felis concolor*), are found in the mountain habitats than elsewhere in Canada, for east of the Rockies these magnificent felines have either been entirely eliminated or they are rare. The cougar is North America's most specialized mammalian land predator, having the agility and armaments of the domestic cat, but attaining the size and power of a leopard. Large males have measured almost 2.5 m (8 ft.) in length from nose to tip of the long tail and have weighed 102 kg (225 lb.).

The cougar's thick tail, which may reach 90 cm (3 ft.) in length, is primarily used as a balancing organ during the big cat's prodigious leaps, or while climbing rocks and trees. Solitary except during mating times, or when females are raising their young, the mountain lion lives in a selected territory that is marked by fecal mounds and urine sprays,

▲ **Round-leaved sundews** are 10 to 23 cm (4 to 9 in.) tall. Their leaves are covered with reddish glandular hairs which exude droplets of sticky juice. The juice traps insects which are then slowly absorbed by the plant.

OVERLEAF **Dall's sheep** migrate over barren slopes to reach lush grazing at a ▶ higher altitude. These sheep are more slender and a lighter colour than bighorn sheep.

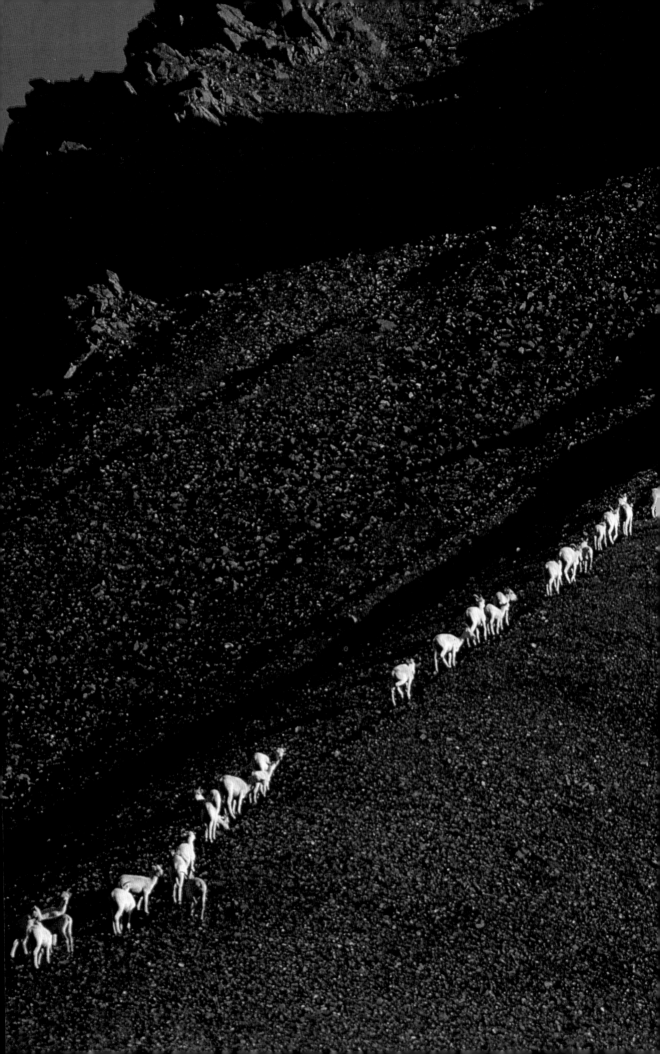

▲ **Cougar**

warnings that keep competing cougars away, or which encourage a male or female during breeding seasons. Female cougars become sexually receptive several times a year if they do not mate and become pregnant during an early oestrus (heat), although there appear to be two peak birth seasons: in late winter or early summer.

Gestation time varies between 90 and 96 days. As few as one kitten, or as many as six are born, but an average litter will be more likely to contain between two and four young. New-born kittens weigh 300 to 400 g (10.5 to 14 oz.); they are born with their eyes closed and are covered by black-spotted, woolly coats; their stubby tails are adorned by black markings that somewhat resemble the rings around the tails of raccoons. The kittens are helpless until their eyes open when they are about ten days old, but after they are gifted with sight they begin to crawl about the den, which may be in a mountain cave, in a crevice among rocks, or in a burrow dug by the mother if no better shelter is available.

Six weeks after birth the little cougars begin to eat meat brought to them by the mother. They are fully weaned at three months. Now, or at most a month later, they follow the mother and eat her kills, although they usually remain hidden while she is actually hunting.

The mountain boreal extends in a north-westerly direction from a point above the Rocky Mountain foothills of Alberta and continues through northern British Columbia, the extreme, western edge of the Northwest Territories, and the Yukon Territory, thence north-westward to Alaska. Within this part of the vast boreal lies some of the most spectacular mountain scenery to be found in Canada, including that encountered in such national parks as Jasper, in Alberta, Nahanni, in the Northwest Territories, and Kluane, in the Yukon Territory, the latter perhaps best typifying the natural admixtures contained by this remarkable ecological system.

The dominant topographic features of the park are two major mountain chains that run parallel to each other in a south-easterly direction. The Kluane Range presents a vista of peaks that rise for some 2500 m (8200 ft.) and are only interrupted by a few large valleys. The valleys are themselves cut by a number of major rivers, three of which are glacier-fed. West of this region lies a narrow trough, the Duke Depression, that separates the Kluane Range from the Icefield Range. This depression contains a number of valleys and large plateaus out of which protrude the tongues of glaciers.

The main feature of the Icefield Range is Mount Logan, at 5951 m (19 524 ft.) Canada's tallest peak. Other towering mountains are St.

THE WESTERN MOUNTAINS

1 Red crossbill	**7** Pocket gopher	**13** Common alpine butterfly
2 Varied thrush	**8** Pika	**14** Bobcat
3 Northern goshawk	**9** Calliope hummingbird	**15** Deer mouse
4 Violet tail	**10** Juniper	**16** Rubber boa
5 White spruce	**11** Long-tailed weasel	
6 Elk	**12** Garter snake	

NOT TO SCALE

Elias, almost 5500 m (18 045 ft.) high; then, in succession: Mount Lucania, King Peak, Mount Steele, Mount Wood, and a number of others, the lowest being Mount Hubbard at 4577 m (15 016 ft.). Forming a massive base for these spectacular mountains is an ice- and snow-covered plateau dating back to the ice ages, which reaches heights of between 2500 and 3000 m (8200 and 9850 ft.).

Snow and ice cover more than half of Kluane's 22 015 km² (8500 sq. mi.), a remarkable region that contains a number of valley glaciers. Among these are Steele, Seward, Hubbard, Logan, Donjek, and Kaskawulsh, all of them imposing, permanently frozen icings. Glaciers move at a slow rate, but the Steele is unusual in that at intervals it moves at an especially fast rate. Dubbed the "Galloping Glacier", it ran downhill for 10 km (6 mi.) in one four-month period during the late 1960s.

The different plant biomes are well defined, but widely scattered in the park. Polar-like areas are found at many levels because of the influence that the glaciers exert on an environment that ranges from alpine tundra to subalpine and boreal, but which also contains extensive marshlands and sand dunes. Tundra vegetation includes lichens, dwarf willows and birches, low shrubs, and wildflowers as well as mosses and fungi; these plants occur at altitudes that vary from 1200 to 1800 m (3900 to 5900 ft.) throughout the park. Timber-line is located at approximately 1200 m (3900 ft.), but the irregular ascent of gnarled trees varies in accordance with temperature and soil conditions. Examples of the prairie-grasslands biome are found in valley bottoms as well as on some south and south-west facing slopes. Here grow such plants as wheat grass, bluegrass, pasture sedgewort, and sedges.

Kluane is home to North America's largest subspecies of moose (*Alces alces gigas*), with bulls weighing as much as 540 kg (1200 lb.).

Grizzly bears abound in the park; some of them attain a weight of 535 kg (1180 lb.) and a length of 2 m (6.5 ft.). *All* bears can be dangeous; they have killed a number of humans in the past and during more recent times, but the grizzly, because of its size and enormous power, and because its behaviour can be very unpredictable, is undoubtedly the most dangerous of all Canadian mammals. Whereas one grizzly may run the moment it scents or sees a human intruder, another may charge. Then again, some bears will charge and stop several metres away from a person, snort and huff, and then back away; others will carry the charge through into an attack that is more likely

◀ **Donjek Glacier**, Kluane National Park, Yukon Territory. In the foreground a thick spread of willow herb splashes a rocky slope with magenta.

▲ Bear pawprints

▲ Bear tracks

than not to end in the death of the victim. Grizzly bears are not good climbers, but a person who seeks refuge in a tree should not stop climbing until he or she is at least 5 m (16 ft.) above the ground. By taking a run at a tree and at the same time reaching upwards with a huge long-clawed forepaw, grizzlies have managed to pull down people who were perched 3 m (9 ft.) above the ground.

Black bears (*Ursus americanus*) while less pugnacious than grizzlies, have also injured and killed humans. On the whole, however, black-bear attacks are less likely to cause death. Nevertheless, because these bears are excellent climbers and can gallop at speeds of 40 km (25 mi.) an hour, running away is less than useless, for predatory animals are encouraged to chase when a person runs. The best tactic to employ when you sight either a black or a grizzly bear is to walk backwards slowly and quietly, putting as much space between you and the bear as possible. If danger is imminent, and trees are nearby, safety can be attained by climbing high; however, because black bears are such excellent climbers, potential victims should select a tree large enough to sustain their weight, but too weak to support the bulk of a heavy bear, and too thin for it to climb! For these reasons, visitors in bear country should afford these animals plenty of room and treat them with the utmost respect.

THE COLUMBIA BIOME

The Columbia River, which flows for nearly 2000 km (1200 mi.) to empty into the Pacific Ocean off the coast of Oregon in the United States, is one of the major features of this irregularly shaped British Columbia biome. Other characteristics include three major mountain ranges, a variety of lakes and somewhat lesser rivers, icefields, and many lush valleys. Indeed, of all the vegetation systems found in Canada, this is the most complex and difficult to delineate, for it does not travel in an easily discernible pattern and it is interrupted frequently by the subalpine biome at various elevations. Because of this, many zones of transition occur in the Columbia biome; and a number of the trees found here also grow in different locations of British Columbia and western Alberta, although they may be taller and of wider diameter in some areas, and may inhabit higher or lower elevations in others.

Such botanical features are, in fact, common to all of the mountain regions of western Canada. Alpine and subalpine biomes occur wherever the mountains rise high enough to be influenced by colder temperatures, while at middle altitudes, along the lower slopes, and in the valleys, species common to a number of other plant systems are likely to be encountered.

The Columbia biome is characterized by five major species of trees.

The western white pine (*Pinus monticola*), one of the tallest ever-greens of this zone, reaches a maximum height of 34 m (110 ft.) and a diameter of more than 1 m (40 in.). Its needles are stiff and sharply pointed and occur in bundles of five; its cones may reach a length of 25 cm (10 in.). This pine also grows on the Pacific mainland coast as well as on Vancouver Island. Within the Columbia biome it may be found up to an altitude of 1000 m (3280 ft.); elsewhere it rarely climbs above 750 m (2460 ft.).

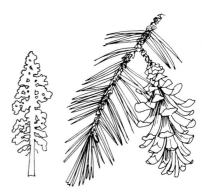

▲ **Western white pine**

Another tall tree of the biome is the western red cedar (*Thuja plicata*). It attains a height of 60 m (200 ft.) and a diameter of 250 cm (8 ft.). This species prefers moist, deep, well-drained soil and favours cool slopes and shady gulches where it may grow singly or in well-spaced groups; it is seldom found in pure stands.

The two Thuja species found in Canada and the United States, although called cedars, belong to a group known botanically as *Arbor-vitae*, a Latin term meaning "tree of life". There are only six known species; the other four are native to China, Japan, and Korea. The true cedars belong to the genus Cedrus; none are native to North America.

▲ **Western red cedar**

The *Arbor-vitae* owes its name to the fact that during the winter of 1535–36 it saved the lives of some of the members of Jacques Cartier's second and ill-fated expedition to the New World. By early winter, the French explorers were suffering from scurvy, a dietary disorder caused by a lack of vitamin C that inflicts on its sufferers extreme weakness, spongy gums, and haemorrhages. Untreated, scurvy is fatal.

Writing about that winter, Cartier noted: "Sometimes we were con-strained to bury some of the dead under the snow because we were not able to dig graves for them, the ground being so hard frozen and we so weak."

At that time, medical science could not account for scurvy, nor could the European doctors of the day find a treatment for it. But the New World natives had discovered a cure! Noting the symptoms among Cartier's men, a number of whom had died by this time, the Iroquois advised the French to eat raw the inner layer of the white cedar's bark. That the natives suggested the *Arbor-vitae* bark as a scurvy cure was a matter of choice, for the sap of all trees contains vitamin C in varying amounts, depending on season. In winter, sap is more readily available from evergreens because the winter hardening process continues to promote growth in such species.

Following the advice, Cartier and his surviving crew for six days ingested quantities of the pulpy cambium layer that lies beneath the tree's outer bark, stripping a cedar that, as Cartier noted, was "as big

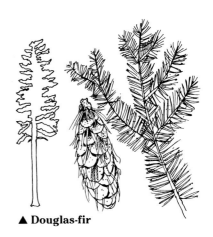

▲ **Douglas-fir**

as any oak in France". The treatment saved their lives and when they returned to France they took with them a number of white-cedar seedlings, the first species of Thuja to be introduced to Europe. Two hundred years later the tree's life-saving properties were immortalized by Linnaeus.

The third major tree species of the Columbia biome is the western larch (*Larix occidentalis*). It attains a height of 55 m (180 ft.) and a diameter of 125 cm (4 ft.), but is confined to the more southerly part of the biome. It reaches altitudes of between 550 and 1220 m (1800 and 4000 ft.). The trunk is slender and clear of branches for most of its length, a characteristic that in those places where the hemlock grows in pure stands, creates an understory that is roomy, shady and easy to traverse and where grow mosses, lichens and a number of small flowering plants.

The western hemlock (*Tsuga heterophylla*) is another large tree found in the Columbia. It attains a height of 50 m (160 ft.) and a diameter of 1.2 m (4 ft.). It occurs in wet regions throughout the interior and in the coastal forests of British Columbia. It is encountered in pure stands at heights of up to 1500 m (4920 ft.), but at lower elevations it tends to form mixed stands with Douglas-firs, red cedars, and Sitka spruce.

The fifth major species of this biome is the blue Douglas-fir. The inland variety (var. *glauca*) reaches a height of 90 m (295 ft.) and a diameter of 4.5 m (15 ft.). This species is found mostly in the southern part of the biome, but it reaches as far north as Babine and Stuart lakes in a region between the Omineca and Hazelton mountains known as the Topley Valley.

Interspersed with the major tree species are birches, poplars, cottonwoods, alders, willows, dwarf and mountain junipers, a variety of shrubs and plants, mosses, lichens, and many species of fungi.

In addition to the river after which this biome takes its name, many lakes, other rivers, creeks, springs and mountain meltwaters maintain a high moisture level in the entire region during the frost-free seasons and attract a wide variety of mammals, birds and insects, including dragonflies and damselflies. Belonging to the order Odonata, these large insects, which have a wingspread of between 7 and 11 cm (2.75 and 4 in.), are especially abundant in this biome, although they are almost equally plentiful throughout the other temperate zones of

This beautiful mushroom is highly poisonous. Known as fly agaric or fly ▶ poison amanita, it may be bright red, orange or yellow.

▲ **A damselfly** rests on a dry cat-tail leaf. The aquatic larvae prey on a variety of bottom dwellers; adults eat many kinds of small flying insects.

our continent and elsewhere in the world, especially within tropical habitats.

Damselflies have been grouped in the suborder Zygoptera and are represented in North America by 12 families, while dragonflies belong to the suborder Anisoptera and are represented by 6 families. Both groups contain some of our most colourful and graceful insects whose members prey on a wide variety of biting insects, including mosquitoes, horse and bot flies, deer flies, blackflies and others.

Distinguishing between the two suborders is simple: dragonflies are larger than their relatives; they are strong fliers with more robust bodies and longer, wider wings than those of the damsels; when at rest, dragonflies always hold their wings in the horizontal position. During fine weather, these insects are almost always on the wing, at times alighting to rest, but most often doing so only after they have captured an insect, when they will settle almost anywhere, including on a human's coat or hat, in order to devour their prey.

Damselflies are slim-bodied and they have more slender wings, which are always folded vertically, over the back, when the insects are at rest. These predators are usually found in the vicinity of water. By and large, outside of mating, damselflies take to the air only to hunt.

Mating of both suborders occurs on the wing after the male clasps the female by the head and transfers a sperm capsule to her as she is being towed through the air. According to the species, dragonfly females lay their eggs on the surface of the water, on the leaves of aquatic vegetation, or within the tissues of some plants. Damselfly females always lay their eggs inside the tissues of aquatic plants, either above or below the level of the water.

After hatching, most nymphs, or larvae, spend from autumn to the following spring or summer in the water, undergoing as many as 15 nymphal stages of growth, a unique aspect of which is a lower "lip", a long and hinged labium used for hunting aquatic prey. Normally folded and fitted over the upper jaw, the extra-long lip shoots out when a nymph is within striking distance of its prey, grasps the insect, the larva, or even small fish, and draws the live food into the mouth, somewhat like a chameleon uses its tongue to secure its food.

After spending up to a year in the water, the nymph climbs up a plant stem, by now unable to conceal the dragon or damselfly shape beneath its outer covering. After some time in the sunlight, the nymphal skin splits and the adult insect emerges. Sitting on the stem while waiting for the sun to dry its wrinkled wings, the insect rotates its head from side to side, its compound eyes evidently already searching the environment for possible prey, or for danger. In due course the wings

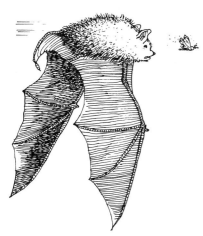

▲ **Little brown bat**

dry and become stretched, gossamer appendages that are heavily veined, resembling rather fine silk mesh. The insect then soars into space, an expert flyer right from the start.

Dragonflies and damselflies themselves serve as food for many species of birds, but there always seem to be enough of them roaming the forests, grasslands, and waterways to bring relief to those animals and humans that are being pestered by the blood-sucking flies.

Insects, including dragonflies, serve as food for a variety of birds, other insects and mammals. Raccoons, skunks, foxes, coyotes, and even wolves eat many kinds of flies and beetles in addition to their more usual foods. During grasshopper season, for instance, wild canids snap up as many of these insects as they can find, evidently enjoying them much as humans do when they snack on peanuts or olives. At times, however, the wild dogs pay for their love of grasshoppers when they become victims of a parasitic gut worm (*Physaloptera rara*), the larva of which may be carried by grasshoppers, crickets, and cockroaches. *Physaloptera* larvae travel to the lower intestines of the host and there attach themselves, feeding on the blood and juices of the animal. If infestations are not severe, the host is not seriously incapacitated, but when many worms are present, the parasites can severely weaken a wolf, coyote, fox, or any other mammal given to eating the larva-carrying insects.

One of the Columbia's smallest insect-eating mammals is the little brown bat (*Myotis lucifugus*), a pygmy insect-eater that measures a maximum of 9 cm (3.5 in.), has a wing spread of 23 cm (9 in.), and weighs a maximum of 12 g (0.4 oz.). This species is found across all of Canada's treed regions with the exception of the northern transition zone and is plentiful in the Columbia and other western biomes because of the longer frost-free seasons at lower elevations and the abundance of insects.

The little brown bat often goes unnoticed as it travels through the night sky with the typical reeling flight adopted by all bats. Like its relatives everywhere, the little brown bat has had some very bad press. It is said to fly into the hair of women and there to become entangled; it is linked with witches and evil and, more recently, is often blamed for outbreaks of rabies. Another myth claims that bats have poor eyesight, a fable maintained to this day by the expression "blind as a bat". In fact, bats can see in daylight and at night.

Because it is so small, the little brown bat can take up temporary residence between spring and autumn in the attics of dwellings, churches, and outbuildings, its squeaks and flutterings often causing distress to the human occupants. Such bats can, indeed, be a nuisance, but since many of them migrate southward in autumn, most property-owners in more northerly areas of Canada can prevent their return the following spring by closing the openings through which the unwanted lodgers gain entry.

A widely held belief has it that bats prey only on mosquitoes, but although numbers of these insects are caught and eaten, most North American bats prey heavily on moths.

It has been known for many years that bats navigate and find their prey by means of sonar-like echolocation. When in flight, they emit a continuous series of high-frequency cries up to 50 000 vibrations per second, that are far beyond the range of the human ear. The returning echoes made when the sounds strike trees, wires, or any other obstruction are picked up by the bat's ears and so it is able to avoid obstacles as numerous as a succession of closely spaced wires strung across a laboratory. Hunting bats scan the darkness by emitting a series of lower-frequency squeaks. When these bounce back from the body of a moth, the flying mammal zeroes in on its target.

With such an efficient hunting system, it would seem that bats ought to be so successful that they would soon eliminate their prey. Not so! Moths, over the millennia, have developed rows of sound-detection organs on both sides of their bodies. Unlike the hearing organs of other animals, however, the sounds picked up by the "ears" of a moth are not synchronized in the brain, but work independently of each other, transmitting vibrations (rather than actual sound) to the insect's brain.

When the sounds made by a flying bat are detected by either the right or left hearing organs of a moth, they cause the vibrations to register instantly on either the left or the right side of its brain. If the bat is approaching from the right, for example, the vibrations are picked up only by the right side of the insect's brain and vice versa. This unusual hearing arrangement enables the moth to determine the direction of its enemy's approach, allowing the insect to take evasive action. But if the bat is approaching from the front, or pursuing from the rear, the ears on both side of the insect's body simultaneously register the enemy's approach. In such cases, instead of dodging left or right, out of the path of attack, the moth folds its wings and drops like a stone to the ground. Such a tactic may have caused many early bats to starve, for, concealed in grass, or within the forest understory, a moth is perfectly safe. But then, with Nature's usual ingenuity, the bat "invented" the science of ballistics! Computing the prey's angle of descent by means of its echolocation, the bat is able to swoop downwards, at the last instant turning the membrane joining its hind legs to its tail into a scoop that traps the falling moth. Undoubtedly bats must miss their

▲ **Stonecrop** is found throughout the Pacific northwest. It forms dense mats in some areas and grows in clumps in others.

targets frequently when using this technique, but they catch a good proportion of their meals this way nevertheless. When hunting other smaller insects, however, bats catch them by mouth, snapping them out of the air with ease.

Seventeen species of bats inhabit Canada between the spring and autumn. The largest is the hoary bat (*Lasiurus cinereus*); it measures up to 15 cm (6 in.) in length, has a wingspan of 44 cm (17 in.), and is found across southern Canada, extending northwards only in Alberta to reach the southernmost part of the Northwest Territories. The smallest includes the little brown, the mouse-eared, and the fringed bats.

Bats are the world's only mammals capable of sustaining true flight — flying lemurs, phalangers, and flying squirrels do not actually fly, but glide downwards for relatively long distances after scrambling to high launch vantages. True flight has only been attained by four kinds of terrestrial animals: the prehistoric reptilian pterosaurs, long extinct, the birds, the insects, and the bats.

In order to attain flight, ancestral bats developed wings that consisted of two layers of skin anchored between the extra-long fingers of each "hand" and running downwards to include the tail. Only the thumbs are free; complete with business-like claws, the digits project out of the wings at points that would nearly coincide with the "wrists" of other mammals.

A bat uses its thumb claws for locomotion during climbing and for turning around while roosting, when it hangs upside down, gripping a support with its clawed feet. Then too, in order to empty bladder or bowels without soiling itself, a bat turns upright and hangs by its thumb claws, a position that a female must also adopt when about to give birth. At such a time, hanging by her thumbs, she folds her tail membrane forward and makes a purse with it. The single infant bat is delivered into the purse when it emerges into its darkened world. Thereafter the bat mother tends her infant much as do all other mammals, except that she once again hangs upside down to do so. Soon after birth, a young bat climbs up its mother's body to reach one of the two teats located on her chest. When nursing or resting, the young bat clings tightly to its mother's body fur.

For the first three or four days after an infant is born, every time that the female must fly out of shelter to hunt she must carry the baby with her. The little bat then hangs crossways on the underside of its mother, its mouth clamped to a teat, its clawed feet gripping tightly to the far side of her body. In this way, the passenger does not upset the female's flight balance. After the infant becomes strong enough to support itself in the nursery, the mother is freed of her burden when she goes to hunt.

That a tiny mammal can exhibit such feats of endurance is remarkable. New-born bats weigh about 2.5 g (0.08 oz.) and measure some 48 mm (2 in.); these figures represent approximately one-fourth of the mother's weight and almost one-half of her length. In human terms, a mother weighing 55 kg (121 lb.) and measuring 1.67 m (5.5 ft.) would have to carry an infant weighing 14 kg (30 lb.) and measuring 83 cm (32.7 in.) while she was engaging in intense physical activity for prolonged periods.

Young bats grow rapidly. At three weeks they can fly, and by the following spring they are sexually mature.

▲ **The roly-poly hoary marmot** has been nicknamed the "whistler" because of its shrill call, which carries a long way.

Other mammals of this biome include the majority of those encountered in other western habitats and some species that are also found across Canada. But there is one mammal, the yellow-bellied marmot (*Marmota flaviventris*), that is absent in other regions of the country (except for a few that inhabit the eastern slopes of the Rockies in Alberta). This large rodent, a relative of the groundhog, is similar to the hoary marmot (*M. caligata*) in many respects, but it is smaller, has longer fur, and the sides of its neck, hips and belly are buff in colour. In its Canadian habitat this marmot lives on low-level mountain slopes, on flat, rocky, open areas, under cliffs, and among rock piles. It eats grasses, sedges and a number of other plants. Dens are always located among rocks, often deep in the ground.

The weasel family (Mustelidae) is represented in Canada by fourteen species. These include: wolverine, the largest; badger; all the weasels; black-footed ferret, believed extinct in Canada — at best extremely rare; river and sea otters; marten, fisher, and spotted and striped skunks. The American badger (*Taxidea taxus*) is the second largest member of the weasel family. This North American mammal is found in the Columbia biome but infrequently elsewhere in Canada. It inhabits a small area in southern Ontario and a second, equally modest region in the extreme south-western corner of that province. It is also found in the south-western corner of Manitoba, in much of south and central Saskatchewan, in a large region in south-central Alberta, and, with a narrow corridor in between, along the southern fringes of the eastern Rocky Mountains. Nevertheless, it is not plentiful in any of its ranges.

North American badgers are somewhat smaller than their Old World counterparts. Males may attain a weight of up to 11 kg (24 lb.) and a length of 85 cm (33 in.), females being about 25 per cent smaller and lighter. Living in burrows and hunting such animals as ground squirrels, kangaroo rats, and mice, this carnivore is adept at digging and is perhaps only second to the wolverine among weasels in its determination and ability to defend itself against larger predators. Mating takes place during August and September in Canada, but, like most other members of the Mustelidae family, soon after the embryos begin to develop, they are held in a state of suspended animation until about the middle of February, not to be born until late April or May.

This survival characteristic is common to predatory mammals that have a high metabolic rate. If females of this group had to nurture growing embryos during harsh northern winters, they might not survive, or they might abort the young. Nevertheless, badgers are unusual among the weasel family in that in the northern part of their North American range they tend to hibernate from November to April, whereas skunks, their distant relatives, den in winter and are sleepers rather than true hibernators. The difference between hibernators and sleepers is that in the former metabolism is greatly reduced and, in mammals, the body temperature drops near to that of the animal's surroundings; but sleepers, although their metabolism is somewhat slowed, maintain body temperatures above those of their surroundings, and will readily awaken if disturbed. Additionally, some sleepers, such as skunks and raccoons, are roused in late winter by the breeding urge.

Among the numbers of impressive mammals that inhabit the Columbia biome, the bighorn sheep (*Ovis canadensis*) is one of the more spectacular and interesting. A relatively large and heavy animal, the bighorn's most distinctive features are the magnificent, curling horns of the rams, massive, brown weapons that arc backwards and downwards and then project their points forward, close to the face. Sweeping out of the forehead, the horns are flat on the top and curve down at the sides and are roughly triangular in cross-section. They give the appearance of being made up of a series of rings, one glued to the other, the largest closest to the head, the smallest at the tips.

Canadian bighorn rams attain lengths of between 160 and 185 cm (5.2 and 6.0 ft.) and may weigh as much as 155 kg (340 lb.); the smaller ewes weigh about 65 kg (143 lb.) and measure about 140 cm (55 in.).

Bighorns favour spring and summer ranges along mountain slopes and alpine meadows, preferably in areas that also offer rocky cliffs. In summer they climb to altitudes ranging between 1800 and 2500 m (5900 and 8200 ft.) while in winter they are more likely to be found at levels below 1500 m (4920 ft.). The sheep feed on the move, cropping grasses, sedges, and herbaceous plants and browsing on fir, willow, bearberry, juniper, and other woody plants, especially in winter.

Because of their climbing ability, bighorns can usually escape from predators such as wolves, coyotes, bears, and lynx if they are in proximity of rocky heights. Lambs in high regions are sometimes taken by

golden eagles, but the cougar is probably the sheep's greatest non-human predator because the big cat is almost as good an alpinist as the animals that it hunts. Since the arrival of firearms, man has been the sheep's greatest nemesis through hunting and because of environmental destruction caused by logging, mineral exploitation, and forest fires.

The breeding seasons vary considerably according to the climatic conditions. In southern regions of the United States breeding takes place during August. In Canada, the peak mating time is December.

Not long before the start of the breeding time, bighorn rams engage in a series of spectacular tournaments, the percussive sounds of which can be clearly heard over distances of up to 1.5 km (1 mi.). These tourneys usually start when two rams begin jostling each other and at the same time kicking swiftly with their front hooves. At a given moment,

▲ **Two bighorn rams** joust prior to the rutting season while two more look on. The winner may be challenged by one or both onlookers. Although the victorious ram will mate with ewes of his choice, the butting duels do not prevent the others from mating.

▲ **Bighorn sheep**

as though the rules had been established in advance, the antagonists separate, turn their backs on each other, and walk away. When each has advanced about 10 m (33 ft.), they turn around. Now they rear upwards on their hind legs, glare at each other and begin to advance slowly, still standing upright. The closer they get, the faster their pace, until at a distance of about 4 m (13 ft.) each ram lunges forward with the hind legs and the two meet head on, causing a sharp, loud crack somewhat like the firing of a small-calibre artillery piece. The impact is so great that it actually causes shock waves to ripple backwards along the whole length of each antagonist's body! Neighbouring rams, hearing the altercation, trot over to watch and sometimes to join in the fray, creating a scene reminiscent of medieval knights engaging in a tourney free-for-all.

Lambs are born during May after a gestation time of 180 days. They are dressed in soft cream and fawn wool and have pleasant, friendly little faces and large, appealing eyes.

The sheep are highly social. Led by an elderly ewe, they gather in small bands of from a dozen to as many as a hundred, usually when they are joined by the mature rams in winter. The latter form their own "bachelor clubs" after the mating season. Despite the fact that they bond socially in small groups, bighorns are not territorial, behaving in friendly, tolerant fashion when several bands gather on particularly appealing pastures. Interestingly, although at breeding time rams appear to be very competitive, they never challenge the authority of the ewe leaders.

On the whole, bighorns are calm animals and will readily accept human presence if they are not interfered with. They are extremely curious and alert at all times, characteristics exhibited by the great majority of wild animals, all of which must constantly depend on their senses if they are to survive in their world, be they prey species, or predators.

The Spanish explorer, Francisco de Coronado, was the first European to see bighorn sheep, while travelling through south-western North America in 1552. It was not until the early 1800s, however, that the species was scientifically named following a description given by a member of one of fur-trader–explorer David Thompson's expeditions to survey the Canadian Rockies for the Hudson's Bay Company.

THE MONTANE BIOME

This biome occupies a compact region in the mid-central part of British Columbia, extending in a narrow point northward on a line with the Queen Charlotte Islands and southwards to the border of the state of

Washington. Within its southernmost part grows the Ponderosa pine (*Pinus ponderosa*), a regal tree that reaches heights of between 49 and 52 m (161 and 170 ft.) and is not found elsewhere in Canada. It grows in the drier portions of the biome and extends as far north as Vavenby on the North Thompson River, preferring well-drained slopes; it grows at altitudes of up to 700 m (2300 ft.) in most locations but climbs to 1000 m (3280 ft.) on exposed, south-facing slopes.

Most of the montane is characterized by white, black, and Engelmann spruces and lodgepole pine (*Pinus contorta*), a western evergreen that for the most part favours mountain altitudes of between 600 and 1800 m (1969 and 5900 ft.) on the Alberta side of the Rockies and in British Columbia and the Yukon, where it mixes with the boreal biome in some areas. A few pockets of lodgepoles are also found in extreme northern Alberta, one pocket extending into the southern part of the Northwest Territories. Perhaps the tree's most unusual habitat is the Cypress Hills, an "island" of small mountains that straddles the southern border of Saskatchewan and Alberta.

The Cypress Hills are, in effect, a mini montane zone totally surrounded by the grasslands biome. Their presence in the predominantly flat plains country is due to a caprice of the ice-age glaciers, which for unknown reasons flowed around the hills, leaving them intact and giving some idea of what the rest of the prairies must have been like before the great freeze arrived. Today, parts of the Cypress Hills have been declared provincial parks, the western third under the care of Alberta, and the eastern two-thirds administered by Saskatchewan.

Lodgepole pines are medium-sized trees with slender, straight trunks, which in forest habitats sport crowns of small branches enhanced by stiff, short needles. When growing in pure stands, or mixing with other species in forested regions, lodgepole trunks are devoid of branches from the ground to the crown, but in open locations the limbs grow all the way down the tree, almost touching the soil. The non-scientific name of the species derives from the fact that the Plains Indians used the pine's saplings as lodge supports. This pine grows to heights of between 15 and 30 m (49 and 98 ft.) and attains a diameter of about 70 cm (27.5 in.).

The plants, topography, and climate of the montane furnish ideal conditions for mammals and birds within diverse habitats, from low,

OVERLEAF **The Cypress Hills** of Saskatchewan offer some idea of what the ▶ plains country must have looked like before glaciation bulldozed the terrain. It is believed that the ice mass split around the hills, leaving them intact.

lush valleys to mid-level slopes and upwards to the subalpine zone. To the east, the biome blends in transition with the Columbia, while its western boundaries combine with the coast biome to form yet another transition zone.

North of the ponderosa-growing zone the montane contains two regions of British Columbia known as the Chilcotin and the Cariboo, lush country where cattle ranching and wilderness still cohabit in relative accord on the enormous Fraser Plateau. This area of relatively flat land is drained by the turbulent Fraser River, which empties into the Pacific Ocean at Vancouver after coursing more than 1770 km (1100 mi.). On the plateau itself, a number of rivers travel eastward to feed the Fraser. Tall peaks virtually ring the entire region, many of them topped by glaciers of blue ice, others keeping their caps of snow the year round.

Birds are numerous everywhere during the frost-free seasons, including five species of grouse and the smallest of all Canadian birds, the minute rufous (*Selasphorus rufus*) and calliope (*Stellula calliope*) hummingbirds, both of which belong to a large family (Trochilidae) confined to the New World.

Between Alaska and Patagonia, at the southernmost tip of South America, live more than 300 species of hummingbirds, the great majority inhabiting the tropics. North America has 18 species, only 4 of which migrate to Canada every spring. The ruby-throated has the widest range in this country, extending along a corridor of varying width in southern Canada from Nova Scotia to the foothills of the Rocky Mountains in Alberta. The other three species, the black-chinned, rufous, and calliope are found only within the western mountains, the former a rare visitor to the southern part of the montane, the second breeding throughout British Columbia, and the last being mostly confined to the entire montane biome, although some of its members probably spill over into the western edges of the Columbia and the eastern fringes of the coast zones.

Most hummingbirds do not migrate long distances, but the ruby-throated and the rufous fly about 3000 km (1900 mi.) from their winter range to their breeding grounds, a return journey of some 6000 km (3800 mi.) undertaken by birds that measure between 7.5 and 9 cm (3 and 3.5 in.) in length and weigh only a few grams! Crawford H. Greenewalt, of the American Museum of Natural History, has established that hummingbirds can attain a top speed of slightly less than 48 km (30 mi.) per hour, beating their wings during what may be termed normal flight at a rate of 50 strokes a *second*, but evidently able to considerably speed up that rate when going "flat out".

Hummingbirds can hover, go straight up or down, fly backwards, or zoom away on a straight course almost faster than the eye can follow. During the breeding season from April to June, depending on latitude and elevation, males compete strongly for the favours of the females, often engaging in aerial dog-fights. During these displays, they fly to heights of 15 to 20 m (49 to 66 ft.) while executing sweeping arcs, zooming up and down, and emitting their chattering little cries.

▲ **Ruby-throated hummingbird**

Because of their exceptionally high metabolic rate, these tiny birds must eat every 10 or 15 minutes from early morning to late evening, preying on spiders and small insects and sipping nectar from flowers. They are strongly attracted to the colour red, but they will feed from any blossom that offers nectar, no matter what its colour. When a hummingbird does not quite get enough to eat by the time that it must roost for the night, it is able to go into a torpor, reducing its metabolic rate dramatically. If it could not do this, it would probably die of starvation or dehydration long before morning.

All female hummingbirds are single mothers. Males have nothing to do with nest building, incubation, or raising the young. Indeed, males usually chase away hungry females during the nesting season, often taking station near a feeder put out by humans and trying to keep all other hummers, male or female, away. Usually while a male is chasing one bird, another quickly zooms in on the feeder and has at least a few brief sucks of sugar solution.

A hummingbird's tongue is tube-like and very elastic. It acts much like a suction pump, being able to probe deeply into the heart of a flower to suck out nectar or minute insects. This organ is also used to feed the nestlings. The mother thrusts her beak deep into the gullet of a young bird and pumps food into its crop with her tongue.

The nests of Canadian hummingbirds are cup-like, located at various heights from 1.5 to 15 m (5 to 49 ft.) from the ground, usually in the shelter of evergreen needles, or other shrubby plants, including hawthorns. The female gathers bits of plant material with which to weave the cup, then searches for any kind of down with which to line the inside chamber. Next she collects spider-web silk to use as bindings on the outside, wrapping this around the structure. Some hummingbirds perform this task by first affixing the sticky material to one part of the nest, then holding the remainder in the beak, flying circles around the cup. The nest is about 5 cm (2 in.) in diameter by slightly less than 4 cm (1.5 in.) deep on the outside, and about 2.5 cm (1 in.) in diameter by 2 cm (0.8 in.) on the inside.

When the nest is complete, the female will lay two minute, glossy white eggs, each measuring perhaps 13 mm (0.5 in.) in length, and 8 mm (0.3 in.) in width. Ruby-throats incubate the eggs for 16 days;

black-chins for between 13 and 16 days; rufouses and calliopes for about 15 days.

The tiny young are *altricial* — in need of long-term parental care — and are either entirely naked, or nearly so when they hatch from their eggs. Ruby-throat and rufous chicks are born with their eyes closed and remain blind for the next six or seven days; the other two Canadian species may also emerge sightless, but no information on the presence or absence of this characteristic is available at present. Young hummingbirds are ready to leave the nest between 20 and 23 days from birth.

Unlike the hummingbirds the ruffed, sharp-tailed, blue, spruce and sage grouse and the white-tailed and willow ptarmigan that inhabit the montane biome are all permanent residents in Canada. The two ptarmigans, together with the rock ptarmigan, are birds found only in the western mountains or in the northern regions of the country. The blue grouse (*Dendragapus obscurus*) is distributed from the eastern side of the Rocky Mountains westwards across British Columbia, including Vancouver Island and the Queen Charlotte Islands, and north to southern Yukon Territory. Small numbers of sage grouse (*Centrocercus urophasianus*) a species generally found in the United States, live in the extreme south-central part of the montane biome and in south-western Saskatchewan and south-eastern Alberta in an area confined to the Cypress Hills and vicinity.

The sharp-tailed grouse (*Tympanuchus phasianellus*) is widespread in Canada, being found from south-western Quebec to the edge of the coast biome and north into the Yukon and Northwest Territories, almost to the Beaufort Sea coast.

The spruce (*Dendragapus canadensis*) and ruffed grouse (*Bonasa umbellus*) are the most widely distributed in Canada. The former occurs from Nova Scotia and eastern Labrador right across the country, from the northern transition zone south to the U.S. border, except for a large portion of the central plains. The range of the ruffed grouse is similar, but generally does not extend as far north except in the Yukon and in the extreme western part of the Northwest Territories; the ruffed grouse is also found in the Cypress Hills.

The ruffed grouse, or "The Drummer", as it is often called, is perhaps the best known of all North American members of the Tetraoninae family, of which there are nine species in Canada, and it is one of the woodland birds most sought by human hunters. The males of this species have attained wide notoriety because of their habit of standing or strutting back and forth on a log, deep in the shelter of the forest, while beating their wings, producing sounds very much like those made by a just-being-started two-stroke gasoline engine heard from afar. A cock begins his drumming with a few vigorous, but slow beats, creating measured thuds that soon increase in tempo and after several moments die away in a muffled roll. For many years it was believed that the grouse actually struck a hollow log with his wings, but in more recent years it has been established that the wings do not touch the cock's drumming perch. The powerful beats displace air with such force that the hollow, booming sound is produced.

Ruffed grouse are wary birds. Excellent flyers, they nevertheless spend a lot of their time on the forest floor as they forage during the frost-free seasons, eating berries, insects, and seeds. If approached by an enemy, they emit alarm calls, little whistles that echo around them so that it is often difficult to pinpoint the bird by the sound that it is making. As they whistle, the birds crouch low and strut away stealthily, their sharp eyes monitoring the cause of disturbance. At other times, a grouse will crouch in the underbrush, immobile and well camouflaged by its woodsy-coloured coat. If an intruder comes too close, the bird explodes into action, making a loud noise with its strongly beating wings and racing swiftly away from danger, but being careful to keep trees and other concealing vegetation between itself and the animal or human that has disturbed it. Apart from enabling the bird to effect a rapid escape, the sudden and noisy flight is calculated to startle an enemy; and it almost invariably achieves that result, as human hunters and hikers can testify.

In the autumn, the ruffed grouse prepares itself for winter by growing a series of closely in-line horny projections on both sides of all of its toes. These function as small snowshoes and allow the bird to walk on top of the white cover. In spring, the projections are shed.

When deep snow lies within the forest and temperatures drop sharply after sunset, the grouse dives into the white blanket, shuffles its body to make a small chamber while at the same time shaking loose snow into the entrance hole, and sleeps comfortably through the night within its impromptu igloo. This technique at times backfires on the bird, however. In early winter and, especially, in late winter–early spring, it is not uncommon for a thaw to descend on the wilderness during the early part of the night, melting a centimetre or two of the surface snow. If the warm spell is short-lived and is immediately followed by a hard freeze, a strong layer of ice forms over the grouse, often trapping the bird within its snow chamber. Sometimes it can break through the ice cover, at other times it becomes entombed in its erstwhile shelter, there either to freeze to death, or to be picked off by a fox, lynx, bobcat, or coyote. By and large, however, the grouse's snow

▲ **Ruffed grouse**

shelters serve it well in latitudes where the thermometer can plunge down to $-40°$ (at this mark, Celsius and Fahrenheit readings coincide) or lower.

M ajor mammals of the montane zone include moose, elk, mule deer, small numbers of bighorn sheep, beaver, cougar, grizzly and black bears, wolves, wolverine, lynx, bobcats, coyotes and badgers. Most of the smaller mammals found elsewhere in the mountainous regions of the west, such as mice, shrews and tree and ground squirrels, also inhabit the biome.

It can be fairly said that the early exploration and settlement of Canada and the United States was greatly facilitated, if not actually spurred, by the beaver (*Castor canadensis*), the large, buck-toothed and ingenious rodent whose pelts were at one time referred to as "hairy banknotes".

In 1670, Prince Rupert, cousin of England's King Charles II, established the Governor and Company of Adventurers of England Trading into Hudson's Bay, later to be known as the Hudson's Bay Company, an enterprise dedicated to general trade, but especially interested in beaver fur. At the time, the French in Canada and the British in the American colonies were actively trapping the animals and shipping pelts to Europe on an "every-man-for-himself" basis. The Hudson's Bay Company was the first to really organize the trade and to systematically encourage wilderness exploration more than a hundred years before the American Revolution, no doubt spurred by European hat makers, who were clamouring for beaver "felt", the animal's fine woolly underfur. By 1750, beaver had become rare in New England, sparking exploration of other wilderness areas. In 1763 more than 75 000 beaver skins were exported from across North America. The trapping of beaver had begun in earnest.

In modern times, the "hairy banknotes" are in greater demand than ever; so are the pelts of many other mammals. Between 1976 and 1978, more than 800 000 beaver were killed by trapping in Canada and a further 400 000 died by the same means in the United States; and during the 1977–78 trapping season, nearly 3.5 *million* animals belonging to 29 species were killed for their fur in Canada, including nearly 400 000 beaver. The value of the catch was $44 139 363. Trappers in the United States did much better in that year; they killed almost 19 *million* animals belonging to 26 species, including more than 200 000 beaver. Value of the catch: in excess of $268 million.

That the beaver, Canada's national emblem, continues to survive in the face of such intense human persecution — referred to euphemistically as *harvesting* by some — is a tribute to this animal's ingenuity

and extraordinary abilities, especially in view of the fact that adults and young are also hunted by cougar, wolves, coyotes, lynx, bobcats, wolverine, bears, mink, golden eagles, some hawks that take small kits, and even such fish as northern pike, large specimens of which are 122 cm (48 in.) long and may weigh up to 20 kg (44 lb.); to such fish, a beaver kit is but a good mouthful. On the other hand, logging, industrial development, and agriculture have created many habitats that are ideal for beaver settlement, allowing more range for the species to populate. Ironically, when beaver do as nature intended and cause flooding on roadways and resort property, or if they dare to take a tree growing on a cottager's beach front, owners and highway maintenance officials clamour for the removal of the animals. These complaints are usually heeded and the "nuisance" beaver are trapped for their fur because killing them is quick, cheap, and financially rewarding. Live-

▲ **Against a backdrop** of British Columbia mountains already covered by early autumnal snow, a beaver carries fresh-cut poplar to its underwater larder, located in the mud near its lodge.

trapping and relocation takes time, costs money, and does not yield a dollar profit.

Beaver are social animals. A family will probably include mother, father, last year's young, one or two "aunts", and the current year's litter for a total (in untrapped ponds, rivers and lakes) of about one dozen animals, depending on the size of the home pond and the amount of fodder contained in it and on the surrounding shores.

Just as myths have grown up about a number of animals, so have many fables been woven around the biology of beavers. At one time the animal was said to gather mud and rocks, place the load on its tail, and then swim to an under-construction dam or lodge. Unloading at the site, it was said to use its tail as a trowel with which it plastered the mixture on the dam or lodge. Beaver are also believed to cut down trees in such a way as to cause them to fall into their ponds deliberately; then too, it is still generally believed that these animals slap their wide tails sharply on the water so as to alert others of their kind to the presence of danger. These and some even more ludicrous tales still survive in the late 1980s.

In reality, when it comes to beaver biology, the truth seems even stranger than the fiction, for this animal is probably the best environmentally adapted of all North American mammals.

Unlike cud-chewing animals, such as deer and domestic cattle, that have special stomachs designed to break down plant cellulose, the beaver cannot digest its cellulose-high food during the first "sitting" and must excrete partly digested vegetation and re-ingest it a second time. To the human mind, this may seem a somewhat unhygienic way of obtaining sustenance, but it works well for the beaver, which deposits its wastes in the water of its habitat, rather than on land, and quite separately from the porridge-like food. This is stored in the animal's exceptionally large appendix, and when this organ is full, the contents are excreted, but only when the colon is empty of feces. By twice routing its food through its digestive system, the beaver breaks down the cellulose and derives nourishment from the vegetation that it consumes.

From spring to autumn, beaver feed mainly on shoreline and aquatic plants, taking waterlily roots, pickerel weed, arrowhead weed, a few sapling trees during spring, and tender succulents. By autumn, beaver begin to cut down trees, selecting poplars, maples, birches and a variety of other deciduous species and dropping them by making alternate cuts at the top and bottom of a selected area on the trunk. When both notches have been made, the animal grips the intervening wood with its long, orange-coloured incisors and, giving a powerful pull while twisting its head away from the tree, tears out the wooden wedge. Bite by bite and rip by rip, it deepens each notch as it works around the tree; eventually, just before the tree begins to topple, the gnawing and tearing has created an effect somewhat similar to that which would be obtained by placing two sharpened pencils together, point to point.

Sometimes, if a tree happens to be leaning towards the water, it conveniently drops into the pond; most often trees will fall in any direction and, occasionally, may actually come down on top of a cutter. Such accidents, however, are more unusual than usual, for beaver are quick to run for the pond at this stage, doing so not only because of the danger posed by the falling tree, but also because they know that the crash made by its landing may well attract predators.

After a tree has been felled, the beaver clan, generally led by a top ranking female, cuts up the upper branches and as much of the trunk as it can manage (the main stems of some felled trees are too large to be cut, for the beaver cannot get to that part of them resting on the ground). The cut sections are laboriously towed to the water and carried beneath the surface to a "pantry" area, where they are anchored in the bottom mud as supplies for the winter. It should be noted, however, that the animals consume the bark and cambium layer only: they do not eat the actual wood.

When they can get it, some beaver also take animal protein. If they happen to live in a habitat that is well supplied with fresh-water clams, they feed heavily on the molluscs the year round, cutting down and storing far fewer trees in autumn. Similarly, if the reasonably fresh carcass of an animal is encountered in their habitat the beaver will eat parts of it.

Other unusual beaver characteristics include: ear and nose valves that close as soon as the animal submerges; extra "eyelids" that cover the eyes to keep out debris when under water; loose, well-furred lips that can close behind the long incisors, allowing the animal to feed under the surface without swallowing water; the wide tail, used as a rudder when swimming, as a prop when sitting upright, especially when gnawing at a tree, as a mat when grooming, and as a makeshift "plate" when feeding on excreted, partly digested food on shore or in the lodge chamber; hand-like front paws that have elongated, delicate fingers and slender claws for handling food; back feet, the first two toes of which have horny pads used for "brushing" the coat, and claws with serrated edges that are used for combing. The remaining toes have flat, blunt claws useful for climbing and digging.

Beaver have two sets of glands in the anal area. Discharging into the anus are two musk glands that advertise the beaver's sex and its presence in the territory; the second pair, somewhat behind the anus, are oil glands that discharge their contents through minute pores onto the

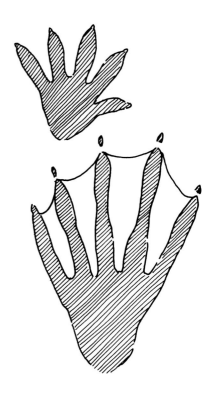

▲ **Beaver pawprints**

▲ **Beaver tracks**

▲ **Beaver lodge**

surrounding fur. This oil is of great importance to the well-being of the animal. After it emerges from the water, either in the lodge or on land, a beaver never fails to sit on its tail and brush oil over its entire body with a back foot, using the horny pads below the claws and in this way keeping itself waterproof. When this task has been accomplished, a beaver will spend a great deal of time combing its fur with serrated claws.

Beavers build their lodges rather simply, but soundly. Selecting a location shallow enough to minimize the work, but deep enough to allow for at least two entrances that will remain under the surface during low water, they pile mud, stones, and branches to first make a base. On top of the foundation, they continue to add the same materials until the somewhat conical structure has risen a suitable distance above the water. This done, they dive and begin chewing their way into the centre of the mound, cutting out a roughly circular space at a level likely to remain above high water. Then they cut another doorway at an angle to the first. Some lodges have three entry-exits.

The family sleeps and rests within the lodge chamber which may be 2 m (6.5 ft.) in diameter and has a sloping, domed roof that is often finished with shredded bark, usually willow, to make the home waterproof. Above the middle of the chamber, interlaced branches that have not been plastered with mud furnish an irregular vent for intaking fresh air and removing exhaled gasses. When winter comes, the outside of the lodge becomes frozen, turning the shaggy mound into a fortress that a bear can broach only on rare occasions.

Beavers build their dams with the same kind of materials that they use for their lodges. They begin by making a base along the bottom for the entire length of the gap to be filled. On top of this they pile more mud, stones, small logs, branches, and assorted vegetation, building upwards with the current until they are satisfied that the structure will give them a sufficient depth of water for their needs. During high-water conditions, the beavers broach the dam, allowing water to escape so that their lodge chambers will not be flooded; in face of drought, they raise the dam higher, trapping more water behind it. Some old dams are so wide and strong that it is possible to drive a team of horses over them. The longest beaver dam ever recorded was one located on Jefferson River in Montana: it measured 652 m (2139 ft.)! Usually dams are much shorter than that whopper; some are even tiny, perhaps measuring only a couple of metres.

Beavers usually mate in late winter/early spring and gestation time is just under four months. Most kits in Canada are born in late May or early June, the number in each litter varying from two to six. Newborns weigh between 225 and 700 g (7.9 and 24.7 oz.). The kits are born fully furred and with their eyes open. They must be taught how to swim by

the adults, but they take readily to the water and play joyously around the lodge or near the bank under the watchful eyes of their mother. Usually, the kits remain with the parental group for two years, although some may leave during the summer following birth and others may remain with the family for a number of years. Beavers have been known to weigh 45 kg (99 lb.) but most probably average between 22 and 28 kg (48.5 and 62.0 lb.).

Mud and stones are carried by the front paws, hugged to the chest; when a loaded beaver reaches the lodge or dam with building materials, it must scramble out of the water by standing upright and using its back legs and feet. Beaver plaster mud with their hands, not their tails; and they do not slap their tails on the water as warnings to other beaver, although at times the staccato report may have this effect. The main intent of the sudden action and ensuing noise is to startle a would-be predator into identifying itself, or to put it off its stroke for a few vital seconds while the beaver escapes under water. Indeed, the only predator capable of harming an adult beaver while it is swimming on pond, river or lake, is man, who may use a gun, or traps. If the tail slap really were intended as a warning, the most logical place to thump would be on land, where beavers are most vulnerable to predators.

Nine different kinds of beaver are recognized in Canada. All look alike and behave in much the same way, but subspecies have been classified according to certain anatomical differences. With the exception of the extreme northern regions and a relatively small area of the prairies, beaver are found across Canada. Four subspecies live within the western mountains.

▲ **The yellow-bellied marmot,** related to the hoary marmot and to the groundhog, has limited distribution in Canada, being found only in the dry, south-central interior of British Columbia and in extreme southwestern Alberta.

MOUNTAIN IMAGES

◀ **Wind and weather** often combine to oxidize the minerals contained in surface rocks, altering their hues and painting the landscape. This aerial photograph was taken in Mount Edziza Provincial Park, British Columbia.

▲ **Coyotes**, in some parts of Canada commonly called "brush wolves", have considerably increased their range and their numbers in recent times. This ecological change is largely due to alterations of the environment by humans, including the drastic reduction of wolves, the coyote's natural control.

▲ **Most of the high peaks** of the St. Elias Mountains, Yukon Territory, remain snow- or ice-covered the year round.

From the top of Mount Temple, ▶ Banff National Park, the western mountains march to the horizon in serried ranks, their dragon's-teeth peaks surrounding an observer.

◀ **Evergreens and aspens** colour
the wilderness in autumn in the
Kananaskis Range, Banff National
Park, Alberta.

▲ **The emerald hue** of Lake O'Hara,
Yoho National Park, British
Columbia.

▲ **A half-grown lynx kitten** stares curiously at the photographer. These solitary hunters are found over most of Canada with the exception of the far north, the prairies, coastal British Columbia and along a narrow band from southern Nova Scotia to southern Ontario.

◄ **A great spangled-fritillary** at rest on a plant. Butterflies feed on a variety of materials, including nectar, carrion and the droppings of birds and mammals.

▲ **Mountain goats** at rest in Yoho
National Park, British Columbia.
Superlative alpinists, these goats
have concave hooves with spongy
pads that provide good footing on
slippery rocks, allowing the exceptionally agile animals to climb to
some of the highest and steepest
crags.

Alpine flowers in Bugaboo ▶
Glacier Provincial Park, British
Columbia.

◀ **Various kinds of cotton grasses** grow in our western regions. Habitats range from seashores in British Columbia to alpine meadows in Alberta, the Yukon Territory and in western regions of the Northwest Territories. The white, cottony balls of this sedge conceal tiny flowers.

▲ **Mount Assiniboine** raises its Matterhorn-like peak over a vista of evergreens and snow in Mount Assiniboine Provincial Park, British Columbia.

The yellow monkey flower is as ▶ much at home growing at sea level as it is at high altitudes. *Mimulus* is found from the Yukon Territory to southern British Columbia.

THE GRASSLANDS

 THIS BIOME BEARS LITTLE RESEMBLANCE TODAY to that which existed before the arrival of European settlers, when native prairie grasses predominated in a major portion of the zone and such animals as bison, elk, mule deer, antelope, black and grizzly bears, wolves, and coyotes were abundant. Most of the wild prairie has now been planted with crops such as wheat, oats, and barley, while a wide belt of aspens has developed across the top of the biome, a park-like region where the trees grow on sandy, almost desert lands.

Before the establishment of agriculture in the late nineteenth century, the grazing of countless bison and dry summers accompanied by prairie fires ignited by lightning, prevented the aspens and other trees from colonizing the land, but enhanced the development of grasses. Blue grama, rough fescue, little blue-stem, and other nourishing wild grasses in lush seasons grew tall and fed a host of herbivores, birds, and rodents. During this pre-settlement period, black-billed magpies (*Pica pica*) maintained a close association with the bison, following the great wild cattle, feasting on the remains of those old and sick individuals that had died on the move, eating the birth residues after cows had calved, and, between times, feeding on the insects that always surrounded the herds in clouds. The birds often perched on the backs of their shaggy benefactors and even foraged among their droppings, which, when fresh, usually contained undigested seeds, and, when old, furnished a supply of large carrion beetles that were avidly sought by the magpies. Such was the relationship between the two disparate species that when the bison were almost exterminated, the magpies declined dramatically. Years later, however, prairie ranches unwittingly came to the rescue of the birds when they introduced cattle to the range. Soon afterwards the magpies made a come-back, using the domestic cattle much as they had used the bison.

Magpies are relatives of the ravens, crows, and jays. They are between 30 and 33 cm (12 and 13 in.) long, and their exceptionally long tails account for almost one-third of the total length. Glossy green-black is the predominant colour of these tough and intelligent birds, but the dark plumage is vividly broken up by bands of white over the back and sides and on the primary wing feathers. They have long, slightly hooked black beaks and strongly clawed feet, allowing them to prey on small rodents, other birds, and large insects, besides making

◄ **In the Frenchman River Valley**, Grasslands National Park, Saskatchewan, the land rolls gently towards the horizon while big blue skies studded with white clouds give a sense of infinite space.

A MOUSE THAT HUNTS GRASSHOPPERS

The northern grasshopper mouse (*Onychomys leucogaster*) is a predatory mouse. This stocky and well-muscled rodent has a short, tapering tail that is quite thick at the base, and a coat that may be grey, dark brown, reddish brown, or light cinnamon on the upper parts and flanks and pure white below on the underside. Measuring between 14 and 16.5 cm (5.5 and 6.5 in.) and with a mass of about 56 g (2 oz.), the grasshopper mouse is a true hunter.

About 50 per cent of its food consists of insects, which it pounces on and devours on the spot, but it also ambushes other mice, enjoys carrion left by other predators, and is even cannibalistic, killing members of its own species when opportunity presents itself. It also eats grasses and grains. Its common name derives from the fact that it devours large numbers of grasshoppers when these insects are in season. For this reason alone, it is valued by farmers, especially so because it also kills a large number of grain-loving mice of other species. This is a

▲ **Northern grasshopper mouse**

western species that inhabits the plains country of Alberta, Saskatchewan, and Manitoba, although it is never abundant in any part of its range.

good use of whatever carrion they can find. Present now in good numbers within the grasslands biome, magpies also range from south-eastern Manitoba, through Saskatchewan, Alberta, and British Columbia and all the way north to the south-western part of the Yukon Territory.

Evergreens such as white spruce and lodgepole pines occur in modest numbers in some sheltered regions and on high lands, but trembling aspens (*Populus tremuloides*), so named because their heart-shaped leaves flutter continuously whenever the wind blows, are the major tree species within the prairie ecosystem. These poplars, in fact, are now abundant on sand dunes and hillsides. Although they grow quickly, usually in dense clumps known as bluffs, they are relatively short-lived. Nevertheless, because they can spread via their root systems aspens are almost impossible to eradicate deliberately, as many early settlers discovered after they had ploughed down the prairie grasses and attempted to grow crops on land that was not suitable for domestic plants. The native grasses, resistant to drought and stimulated by fire, formed a tough carpet that prevented the aspens from growing, but as soon as the "prairie wool", as these plants were collectively termed, was eliminated, the poplars sprang up. Such cleared lands were soon abandoned by settlers and the result was the development of the present aspen parklands, a wide, irregularly shaped and curving belt that stretches across the top of the grasslands from Manitoba to the foothills of the Rocky Mountains in Alberta. The poplar stands are

Aspen groves in southern Alberta during early autumn, photographed from ▶ an aircraft.

picturesque and give shelter to a number of native animals that could not otherwise survive on today's radically altered prairies. The trees, therefore, have formed a natural shelter belt in an otherwise tamed environment; but it is ironic that before human interference, the grasslands system had prospered for many thousands of years, the home of multitudes of bison, deer, antelope, large predators and, during the frost-free seasons, myriad birds belonging to a great many species.

During the second half of the nineteenth century, reports dealing with the fertility of the grasslands biome and published by members of two separate but major Canadian expeditions gave rise to a great deal of confusion. The first report, submitted to the imperial government by Captain John Palliser on his return from conducting the British North American Exploring Expedition (1857–60), stated in part that "in the central portion of the continent there is a region, desert, or semi-desert in character, which can never be expected to become occupied by settlers . . . although there are fertile spots throughout its extent, it can never be of much advantage to us as a possession. . . . Knowledge of the country on the whole would never lead me to advocate a line of communication."

Palliser had encountered the prairies in summer and during a long spell of drought. He assumed that all the lands contained within what has come to be known as Palliser's Triangle, a region that occupies most of the grasslands biome and extends from eastern Saskatchewan to western Alberta, were permanently arid during all frost-free seasons. But John Macoun, of the Sandford Fleming Expedition (1872–75), reported the contrary in 1876: "I fearlessly announced that the so-called arid country was one of unsurpassed fertility and that it was literally the 'Garden' of the whole country."

History has sorted out the facts. Palliser was an explorer; Macoun, a botanist. Each judged the grasslands from his own standpoint. Macoun was undoubtedly overly enthusiastic and Palliser was overly negative. In parts, from eastern Manitoba to the foothills of the Rocky Mountains, the grasslands biome is, indeed, fertile, especially during years of adequate precipitation in the form of rain *and* snow; however, as many prairie farmers discovered during the great drought years of the 1930s, the land and the climate can deal harshly with non-native plants and animals.

The country encompassed by Palliser's Triangle slopes from west to east, with Calgary, at its westernmost terminus, lying at an altitude of 1036 m (3400 ft.) above sea level, and Regina, near its eastern end,

◄ **Full-blossomed prairie roses** grow in silted soil in an area of Grasslands National Park. An indigenous rose species, the hips of this plant, high in vitamin C, were once used as food by Plains Indians.

THE GRASSLANDS

1 Aspens
2 Pronghorn
3 Prairie dogs
4 Great Plains toad
5 Badger

6 White-tailed jack rabbit
7 Coyote
8 Hog-nosed snake
9 Black-billed magpie
10 Grasshopper

11 Click beetle
12 Female and male mallards
13 Northern pintail
14 Northern harrier

NOT TO SCALE

being 580 m (1900 ft.) above sea level. In effect, the entire grasslands biome consists of an enormous plain interrupted by major features in only four locations: in the eastern part, the valley of the Saskatchewan River; in the western part, Alberta's Bow River Valley; in the south-west, the Cypress Hills, and in the south-east the great Missouri *Coteau*, a wide trough that runs southward into Montana and thereafter follows for some distance the route of the Missouri River.

Observed from an aircraft flying from Calgary eastwards, the grass-land biome is evidently now very largely dominated by agricultural fields, man-made lakes (freshwater reservoirs), and domesticated grass-lands for cattle. Apart from a few wild pockets left as provincial parks, or allowed to remain because the terrain is unsuitable for farming, the aerial view continues to reveal a tamed environment until the unfarmed Great Sand Hills are sighted in western Saskatchewan. This rolling semi-desert region begins south of the South Saskatchewan River, interrupting the checkerboard croplands and the golf-course–like pastures. As the flight continues, only three other areas that contain natural forests are to be noted. Spruces and lodgepole pines grow on the north slopes of the Cypress Hills, aspens in a number of other sandy areas, and western species of broadleaf trees survive in Saskatchewan's Qu'Appelle Valley and in southern Manitoba. The most readily apparent tree zone is to be seen in the west, north, and east of the open prairies: the enormous, bow-shaped region containing the aspen parklands.

Unseen from the air, but quickly noted even from a car moving along the Trans-Canada Highway — which travels through the grassland zone — are numbers of introduced plants, some escaped from culti-vation, others weed species brought over from Europe, the most dom-inant of them being Russian thistle and crested wheat grass. Here too are encountered some native animals, such as western badgers; mice; voles; gophers — which are ground squirrels, the colloquial name stemming from French and meaning "honeycomb", after the animal's habit of excavating tunnels under the ground; a variety of birds; and the ubiquitous insects.

Historic natural habitats are those that cannot be farmed, mined, or otherwise exploited for their below-ground resources. Such areas have persisted for thousands of years and are found along river valleys in and around marshes and ponds, on the sand hills, the Cypress Hills,

▲ **Richardson's ground squirrel**

OVERLEAF   **Eroded rocky hills** and coulees, brownish grasses known as ▶ prairie wool, and alkali sloughs are common sights in the south Saskatchewan Badlands. In this photograph, Big Muddy Lake is in the distance.

▲ **Inwood, Manitoba**, located some 73 km (45 mi.) north of Winnipeg, has been made famous by garter snakes, thousands of which emerge in the spring and soon thereafter begin to mate. At this time, males and females twine around each other by the dozens, forming "balls" of snakes.

and within all those plainslands that are too dry, too stony, or too hilly for agriculture.

In the extreme south, the grassland biome has remained relatively undisturbed in a region that has been christened the "Big Muddy Badlands". It is totally unsuited to agriculture and, in many locations, will not even sustain hardy range cattle. This as yet largely natural ecosystem is in Saskatchewan, located south of the cities of Regina in the east and Moose Jaw in the west. It has been named after the Big Muddy River, which begins in Saskatchewan and runs south into Montana, eventually flowing into the Missouri River. This is a haunting, fascinating region composed of sandstone buttes (isolated hills rising abruptly from the prairie), sheer cliffs, and boulder-strewn hogbacks (low, cambered hills). During the late 1800s and early 1900s, it was nicknamed "Station One" on the route travelled by outlaws Butch Cassidy and the Sundance Kid, who at times took refuge in the Canadian West. These renowned criminals were not alone in this practice for the Big Muddy Badlands were havens for many other outlaws, horse thieves, and cattle rustlers, offering very tough terrain, caves in which the men could shelter, and proximity to the border of the United States.

Alkali lakes and sloughs, small, marshy pools, dot the Badlands landscape and elsewhere in the south of the biome; these contain water high in soluble mineral salts, which are detrimental to the growth of most plants. One such body of water, Old Wives Lake, located some 40 km^2 (25 mi.) south-west of Moose Jaw and about 400 km^2 (154 sq. mi.) in extent is said to be haunted! Legend has it that more than a century ago a group of Sioux that included three elderly women were at camp on the lakeshore when surprised by a Cree war party. To make good their escape, the Sioux abandoned the three old wives, who were killed by the Cree. Since then it is said that at certain times the spirits of these women return to the lake during moonless nights to bemoan their fate by screaming mournfully. However true this may be, the waters of Old Wives Lake and most other ponds and sloughs of the region contain too much alkali to sustain around their perimeters the majority of grassland plant species, neither can they be used for drinking, at least by humans. Typical vegetation found growing in the dry, white margins of sloughs are red glassworts (*Salicornia* spp.), members of a relatively large family that has developed a high tolerance to salt. Glassworts have succulent stems of a shiny vitreous appearance that, when dry, crunch underfoot.

By summer's end, some of the smaller sloughs are completely dry, their entire area covered by a white alkali crust and colonized by glassworts. Farther from the sloughs, but also thriving in soil that has a high salt content, grow clumps of dark green greasewood (*Sarcobatus vermiculatus*), shrubby plants the normal habitats of which are the semi-desert regions of Colorado and Utah in the United States. Poisonous to domestic livestock, greasewood is often eaten by such wildlife as birds, ground squirrels, and antelopes without causing ill effects.

All of the grassland biome's habitats that rest on a base of sedimentary rock offer a wide variety of sculpted landforms. In the valley of Saskatchewan's Frenchman River, eroded shale left by prehistoric tributary streams has created small, sculptured declivities and shallow caves. Some of these caves contain lignite, an imperfectly formed dark brown coal that was at one time used as fuel by the Plains Indians and early European settlers, especially after the bison had been nearly exterminated and their dry-dung "chips", long used as fuel by the Indians, no longer littered the plains. Bison-chip fires burn hotly. This natural fuel was principally used for cooking, although when millions of buffalo roamed the prairies, Indian women gathered large quantities

▲ **Short-horned lizard**

▲ **An immature pronghorn ante-lope** partially concealed by grasses rests in Grasslands National Park. This antelope is the sole survivor of a prehistoric family that once contained many species. It is unique to North America and not closely related to the African antelopes.

of the hard, spherical droppings during the summer and autumn and used them to heat their tepees in winter, mixing them with whatever lignite and dry wood happened to be available in a land that was mostly treeless. The lignite caves, and old, man-made caverns from which the fossil fuel was mined, can still be found in some parts of the grasslands; nowadays they serve as shelters for western porcupines, skunks, or coyotes.

One feature of the Saskatchewan Badlands, located in the Val Marie area, is the "Sinking Hill", a sandstone dome that for the last 35 years has been sinking at a rate of 30 cm (1 ft.) a year. It is at present slightly more than 10 m (33 ft.) high and thus can be expected to be entirely swallowed by the underground fault into which it is gradually slipping by the year 2022.

WHAT IS A REPTILE?

Reptilians are principally terrestrial and secondarily aquatic. They all share the following physiological characteristics: the skin is protected by scales (the carapace [upper shell] and plastron [lower shell] of a turtle are both formed by heavy, highly modified scales); they breathe through lungs; all except crocodilians have three-chambered hearts; their eggs have leathery shells (in those species that do not "hatch" their young internally); and fertilization occurs within the females. Nearly six thousand species are known world-wide, including alligators and crocodiles, neither of which is present in Canada.

Reptiles are represented in Canada by turtles (order Chelonia), snakes, and lizards (order Squamata, which is divided into two suborders: Ophidia: snakes; and Lacertilia: lizards). In all, 42 species of reptiles are recognized by the National Museum of Natural Sciences. There is a possibility that one more species, the eastern box turtle (*Terrapene carolina*) may live in Ontario, but hard evidence of its presence has not been offered to date.

The only poisonous reptiles found in this country are the rattlesnakes, of which three species are known: the western rattlesnake of British Columbia, Alberta and Saskatchewan, the

▲ **Massasauga rattler**

massasauga rattlesnake of Ontario, and the large timber rattler of Ontario, which is now believed to be extinct in Canada. In common with other pit vipers, these snakes have an indentation on each side of the face, located between the eyes and the nostrils. Within these indentations are located heat-sensing organs that detect the body heat of warm-blooded animals. Fangs are hinged and hollow; when not in use they lie flat against the upper palate. Rattlesnake bites have led to human fatalities, but death does not always follow, even in untreated cases. Anti-venom centres are located in all those areas of Canada where rattlesnakes are found and for this reason few victims need suffer serious effects.

R emnants of the mammals that were once abundant in the grasslands biome include: antelope, mule deer, coyotes, red foxes, gophers, badgers, striped skunk, bobcats in wooded areas, porcupines, and the so-called white-tailed jack rabbit (*Lepus townsendii*), which is really a hare. It derived its common name when early settlers, struck by its large, donkey-like ears, nicknamed it the "jackass rabbit". This hare is slim, has slender legs and a somewhat long, white tail. It may weigh as much as 5.5 kg (12 lb.). When startled, the jack rabbit leaps away, taking jumps that may cover as much as 5 m (16 ft.) at a time; it

▲ **The jack rabbit**, a largely nocturnal hare, is found throughout the grasslands biome.

has been estimated that it can attain a speed of 64 km (40 mi.) an hour during short runs.

An animal that has always been rare in Canada is the black-tailed prairie dog (*Cynomys ludovicianus*). The only Canadian colony is located in the Frenchman River valley of Saskatchewan. This highly social species of ground squirrel once lived in their millions in the vast expanses of the American plains, but farmers and ranchers soon declared war on them and, from a population estimated to have totalled more than 400 *million* prairie dogs, only a few colonies can be found today on our continent.

These interesting animals emit sharp, shrill little barks when alarmed, a sound that prompted their common name and even influ-

enced their scientific name. *Cynomys ludovicianus* meaning "Louisiana dog mouse", is taken from the Mississippi Basin (earlier known as Louisiana), where the greatest concentration of these animals once lived.

In the same area as the prairie dogs are found six threatened species of birds: prairie falcons, ferruginous hawks, greater prairie-chickens, golden eagles, sage grouse, and merlins. During migration times, birds of many species are still plentiful in the grasslands biome, including waterfowl, raptors, songbirds, and two cranes — the sandhills and the endangered whoopers. Plains hog-nosed snakes, rattlesnakes, yellow-bellied racers, short-horned lizards, and the Great Plains toads are relatively common in the southern parts of the biome.

▲**The black-tailed prairie dog** has a limited range in Canada, being found only in the Frenchman River flats of southern Saskatchewan. Highly sociable, these ground squirrels live in colonies, sheltering in underground burrows.

THE COLOURFUL FORESTS

9

 THE GREAT LAKES–ST. LAWRENCE BIOME RUNS from Quebec's Gaspé Peninsula along the north shore of the St. Lawrence River and westward to the east shores of Lake Superior, where it is interrupted by the water and by the southern limits of the boreal zone; it begins again at the western shores of the lake and continues into the south-eastern corner of Manitoba. It ends at the grasslands transition zone.

Great Lakes–St. Lawrence is an irregular system contained in the north by the taiga forests and mixing in the south with the deciduous biome. In some favoured northerly locations, such as in the Gaspé and along both banks of the Saguenay River, up to and surrounding Lake St. John, it invades the boreal zone. Where it encounters the deciduous biome, although there is some form of transition zone, the two systems are difficult to separate, not only because they share natural conditions that are suitable for the development of plants and animals common to both biomes, but also because logging, urbanization, and agriculture have radically altered the environment, creating what are, in effect, unnatural biomes. In addition, a number of boreal evergreens also grow in this zone, although because of a somewhat more favourable climate and a longer growing season, they tend to be taller and of greater diameter.

Typical trees of the biome include eastern white pine; red pine; jack pine; red, white and black spruce; cedar; eastern hemlock; tamarack; aspen; balsam poplar; eastern cottonwood; red and sugar maple, and yellow and white birch. Willows, alders, cherries, and wild plum are also found in this zone together with many varieties of shrubs, wildflowers, ferns and fungi.

As is the case throughout Canada outside of the permanently frozen polar regions, lakes, rivers, creeks, and ponds are scattered everywhere within this biome, including the 1200 km (746 mi.) long St. Lawrence, which carries the waters of Lake Ontario to their meeting with the Atlantic in the Gulf of St. Lawrence. Much has been documented about the biology of the large lakes and rivers, but little lay-oriented material has been written about ponds, those small-to-medium bodies of quiet water that abound in every plant biome, but are often dismissed after their presence has been briefly noted.

Ponds, however, are vitally important constituents of all ecosystems, especially so in densely forested regions outside the influence of major

◄ **Point Pelée National Park**, Ontario, is Canada's southernmost point of land and enjoys a climate similar to that of northern California. The park attracts hosts of birds and is known for its unusual vegetation.

lakes and rivers. By definition, there are two kinds of ponds in Canada (and elsewhere in the world). The largest and deepest usually contain water the year around; the smallest and shallowest are most often seasonal, or *vernal*, as they are properly termed.

Vernal ponds emerge when spring run-off waters and early rains flow into soil or rock depressions. Depending on size and depth they may contain water for a few weeks or several months, but usually dry up before autumn. Nevertheless, during their wet times, these ponds teem with life. Insects, especially some species of mosquitoes, use them as

THE POND ENVIRONMENT

1 Mink
2 Ostrich ferns
3 Water shrew
4 Pondweed
5 Carp
6 Water strider
7 Water lilies
8 Snapping turtle
9 Salamander
10 Dragonfly nymph
11 Mosquito larva
12 Whirligig beetle
13 Star-nosed mole
14 Green frog
15 Cat-tails
16 American bittern
17 Muskrat
18 Marsh wren
19 Eastern kingbird
20 Horsetails
21 Springtail
22 Water flea
23 Backswimmer
24 Milfoil
25 Water snake
26 Mudpuppy
27 Cat fish

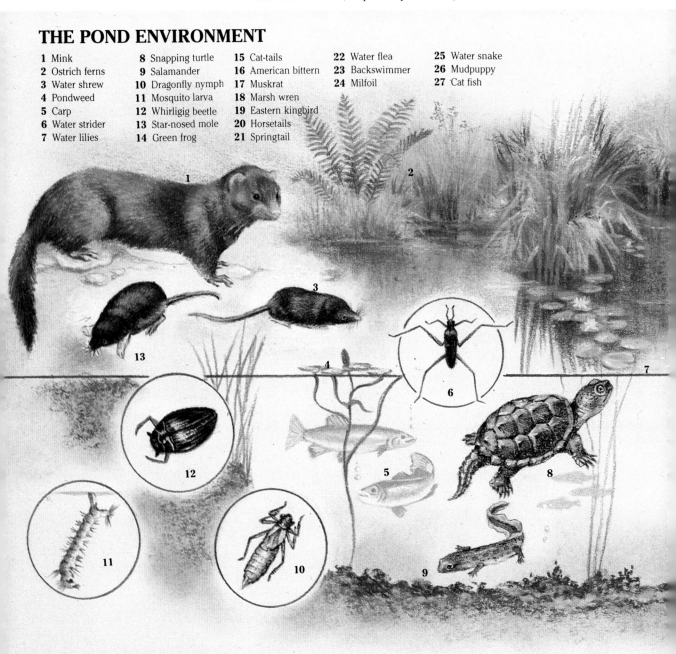

nurseries for their larvae, depositing their eggs in the water; other insects prey on the larvae. Mammals frequent the shorelines in search of prey and drinking water. Multi-hued wood ducks (*Aix sponsa*) which nest in the cavities of forest trees, court on their surfaces and later lead their ducklings to the larger vernal ponds. Frogs and salamanders breed in some of these temporary reservoirs, while forest birds use them as sources of water and food, taking the insects that abound in the surroundings of every pond and the seeds and berries that generally grow in such habitats. Lastly, many species of plants, including large

NOT TO SCALE

▲ Raccoon pawprints

▲ Raccoon tracks

trees, draw on the water that slowly sinks downwards, supplying moisture that may well last underground for the entire growing season.

Large ponds within the Great Lakes–St. Lawrence biome, as in all other Canadian plant zones, are most often made by beaver and probably begin as vernal depressions that offer convenient dam-construction features. Many of these, however, are also fed by small streams in spring, by the rains, and by the snow and ice of winter, but were it not for the indefatigable beaver, most of the stored water would be lost through run-off and evaporation.

Soon after one or more beavers have dammed a suitable area, creating a sizeable pond, muskrats take advantage of the new habitat, constructing their little domed lodges in the shallower parts of the pond builder's domain. As water plants proliferate, and as more and more aquatic animals find shelter in the brown waters, land birds nest in the surrounding trees and among adjacent marshes; waterfowl, including loons and grebes construct their nests in the shelter of cattails and other shoreline plants.

The most characteristic pond flowers are white waterlilies (*Nymphaea odorata*) and their relatives, the spatterdocks, (*Nuphar luteum*) or yellow lilies, also called brandy bottles because their squat seed capsules resemble antique leather flasks and contain alcohol, circumstances that combine to spread the plant's seeds. During the hours of sunlight, the alcohol inside the ripe seed capsules expands, putting pressure on the small containers. By sundown, the capsules cool and begin to contract; but, unable to shrink against the pressure of the expanded gasses, they explode, shooting off their round covers with enough force to cause small, but audible popping sounds and scattering the seeds in a spray.

The wide, floating leaves of both species of Canadian waterlilies become small ecosystems almost as soon as they unfurl in spring. A number of different species of minute insects live on the undersides of each leaf. Some of these feed on the plant's tissues; others obtain their food from floating algae, and yet others are tiny predators that feed on the vegetable eaters. Water mites, very small freshwater sponges, and water snails are some of the inhabitants of the leaves. Frogs and dragonflies perch on top of the green pads, at times merely resting, often lying in wait for flying insects that also alight on the convenient platforms.

Like marine kelps, white waterlilies have flexible stems. During low water, the pencil-thick stalks bend, allowing the leaves to stay on the surface; during high water, the leaves act as floats, and the stems are straightened. The stalks of the yellow lilies are more rigid; during late summer their leaves stand clear of the surface.

Plants "breathe" through their leaves, absorbing carbon dioxide and releasing water through minute pores, or *stomata*. Fresh-water and marine plants, the leaves of which float on the surface, have their pores on the top of each leaf rather than on the underside, as is the rule for terrestrial plants. Without such an arrangement, above-surface aquatic plants would literally drown. Nevertheless, the stomata would not be able to function, despite facing the air, if they became clogged by water and it is for this reason that their leaves are coated with a wax-like material that makes them waterproof. During heavy rain, or when the surface of the pond is stirred by wind, the upper surfaces of the leaves shed water; and when the weight of a frog submerges part or all of a leaf, the others continue to function.

Another characteristic plant of the pond environment is the touch-me-not, or jewelweed (*Impatiens* spp.), two species of which are found in Canada, one yellow and more likely to inhabit wet mountainous

▲ **A green darner dragonfly** newly emerged from its nymphal skin. Sometimes called "mosquito hawks", dragonflies eat many small insects including biting flies; developing in ponds and marshes, their robust nymphs prey on a variety of small aquatic animals, including the fry of fish.

areas, the other spotted and of an orange cast. It is generally believed that the name "jewelweed" was prompted by the shape and delicacy of the blossoms. In fact, the term refers to the leaves which, when submerged, are covered by minute air bubbles that catch the light and give off silvery sparkles. This plant's second common name, "touch-me-not", relates to the fact that its seed capsules explode when touched, a means of propagation similar to that of the yellow waterlily, but depending on contact rather than on atmospheric temperatures.

In the marshy areas that adjoin most ponds grow rushes, sedges, and a variety of grasses, all of which contribute to the aquatic ecosystem. Identification of the many species of these plants that grow in pond-created wetlands in the Great Lakes–St. Lawrence biome and in similar habitats found everywhere in Canada can sometimes be confusing, but, although a particular species may defy casual recognition, the distinctions between each plant genus are easily noted. It is said that sedges "have edges", which means that the leaves are keeled, somewhat like the shape of a canoe when seen in cross-section. Many varieties grow in Canada (1000 species are known world-wide), but the most readily recognized are the tussock sedges, the bases of which can support a person's weight and serve as convenient stepping stones in marshy areas. Grasses are more easily recognized by the shape of their leaves, although some are much taller and wider than the kinds that usually grow in domestic lawns. Some wild grasses of marsh and pond-side may well have sharp edges that can slice into flesh with the ease of a razorblade. Rushes are identifiable by their round, often hollow stems.

Cattails, marsh marigolds, scarlet cardinal flowers, wild roses, blue-flowered pickerel weed, white-bloomed arrowheads, ferns, mosses, lichens, and a variety of colourful fungi also grow in the environs of large ponds and their adjacent marshlands. On somewhat drier parts of a pond's ecosystem grow plants that are the sole survivors of a pre-historic class, the horsetails (*Equisetum* spp.), the ancestors of which reached a height of 12 m (40 ft.) and lived some 300 million years ago.

Horsetails, have a high silica content; one species, *Equisetum hyemale*, or scouring rush, was at one time used to scrub pots and pans, as nail files, and as fine sandpaper. They grow to a height of about 40 cm (16 in.) and have hollow stems, branches that emerge in whorls and tiny, scale-like leaves. Crowning each of these ancestral plants is a small cone that produces spores that when released develop male and female reproductive gametes. Twenty-five species occur world-wide (except in Australia) from the tropics to the Arctic regions. Despite the horsetail's unappetizing appearance, grizzly and black bears feed heavily on it at certain seasons, as do moose, sheep, squirrels, and some birds.

Aquatic animals commonly inhabiting large ponds in this and other Canadian biomes include the northern water snake and snapping and painted turtles.

The northern water snake (*Natrix sipdedon*) is a stout-bodied reptile with a head that is wide at the jaws; it can attain a length of 1.25 m (4 ft.). It is dark brown in colour — sometimes appearing black, especially when in the water — with darker blotches along the middle back. This snake is not poisonous; it is quite harmless to humans unless handled — when it can bite — but it is often unfairly accused of chasing swimmers and is at times mistaken for the highly venomous water moccasin, a species that does not inhabit Canada. The water snake feeds on fish, frogs, salamanders, and occasionally mice and shrews, hunting on land as well as in the water.

Snapping (*Chelydra serpentina*) and painted (*Chrysemys picta*) turtles inhabit ponds as well as lakes and rivers. The former, which can

▲ **Snapping turtles** are generally said to be "vicious" because they defend themselves when attacked. Left alone, these big turtles are not dangerous. They eat fish, small animals and carrion. In Canada they are confined to southern regions from Nova Scotia to Saskatchewan.

▲ **A toad** perches on a log during its search for insect prey. Toads of a variety of species are common across Canada. Despite a widespread myth, these amphibians do not cause warts. Toads have warty skins; frogs have smooth skins.

attain a length of about 0.5 m (1.6 ft.) and a weight of 18 kg (40 lb.) feeds on carrion, frogs, fish, insects and occasionally will take waterfowl. Painted turtles, of which there are four varieties, are scavengers that also eat water plants and will take live prey, such as fish and frogs when they can get it. These attractive reptiles attain a length of 15 cm (6 in.). Their common name is derived from the colour of their plastron (bottom shell), which is variously patterned with red, yellow, or a combination of both colours.

A number of different species of frogs, salamanders, and toads live in pond-influenced habitats. The largest of these amphibians are the bull-frog (*Rana catesbeiana*) and the green (*R. clamitans*) frogs, the former attaining a length of up to 19 cm (7.5 in.), the latter only slightly smaller. The bullfrog's common name is derived from its deep, cattle-like call.

Hylas, commonly referred to as tree frogs or tree "toads", are arboreal, their "fingers" and "toes" being equipped with adhesive pads that allow them to travel easily along branches and plant stems and even to climb sheer rock faces. They are small, seldom longer than 4 cm (1.5 in.), and live in the vicinity of ponds and marshes as well as in forested areas. Some species are chameleon-like in their ability to change colour from light green to grey or brown, depending on the hues of their surroundings. Another species of *hyla*, the little spring peeper (*Hyla crucifer*) lives in marsh areas and along the shores of waterways. Their calls are sometimes mistaken for the massed voices of chorus frogs, a species that is about the same size as the *hyla*, but is a true frog.

Toads use the water as a nursery for their eggs and young, but as adults live on land; they cannot jump as well as frogs. Their rough, dry skins and a slightly milky, acrid fluid that is discharged when a toad is handled were once thought to cause warts on humans. These useful amphibians feed mainly on insects and slugs, preferring to live in shady, moist habitats, but quite able to travel through dry areas without dehydrating.

In some parts of the Great Lakes–St. Lawrence biome, in relatively deep ponds, live the mudpuppies, or water dogs (*Necturus maculosus*), large salamanders that have bushy, protruding gills. These look rather like reddish plumes and extend outwards and backwards on either side of the head, just behind the jaws. The body is brown on top and speckled below by light yellow, irregular spots. Mudpuppies are carnivores that feed on fish, aquatic insects and other pond or lake dwellers of small size. Unlike other salamanders, the larvae of which develop in water and shed their gills before emerging on land, the mudpuppy, which can grow to 30 cm (12 in.) in length, remains an aquatic larva for its entire life.

Blackflies (*Simulium venustum*) lay their eggs in the downstream side of beaver dams as well as in neighbouring streams, for the hatching larvae require running water in order to develop. Although rightfully detested because of the female's ferocious bites, which cause considerable itching and swelling in animals, including humans, these insects have an interesting aquatic life cycle. On hatching, the minute larvae 5 mm (0.2 in.) long quickly attach their bulbous ends to a rock, securing a hold by producing a sticky substance and by further attaching themselves with a circle of more than a hundred microscopic hooks that radiate from their posterior ends. The head is equipped with two stalked plumes that serve to entrap food in the form of microscopic plants and animals. If a larva becomes dislodged from its anchoring rock, it lets out a silken thread as it drifts and soon pulls itself back to

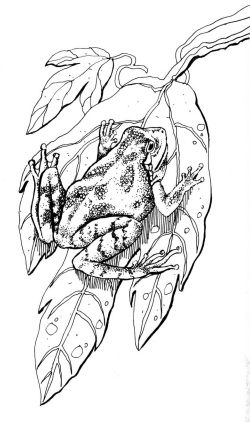

▲ **Common tree frog**

▲ **Turkey vulture**

safety. Depending on the species (1300 different kinds of blackflies are recognized world-wide, although fortunately the majority are harm less), the larvae pupate into adult form after an interval that varies from two to six weeks. They then rise to the surface in an air bubble, which is somehow trapped under water and encases the blood-sucker like a miniature diving chamber.

Some of the birds typical of pond and marsh are great blue herons, bitterns, kingfishers, red-wing blackbirds, marsh wrens and several flycatchers. In the Great Lakes–St. Lawrence biome and elsewhere in Canada, turkey vultures (*Cathartes aura*) glide and wheel above forest and open country, consummate masters of the air that arrive in late spring and return south before the first frosts whiten the dawn landscapes.

These large, black birds with naked, red heads can in no way be described as beautiful when viewed at close quarters, but their domi nance of the air is magnificent. With wings that span almost 2 m (6.5 ft.), the vultures take advantage of the thermal updrafts, gliding through space with outstretched wings that may not be seen to flap for many minutes at a time. Rising, wheeling, and dropping, their scarlet heads keep turning from side to side as their keen eyes search the wilderness for dead animals. Some people believe that turkey vultures prey on young animals, especially on domestic lambs. This is non sense. The vulture's feet are relatively clumsy; it has fairly long, stout claws, which, unlike those of other raptors, cannot grasp and stab prey, serving instead to hold down carrion while the bird tears at it with white, rather straight beak, only the tip of which is curved and pointed.

Turkey vultures do not build nests, but lay their eggs (usually two, sometimes only one, rarely three) on the ground, among rocks, under downed trees, on cliff ledges, or inside caves. After a period of incu bation by both parents, chicks hatch between 38 and 41 days after the eggs are laid; their eyes are open and they are dressed in downy, white plumage, their heads bare, but black at this stage. The young vultures are fed regurgitated carrion and do not fly until they are 11 weeks old, which is near the time they must migrate south.

Mammals of the Great Lakes–St. Lawrence biome include moose, white-tailed deer, small numbers of woodland caribou in a few areas, black bears, wolves, coyotes, red foxes, lynx and bobcats, pine martens and fishers, eastern porcupines, striped skunks, shrews, moles, several species of bats, and a variety of rodents, such as deer mice, red squirrels, and chipmunks.

FIREFLIES

Fireflies (family Lampyridae) are not flies, but rather beetles. To date 1700 species of fireflies have been identified world-wide, a number of which are found across Canada. Also known as lightning bugs, the nocturnal displays of green light emitted by both sexes during warm nights are well known and admired features of a Canadian summer. Males have several luminous organs on their abdominal segments and produce the most light; females, flightless in most species and known as glow worms, usually have only one luminous segment located on the underside, at the very end of the body.

Fireflies emit their flashes to attract each other during the mating season. Flashes of males and

▲ Fireflies

females can be distinguished because those of the males are above ground and never emitted from the same place twice, while those of the females are static and noted within foliage, or on the ground.

The almost totally cold light produced by these insects results when a firefly simultaneously discharges a cell product, luciferin, and an enzyme, luciferaze. The ensuing chemical reaction produces the light. Scientists have managed to synthesize such light in the laboratory, but no one to date has been able to produce practically heatless light for industrial or domestic needs, despite the enormous advantages that such luminescence would offer.

Two of the smallest and most inconspicuous mammals of this and other Canadian biomes are the water shrew (*Sorex palustris*) and the star-nosed mole, the former distributed right across the forested regions of the nation, the latter inhabiting a wide range between the Atlantic seaboard (but not including Newfoundland and Prince Edward Island) and the south-central part of Manitoba, excluding the prairies.

The water shrew is 15 cm (6 in.) in length counting the tail and has a soft, velvety coat that is charcoal black on top and silver-white tinged with brown on the undersides. These shades run along the tail, bisecting it, dark on top, silver below. This shrew's relatively large back feet have a fringe of short, stiff hairs; the middle toes are partially webbed. The back feet and the fairly long, well-furred tail with its closely piled fur give the shrew the ability to walk on still water, the webs on its feet aided by air bubbles trapped by the fringe of hairs.

▲ Water shrew

The water shrew emits a high-pitched, shrill little cry when startled and, never far from water, it is quick to dive below the surface, its downward progress marked by a trail of silvery bubbles. Like all of its kind, this animal is a hunter with an insatiable appetite. Its major food consists of a variety of aquatic insect larvae, especially those of caddisflies, stoneflies, and mayflies, which constitute almost 50 per cent of its diet. In addition, it eats worms, small fish, and at times fish eggs

THE EASTERN FOREST

NOT TO SCALE

▲ **Star-nosed mole**

as well as water snails, salamander larvae, and frog spawn. In return, the shrew is hunted by great blue herons, large fish, such as northern pike and largemouth bass, and loons and mergansers. Typical of shrews, its metabolism is rapid: it may die of old age at 16 months!

Little is known about this animal's gestation time, but breeding usually takes place in late February and it is believed that two or three litters are produced each year. Nests are made of grasses and other plant fibres and are usually about 10 cm (4 in.) in diameter; they may be made inside a hollow log, underground along a stream bank, and even inside a beaver lodge above the high-water mark, although how the shrew can tell when its nest is going to be safe from flooding is unknown. The beaver do not seem to object to their uninvited guests, however, perhaps because the shrews pay rent by ridding the den of unwelcome parasites.

The star-nosed mole (*Condylura cristata*) differs from all its North American relatives in a variety of ways and has the distinction of being one of the most anatomically odd mammals inhabiting the continent. It measures 20 cm (8 in.) in length, but its tail accounts for one-third of the total and is therefore long for a mole. But this appendage is unique in other ways also: it is thick, scaly, and during the summer and autumn is dressed in black hair; at the start of winter, however, the tail begins to store fat, eventually thickening to four times its earlier diameter. Now the hair becomes sparse and greasy, and the scales separate to reveal the pink skin, which is greatly stretched.

This mole's most extraordinary feature, and the one from which it has derived its common name, is its nose. The tip of the long snout is furnished with a radial arrangement of pink, fleshy tentacles, 11 to a side, that encompass the nostrils and act as tactile sense organs. Combined with its sense of smell, they at least partially make up for the mole's small, weak-visioned eyes, which are further hindered by facial hair.

The star-nosed mole spends more time on the surface than do its relatives, but it does dig tunnels with its fairly broad, sturdily clawed front feet. During this kind of activity, the tentacles are folded over its nose so as to prevent dirt from entering the nasal passages. When foraging, above or under the ground, it relies on its sense of smell, its hearing, and the touch sensitivity of its pink "feelers". It also hunts in water, being an excellent swimmer and diver. During such aquatic foraging, it must use its eyes to a certain degree, but relies greatly upon the tentacles, which, as it scuttles along the bottom, pick up the vibrations of the small prey animals against which they come into contact. The star-nose eats large numbers of aquatic worms, leeches, crayfish, insect nymphs, and larvae.

THE DECIDUOUS BIOME

The greater part of this biome, which is our most southerly, lies within the province of Ontario and contains more species of trees than are found in any other Canadian plant zone. Apart from the various kinds of evergreens that grow in the Great Lakes–St. Lawrence system, tolerant hardwoods typify the deciduous region. Some of these trees grow as far east as south-western New Brunswick, others have extended their range northwards and westwards, but, by and large, most species are found within those temperate areas that lie in a belt between the border of the United States and a northern latitude that roughly travels along a line between Montreal, Quebec, and Sault Ste. Marie, Ontario.

As noted earlier, however, the boundaries of the deciduous biome, mingling as they do with the Great Lakes–St. Lawrence, are extremely irregular. Additionally, because of farming, logging, urbanization and its consequent population pressure, the most extensive highway system in Canada, mineral and industrial development, and a variety of atmospheric and water-borne pollutants, this plant system has been radically and adversely altered. It bears but scant resemblance to the natural environment that existed when the first European colonists settled the land.

In addition to birches, a total of 56 species of hardwoods grow in this biome including: chestnut, walnut, hickory, beech, oak, maple, ash, elm and a variety of trees found only in this plant zone.

The one species of chestnut native to Canada (*Castanea dentata*) is practically extinct, having been devastated by a fungal disease soon after the turn of this century. This tree attained a height of 30 m (100 ft.) and a diameter of 1 m (40 in.) and was native to southern Ontario from the Niagara River and Lake Ontario westward to Lake St. Clair.

Two species of walnuts grow here: the black (*Juglans nigra*) and the butternut (*Juglans cinerea*). The former grows in the region of southern Ontario that borders lakes Erie, Ontario, and St. Clair; it reaches a height of 27 m (90 ft.) and a diameter of about 1 m (40 in.). The latter is found from the valley of the St. John River in western New Brunswick, to the lower St. Lawrence Valley and thence west throughout the hardwood areas of Ontario and Quebec.

The four species of hickory (*Carya* spp.) — bitternut, pignut, shagbark, and shellbark — are medium to large trees that have compound, alternate, and somewhat aromatic leaves. The nuts of the last three species are edible; those of the bitternut, as the tree's name implies, are inedible. Canadian hickories are confined to southern Quebec and Ontario.

Beeches (*Fagus grandifolia*) are among the most stately hardwoods commonly found in the deciduous biome. They reach a height of 24 m

The Indian pipe is parasitic and ▶
saprophytic. It has no green chloro-
phyll and must feed on the roots of
live plants or on decaying matter. It
is found in forests from Newfoundland to southwest British Columbia.

(80 ft.) and have a trunk diameter of 1.2 m (4 ft.). The trunks are usually straight and erect when the trees grow in dense stands, the branches forming an elegant canopy crowned by oval, serrated, sharp-pointed leaves. The smooth, bluish, tight-fitting bark on the trunks is attractive and unmistakable. Beeches, especially young ones, usually retain most of the dead leaves throughout the winter, creating pleasing vistas of golden colour when seen against the background of evergreens and snow. These trees are found from Nova Scotia's Cape Breton Island westward (except on the Gaspé Peninsula) to the north shore of Ontario's Georgian Bay in Lake Huron.

Eight species of oak (*Quercus* spp.) grow in this plant zone: white, bur, swamp white, dwarf chestnut, chinquapin, red, black, and pin. Most are confined to Ontario's southern peninsula and reach heights that vary between 15 m (49 ft.) and 24 m (80 ft.) with diameters up to 1.2 m (4 ft.).

Throughout the northern hemisphere, 150 species of maple (*Acer* spp.), a red leaf of which is emblazoned on Canada's flag, are found, being abundant in eastern Asia, especially within the Himalayan Mountains and in some regions of China. Ten species grow in Canada. The vine maple and the broadleaf maple are confined to the southwestern part of British Columbia; the Douglas maple grows in eastern British Columbia and on Vancouver Island. The sugar, black, red, silver, mountain, and striped grow in the deciduous biome, and the Manitoba maple (*Acer negundo*) ranges from western Alberta east to Ontario. The sap of all maples contains some sugar and during early pioneering times all Canadian species were tapped for this commodity in an age when imported cane sugar was extremely scarce. Later, when production of maple syrup became commercialized, it was not profitable to tap the poorer sugar producers and only the sugar (*Acer saccharum*) and black (*Acer nigrum*) maples were tapped. Depending on the season, almost 200 L (44 gal.) of maple sap are required to produce 4.5 L (1 gal.) of syrup.

Of the 60 species of ash (*Fraxinus* spp.) known to occur in the Northern Hemisphere, 16 are found in North America. Four species grow in Canada; all are eastern trees and confined to the deciduous biome,

▲ **Sugar maple**

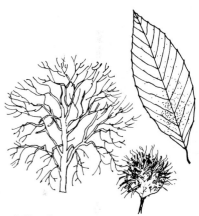

▲ **Beech**

OVERLEAF **Despite cold and heavy snowfalls**, Canada's winter wilderness ▶ offers beautiful scenery. Even though most of the deciduous foliage has fallen from the trees, the few leaves that remain on the snow-bedecked branches add touches of pleasing colour to the forest.

Raccoons are highly intelligent, ▶
dexterous omnivores that have
adapted well to human presence,
being found even in the downtown
parts of some large Canadian cities.
Like bears, raccoons in Canada sleep
through most of the winter.

although the green ash (*Fraxinus pennsylvanica*) has extended its range into southern Manitoba and the black ash (*Fraxinus nigra*) grows into the boreal forest.

Trees that are rare in Canada and found only in this plant zone, but are relatively common in the United States, include: red mulberry, cucumber trees, tulip tree, papaw, sassafras, sycamore, Kentucky coffee trees, hop tree, and black gum.

The white elm (*Ulmus americana*) is probably regarded as Canada's stateliest deciduous tree and one that has unfortunately been devastated by an imported fungus (*Ceratocystis ulmi*), which causes Dutch elm disease. This highly infectious ailment first reached Canada in 1944 and now occurs throughout most of the elm's range in this zone, which extends from Nova Scotia to western Manitoba in a line south of the Great Lakes–St. Lawrence system. The fungus that causes the disease is spread by two species of beetle, one a native (*Hylurgopinus rufipes*) and the other imported from Europe (*Scolytus multistriatus*), which carry the fungal spores from tree to tree. Despite all attempts to halt the spread of the disease, it appears likely that the elms will become extinct, at least in southern Ontario, the only survivors perhaps remaining in the more northerly parts of the tree's range.

Dutch elm disease furnishes a classic example of the problems that arise in an ecosystem when non-native species of plants and animals are introduced. If the newcomer is able to survive and reproduce within the new habitat, it most often proliferates and takes over from native species. Starlings and house sparrows were introduced to North America soon after the turn of this century. They have become pests of native birds and of agricultural crops and appear to be multiplying alarmingly. Conversely, native species that have always been kept in controlled balance by natural forces, may become harmful if an introduced species provides them with a defenceless source of food. Such an event occurred on the North American continent during the middle of the nineteenth century, when a beetle that once fed on plants of the nightshade family and was naturally confined to the banks of the Missouri River was given access to the white potato. Since then this insect (*Leptinotarsa decemlineata*) has become known as the Colorado potato beetle; it is a serious pest of potato plants (which are members of the nightshade family) and has spread to all potato-growing regions on the North American continent. In 1922, the striped, yellow-and-dark brown beetle crossed the Atlantic and became well established in Europe.

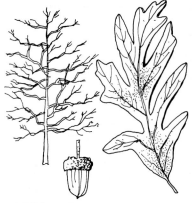

▲ **White oak**

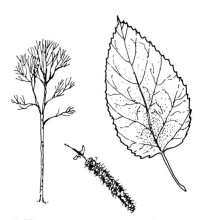

▲ **White birch**

ROOT FACTS

The actual space occupied above ground by a tree or other plant is roughly about half of that occupied by its root system, but if all the main roots and the millions of tiny root hairs that project from them are measured and the result added, it is to be noted that roots travel enormous distances. One experiment conducted a number of years ago established that a rye plant growing in a box 30 cm (12 in.) square that had attained a height of 50 cm (20 in.), had 516 km (320 mi.) of main roots. When the root hairs were laboriously counted, they would have covered a straight-line distance of 8284 km (5147 mi.) if placed end to end. The combined total added up to 8800 km (5468 mi.)!

With such extensive networks of hold-fasts, plants can withstand the buffeting of even the strongest gales if they are growing in deep soil. More than that, however, the network of roots furnishes a constant supply of nutrients that are extracted from the ground. They also serve as conduits for water and oxygen while combining with the soil to form vast, spongy masses that channel excessive moisture, spreading it into other areas and

serving as reservoirs for rain and melt-water for use during the many dry periods that occur over the course of a growing year.

Although an integral part of the deciduous biome, Point Pelée National Park, located in Ontario, is one of Canada's most unusual ecosystems. It is the nation's southernmost point of land and lies at the same latitude as northern California and the Costa Brava in northeastern Spain; it is further distinguished by having the warmest climate of all Canadian biomes.

Point Pelée is composed of a foundation of sand and gravel that is 3.5 km (2.17 mi.) wide at its northern base and slightly more than 17 km (11 mi.) long, its terminus a curving, sharply pointed spit that thrusts into Lake Erie south-east of Windsor, Ontario, and points to the state of Ohio across the water. Geologists believe that the landspit first began to form some 10 000 years ago as glacial melt-waters carried sand and silt and deposited these minerals along a submerged limestone ridge that extended from what is now Ontario to the opposite, U.S., shore.

Where the sandspit bites into the lake, it is beset by strong currents that alter its shape continuously, at times lengthening the tip, at others shortening it while altering its curvature and sweep. During the moist

Prickly pear cactus in bloom in Point Pelée National Park, Ontario. Nowhere ▶ plentiful in Canada, the prickly pear is also found in some regions of British Columbia.

▲ **A grasshopper** feeds on a sausage-like cat-tail head. These insects can severely damage wild plants and crops when populations increase explosively. Otherwise, they are preyed on by a variety of mammals, birds and other insects.

springs common to the point, the land produces lush, jungle-like lowland vegetation overlooked by a variety of deciduous hardwood trees, including basswood, hackberry, oaks, red ash, and silver maples, many of which are covered by lianas of wild grapes, poison ivy, and Virginia creeper. This is one of the country's few remaining stands of deciduous or Carolinian forest.

Undergrowth is luxuriant and thick during the spring, but dies off and is replaced by other lowland plants during the hot dry spells of mid-summer, when prickly pear cactus (*Opuntia humifusa*) thrives, producing showy, rose-shaped yellow blooms.

Point Pelée is most famous for the numbers of birds that are seen there during the nesting season and, especially, during spring and autumn migration flights, when two major flyway routes overlap at the park. More than 332 species have been counted during the height of migration and some 90 species are known to nest on the point.

L arge mammals, such as bears and moose, are no longer encountered within this biome, much of which now consists of agricultural/urban land. Coyotes (*Canis latrans*), not known in eastern Canada until about 60 years ago, have become problem animals in some areas, not only because they prey on domestic sheep and on the young of other livestock, but also because they are interbreeding with feral or wild dogs and producing what is in effect a new species, animals that are often larger than their wild progenitors and far less shy of humans.

Smaller, highly adaptable animals have become numerous because of the changes made on the environment by humans. In large areas, native forests have been replaced by vegetable, fruit and seed crops that supply abundant food for groundhogs, mice, voles, and the omnivorous raccoons. Skunks, although largely carnivorous, also take advantage of crops such as strawberries and other fruits; in addition, they may prey on domestic chickens. Because wolves have been eliminated in large parts of this biome, white-tailed deer (*Odocoileus virginianus*), taking advantage of agricultural crops as well as an abundance of saplings and other wild plants, have overpopulated, in some areas causing damage to wild plants and agricultural crops, as well as causing highway accidents. Birds of some species are also abundant in other regions because of the altered habitat and food supplies, especially gulls, starlings, grackles, house sparrows, and feral domestic pigeons.

In the remaining natural forests, in and around lakes and streams, and in the marshlands, many of the mammals, birds, amphibians, reptiles, and insects found in other temperate biomes are present.

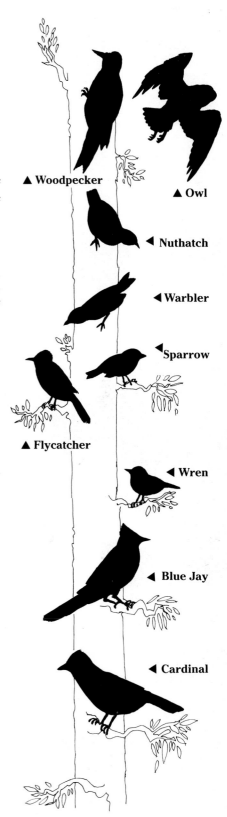

▲ Woodpecker

▲ Owl

◀ Nuthatch

◀ Warbler

◀ Sparrow

▲ Flycatcher

◀ Wren

◀ Blue Jay

◀ Cardinal

FOREST IMAGES

◀ **The showy lady's-slipper**, one of Canada's most beautiful members of the orchid family, inhabits wet woodlands from Ontario to Newfoundland. Other slipper varieties range over most of the nation.

▲ **Porcupines** are Canada's second largest rodent next to the beaver. Adult males measure about 90 cm (3 ft.) in length and weigh up to 11 kg (25 lb.). Myth to the contrary, a porcupine does not throw at an enemy any of its approximately 30 000 quills.

◀ **The upland sandpiper** inhabits grassy uplands, prairies and pastures.

Autumn colour on Beausoleil ▶ Island, in Lake Huron's Georgian Bay, Ontario.

◄ **The red eft** form of the red-spotted newt. These newts are born in the water but live for one to three years on land before returning to pond or marsh.

◄ **A sphinx moth** showing the intense colour of its hind wings. Most of these moths feed at dusk or at night.

**Quebec's Laurentian deciduous ►
forests** in autumn, photographed from the air. Sugar maples provide much of the colour in the fore-ground.

◄ **Goldenrods** of many different species abound in Canada. Sometimes mistakenly called butterfly weed, perhaps because butterflies do alight on them, it has been estimated that between 62 and 69 different goldenrods are found on this continent, many of them in our nation.

▲ **The swallowtail** family includes our largest butterflies. Colour and markings vary among the species.

◄ **Blue jays** have many calls, some harsh and noisy, others soft and cooing. Nesting in forest trees, usually conifers, they raise from four to six young. Blue jays eat seeds, fruit, insects and the eggs and fledglings of other birds.

▼ **Five species of chipmunk** live in our country. Members of the squirrel family, these striped rodents are indefatigable hoarders of seeds.

Northern saw-whet owls are ► permanent residents in forested regions across extreme southern Canada. Their common name derives from their repetitive, high-pitched and rasping calls, which sound somewhat like a file being passed over the teeth of a saw.

THE ACADIAN BIOME

 THIS BIOME ENCOMPASSES CANADA'S FOUR MOST easterly provinces: New Brunswick, Nova Scotia, Prince Edward Island, and some areas of Newfoundland. White, red, and black spruce, balsam fir, yellow and white birch, white and red pines, larches, red maple, trembling aspen, and balsam poplar grow in all four provinces, while sugar maple, jack pine, eastern hemlock, and beech are found in the first three provinces (scarce in Prince Edward Island), but not in Newfoundland.

The Eastern maritime forests are strongly influenced by the Atlantic Ocean, particularly so in Newfoundland, the craggy coasts of which dive inland in many locations where forests and sea literally meet. Similarly, although there are fewer coastlines, trees and ocean frequently come together in Nova Scotia and New Brunswick, while Prince Edward Island, largely comprising rolling lowland, presents to the Atlantic many stretches of beaches where salt-resistant plants encounter the brine and waves and offer shelter to sea birds and some marine organisms, such as crabs, during high tides.

From the standpoint of its major species of trees, parts of Newfoundland rightfully belong to the Acadian biome. Geologically and biologically, however, this island, which covers an area of more than 400 000 km^2 (154 440 sq. mi.) and is unique in North America, represents three prehistoric geological formations and the three plant biomes (boreal, tundra, and Acadian). Further influenced by the Atlantic, these formations have produced a number of unusual ecosystems.

The theory of continental drift, which postulates that Africa, Europe, and North America drifted together many millions of years ago, was largely discredited when it was proposed by German geologist Alfred Wegener (1880–1930) in 1912. More recently, however, it has become an accepted hypothesis based upon findings which suggest that the earth's crust is supported by a series of *tectonic* (Greek *tektonikos*: "construction") plates, or slabs, which float on a mantle of molten rock deep within the globe. Drifting and shifting at an *extremely* slow rate, the plates brought the three continents together some 450 million years ago. When they began to drift apart again about 200 million years later just as slowly as they had originally travelled, the evidence suggests that a piece of North Africa remained fixed to Newfoundland, leaving behind a region that now includes the land lying east of an imaginary line between Bay d'Espoir, in the south, and Bonavista Bay, in the north-east, and incorporating the Avalon Peninsula.

◀ **A Gros Morne, Newfoundland, "fjord"** seen from the air in May. Formed by glaciation, these "fjords" were cut off from the sea by the rising land.

However this may be, the landscape and topography of Newfound-land show three definite variations, including the remnants of the Appalachian Mountains, which, over millions of years, have been reduced by erosion in the four maritime provinces. In the region encompassing the Avalon Peninsula, the rocky landscape is relatively low, but punctuated by long fjords; some of these cut deeply into the land. On the island's west coast, striated beds of shale, their seaward faces eroded and left naked, their arched brows covered by a thin topping of soil that supports hardy red pines, graphically demonstrate the power of the elements. In the north-west, at the tip of the Great Northern Peninsula, the boreal biome is encountered, in places inter-rupted by tundra-like vegetation; and in the central regions a mixture of basalt rock, muskeg bogs, dense forests of spruce and pine, and a profusion of wildflowers in sheltered valleys alternate at frequent intervals.

Many of the smaller plants, sedges, grasses, and shrubs are of the same species as those found in other northern and eastern biomes, but some, like the insectivorous pitcher plant (*Sarracenia purpurea*), grow particularly well on the island.

Mammals native to Newfoundland include only 14 species, of which woodland caribou are the most significant. Some of the others are black bears, lynx, river otters, beaver, foxes, pine martens, weasels, and Arc-tic hares. Wolves were native to the island, but were exterminated by 1910. Meanwhile, some mainland mammals, such as moose, snowshoe hares, chipmunks, and red squirrels, have been introduced.

Prince Edward Island has a total area of only 5650 km^2 (2181 sq. mi.), just 0.01 per cent of the nation's total land area. Today it hosts few examples of its original Acadian biome and fauna, most of its rich soil regions having been cleared and taken over by agricultural crops, especially potatoes, for which Canada's smallest province is famous. The same holds true for the small number of terrestrial mammals that originally inhabited the forests and clearings found when Cartier landed on the north-west tip of the island in 1534, although sea and land birds are plentiful there, as they are in the entire Acadian biome. More than 300 different species of birds have been reported, a large number of them also being found off the Quebec coast in the Gulf of St. Lawrence.

One of the most spectacular seabirds of this region is the goose-size northern gannet (*Sula bassanus*), a superb flier and diver with a wing-spread of almost 2 m (6.5 ft.). At one time it bred in enormous colonies along the entire east coast. Senseless slaughter had brought the species to near extinction by 1904, at which time the Canadian government invoked protection laws. Today about 30 000 gannets breed in the

▲ **Pitcher plants** are found from Newfoundland to Saskatchewan. The pitcher-like leaves usually remain half-filled with water, while their flaring lips are lined with downward-pointing bristles that help to trap insects, which are absorbed by the plant.

region. The largest colony, numbering about 15 000 birds, is located on Bonaventure Island, off the Gaspé Peninsula in Quebec.

Great and double-crested cormorants, razorbills, Atlantic puffins, great black-backed gulls, guillemots, Arctic and common terns, lesser golden-plovers, sandpipers, murres, bald eagles, great horned owls, and many other species make this biome a bird-watcher's paradise, for, unlike the west coast — which also has many species of interesting birds — the Atlantic shores are far more accessible to boaters and hikers. For the same reason, whale and seal watchers have ample opportunity to observe these great marine mammals during those times when they travel and hunt in the Acadian zone's waters.

Canada's marine mammals belong to four groups: Odontoceti, or toothed whales; Mysticeti, or baleen whales; Pinnipedia, or seals and walruses; and *Enhydra lutris*, the sea otter, which is not native to the Atlantic seaboard.

A total of 33 species of cetaceans occur in Canada, although some are sighted infrequently and others may rarely visit the nation's shores. Of these 25 are toothed whales, the remaining 8 are baleen whales.

Some odontoceti, such as the large sperm whale, have rows of conical teeth in the lower jaw that fit into sockets in the upper jaw; others, like the orca — killer whale — have strong, conical teeth in both jaws. All toothed whales, including dolphins and porpoises, are carnivorous hunters. The sperm whale (*Physeter catodon*), immortalized by Herman Melville (1819–91) in his book, *Moby Dick*, is the largest member of this family, reaching a length of more than 15 m (49 ft.) and a weight of more than 47 t (52 tons). It is a regular visitor to both the Atlantic and Pacific coasts and a tenacious hunter of giant squid (*Architeuthis harveyi*), relatives of the octopus and cuttlefish, some of which have been reported to grow up to 18 m (59 ft.). Harpooned sperm whales, on examination, have been found to contain in their stomachs pieces of squid which suggest that some of these ten-armed creatures may exceed 18 m, but to date only one sperm-whale stomach has yielded an entire squid: it measured 10.5 m (34.5 ft.) and weighed 184 kg (405 lb.). Sperm whales, which also feed on fish and sharks, are capable of diving to great depths, the known record being 1134 m (3720 ft.).

In addition to the sperm whales, some of the toothed whales known to visit the coastal waters of Canada's three oceans at different times of the year include: giant, Sowerby's, and Blainville's beaked whales;

▲ **A beluga**, or white whale, "stands" on its tail to get a better view of its surroundings while two companions show their backs as they swim partly submerged.

◄ **Common murres** on a cliff edge in Newfoundland. Related to the puffins and to the extinct great auk, this diver/swimmer breeds farther south than the thick-billed murre, nesting along coasts and islands of the North Pacific and North Atlantic.

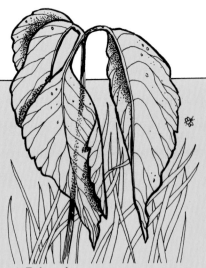

▲ Poison ivy

LEAVES OF THREE, LET IT BE

Poison ivy (*Rhus radicans*) is abundant throughout wooded and shrubby areas of Canada below the tree-line. The plant grows in rather specialized locations, which aids in its detection: it often clings to roadside shrubbery, or on the edge of woodlands; but it can also grow within relatively open forests in locations where it can get at least some sunshine. The rhyme *leaves of three, let it be* will help to recognize poison ivy's characteristic foliage: three wavy-edged, or toothed leaves that grow at the ends of many long stalks, their upper surface being variously glossy or waxy dull, depending on the plant's age and growing location. Although the ivy sometimes climbs on other plants, fence wire, or trees, it often grows unsupported on the ground. The twigs are brown. Leaves reach a length of between 5 and 7 cm (2 and 2.75 in.) and ground-growing plants attain a height of about 46 cm (18 in.).

The juice from all parts of this plant (including from its roots) contains a poison that causes a serious irritation on the skin. In some individuals especially sensitive to the poison, the rash is hard to cure; even when seemingly neutralized, it may recur weeks or months later without further contact with the ivy. If it is necessary to hand-clear the plant from a location, protective clothing and gloves should be worn. Poison ivy should *never* be burned: its smoke is poisonous and can seriously irritate the lungs of those who might inhale the fumes.

northern bottlenosed whales; white whales (beluga); narwhals, the males and rarely females of which have a long, spirally twisted tusk projecting from their upper jaw, whose use has not yet been determined; blue dolphins; common dolphins (rarely); bottlenosed dolphins (rarely); white-sided dolphins; orcas; pilot whales; harbour porpoises, and Dall's porpoises.

The great blue whale is the most impressive of those mysticetis that visit Canadian waters. The others are: gray, fin, sei, minke, humpback, right, and bowhead. All of these whales feed on planktonic organisms that consist of minute larvae and fry (young) of many different species, some small fish, and an undetermined amount of marine algae, although whether the latter actually serves as nourishment is not known. Baleen whales swim through "clouds" of plankton, some with their mouths open, scooping up great quantities of food during each pass. When the mouth is full, they close the jaws and strain out the water through numerous panels of baleen, which take the place of teeth and make efficient filters. Baleen is the material commonly called *whale bone*. Actually, it is not bone at all, but is composed of a hard protein called *keratin*, which is the same material that forms the hair, wool, nails, and other similar structures in animals, including humans.

Four species of seals inhabit Canada's Atlantic waters: gray seals, harbour seals, harp seals, and hooded seals. The harp species (*Phoca groenlandica*) has been the primary target of Canada's annual seal hunt since the mid-eighteenth century, when sailing vessels and sealers from a number of nations first began gathering off the Newfoundland coast to reap the harvest of adult and pup seal pelts. Between 1820 and 1860, an average of 0.5 million seals were killed annually; the greatest number killed in any one year was in 1831, when 300 ships manned by 10 000 sealers killed a total of 687 000 harps. In this century, killing of seals continued under federal government supervision until the early 1980s, when opposition to the annual hunt voiced by many in North America and elsewhere caused Europe to ban the importation of seal pelts. Since then seal hunts have taken place each season, but on a far smaller scale than ever before.

All marine mammals can spend a long time under the surface — as much as 90 to 120 minutes in some cases — and at great depths without suffering ill effects. Humans, by comparison, can only spend between two and four minutes while free diving at depths of no more than 100 m (328 ft.).

Before a dive, whales and seals first prepare themselves by deep breathing, an exercise during which they can fill their lungs to between 80 and 90 per cent capacity: humans, in comparison, can only use half their lung capacity. While deep breathing, they are also "loading" their muscles with large amounts of oxygen-rich myoglobin, which is a form of hemoglobin, the breathing pigment of the red blood cells. In addition, marine mammals can re-route their blood supply from uncritical parts of their bodies and pump it in large amounts to the nervous system and heart, and their muscles are capable of functioning efficiently without oxygen for prolonged periods.

While diving, the heart rate of whales and seals drops dramatically: in seals, from 120 beats a minute down to only 10 beats a minute; in dolphins, from 110 beats a minute to 50 beats a minute. Then, too, during deep dives their lungs collapse under the pressure of water, thus preventing nitrogen bubbles from entering the bloodstream and creating the "bends", or nitrogen narcosis, which in humans can be fatal unless a diver can quickly be placed in a decompression chamber and allowed to recover slowly. As these mammals begin to rise towards the surface, the lungs gradually re-inflate.

As soon as their heads emerge from the water, whales "blow" or "spout". Many people still believe that this characteristic cetacean display is composed of exhaled water. This is not so. In fact, as they clear the surface, they exhale through narrow nostrils (in some species, only one "blow hole" is present). The stale breath, emerging under pressure and warmed by the animal's internal temperature, expands rapidly,

▲ **Harbour seal**

▲ **Hooded seal**

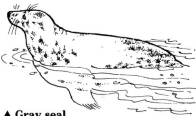

▲ **Gray seal**

▲ **Harp seal**

OVERLEAF **New Brunswick in autumn** is a province filled with riotous ▶ colours.

▲ **American woodcock**

WOODCOCK EYES

Measuring a total length of between 25.4 and 30.5 cm (10 and 12 in.), the American woodcock (*Scolopax minor*) is unusual among birds in that its large eyes are located high on the head, practically above its brain. The woodcock feeds primarily on earthworms as well as on other underground life forms and the unusual placement of its eyes allows it to stay in visual touch with its environment while its head is lowered to ground level and its beak, which has a flexible tip, is deep in the soggy ground, searching for food.

This stout-bodied, cinnamon-coloured bird with the long beak belongs to the sandpiper family of shorebirds, the Scolopacidae. Although technically a shore bird, the woodcock is most usually found within, or just outside the forest. In Canada it ranges from Newfoundland along a relatively narrow, southerly band of territory that extends through the maritime provinces, southern Quebec and Ontario, and westward to southern Manitoba. Woodcocks are among the earliest birds to return to Canada in spring, often arriving while patches of snow still decorate the forest floor. At dusk, during the spring breeding season, males strut about while emitting sharp, nasal calls similar to the cries of the common nighthawk. At intervals, the birds whir upwards, beating their wings so rapidly that, as the stiff flight feathers displace air, they produce a rapid series of loud, musical whistles. Rising high, a male woodcock next dances acrobatically on its extended wings, then dives back to earth and resumes its intermittent *peent* calls.

cooling instantly and converting to vapour. Large whales may exhale up to 2000 L (440 gal.) of moisture-laden breath, emitting the characteristic misty cloud that disappears soon after it has formed.

Sea water can transmit sound between five and six times faster than air. At sea level, sound travels through air at a speed of 335 m (1100 ft.) per second. In the sea, sound travels at speeds of between 1675 m (5495 ft.) and 2011 m (6598 ft.) per second. This circumstance has allowed marine mammals and fishes to develop echolocation to a high degree. Toothed whales, some baleen whales, and a number of seals use this skill when seeking prey and for navigational purposes, somewhat like bats. Additionally, at least some whales communicate with one another by this means. When echolocating, or "talking" to one another, cetaceans emit low-frequency sounds in the form of clicks and whistles that can reach a range of 150 kHz or 150 000 cycles per second, especially when an animal is tuning in to its prey. By actual test, an Atlantic bottlenosed dolphin (*Tursiops truncatus*) was able to distinguish the difference between a steel ball 5.4 cm in diameter (2.13 in.) and another that was 6.35 cm (2.5 in.) in diameter.

Mammals found on the mainland regions of the Acadian biome include the majority of those native to other Canadian ecosystems. In addition to mice, voles, moles, and squirrels, Arctic foxes are found in extreme north-western Newfoundland and, more rarely, in the eastern part of that province and in Nova Scotia's Cape Breton Island. In spring, polar bears (*Ursus maritimus*) riding spring pack-ice rafts reach the northernmost shores of Newfoundland, some of them continuing to float through the Strait of Belle Isle into the Gulf of St. Lawrence, from where they may travel along the Quebec shore as far as Anticosti Island.

Cougar (*Felis concolor*), the eastern species of which was brought to the very edge of extinction soon after the turn of this century, has in recent years made a modest come-back. Sightings have occasionally been made in New Brunswick, Ontario, and parts of Quebec, and tracks and scats have been reported.

Variously called mountain lion, catamount, cougar, and a variety of other colloquial names within its range, which extends from Patagonia to northerly regions of British Columbia, this big cat has been known to attain a length of 2.5 m (8.2 ft.) and a weight of 79 kg (174 lb.), but is usually somewhat shorter and lighter. Because in more recent years logging and farming in eastern Canada have created near-ideal habitat for white-tailed deer, cougar have evidently been able to survive in suitable forested regions, although their numbers are probably small.

Despite its size, the cougar is a silent, secretive animal that may live within a short distance of human habitations without attracting attention unless it takes to killing domestic stock, which is something that it rarely does if its natural prey is readily available.

Feared by many, the cougar does not usually attack humans, although it has done so on rare occasions. Most often it takes good care to keep away from people, its big, soft pads making hardly a whisper as it slides through even the deepest wilderness. About the only time that this cat makes noise is during the mating season, when a female may cut loose with an unearthly shriek capable of striking fear in even the most seasoned forest travellers. Males, on the other hand, resort to soft whistles when wooing a mate, who, if she is receptive, may often respond in kind. The sight and sounds of two cougars engaging in a whistling duet is fascinating. Alternately purring loudly, rubbing against each other, scent-marking trees and rocks with sprayed urine, and emitting soft, cooing whistles, the big cats behave quite sedately, seemingly out of keeping with what might be expected from two such powerful animals.

▲ **Red maple leaves**, ferns, lichens on the tree trunks and green leaves make a patchwork of early autumn colour in a section of Acadian woodland.

AFTERWORD

 NO BOOK ON THE NATURAL HISTORY OF Canada can be complete without a review of the negative pressures that are being exerted on the nation's environment. At a casual glance, any country that has been blessed with so much wild land on which live so many species of plants and animals and which is further enriched by an abundance of potable water should not have to worry unduly about habitat and species destruction, especially when its human population is smaller than that of most other industrialized states. Closer scrutiny, however, quickly shows that the largely uncontrolled damage inflicted on the environment by over-exploitation and pollution is, indeed, a cause for serious concern.

After devoting more than half of my life to a close study of Canada's natural world and, especially, after having examined in this book the biology of our land, I conclude with many misgivings that are yet somewhat tempered by hope for the future.

My misgivings stem from the undeniable fact that Canada's natural environment is being systematically raped in the name of progress, sport, or entertainment, its resources "harvested" without concern for the future and without real awareness of the havoc that is being created by unbridled exploitation.

My hope for the future emerges from the knowledge that more and more people share those concerns and are actively seeking to protect the natural state. In this regard, I receive a great many letters from readers, all of whom express a profound interest in, and a love for, nature. Such correspondence is addressed to me by people of all ages and condition who live on this continent and elsewhere in the world. The great majority of writers invariably ask: "What can I do to help?"

In part, this afterword will attempt to give a collective answer to all those who have phrased that question. In part, I propose to examine some of the major abuses to which our environment is being subjected. Then, too, I will examine some of the theories of conservation as espoused by the Society of Conservation Biology, a recently formed international forum that seeks to promote what is, in effect, the new science of the scarcity and diversity of terrestrial and aquatic species with a view to changing the present exploitative attitudes before it is too late to turn back. Michael E. Soule, of the School of Natural Resources, University of Michigan, who is president of the board of governors of the society, has warned of the probable extinction of the majority of the world's natural species during the next 50 to 100 years.

◄ **Autumn leaves** cover the forest floor in Algonquin Park, Ontario.

Soule is not saying that such a grim prospect is inevitable, of course. Like many other informed conservationists, he sees a time in the future when, as species after species become extinct, more and more people will realize that the right to life of non-human entities is as important as the right to life of mankind. They will then join forces to protect what is left of the natural environment and, one hopes, in time to redress at least some of the balance.

I agree with the scenario drawn by Soule, especially in view of the fact that scientific research has already forecasted that massive species extinction will occur by the year 2000. I am also sanguine in the belief that the runaway rate at which the despoliation of our environment is continuing will be at least slowed *before* the turn of the century by the outraged protests of an informed public.

T he first law of ecology states that in nature *everything is connected to everything else.* This means that when one thing is removed by unnatural means a negative chain reaction takes place. Such a reaction may entail the extinction of a species, or, conversely, it may entail the overpopulation of a species. In either event, any ecosystem so disturbed will in due course become negatively altered and may well collapse. To illustrate: when wolves were eliminated from the greater part of the United States and, to a somewhat lesser extent, from southern Canada, deer in the north-eastern parts of the continent overpopulated their range. On the surface this was good news for hunters and for those government biologists who were in charge of "managing" the so-called renewable resources. But, given the fact that human hunting is unable to deal with massive overpopulation, deer have become an actual pest in some regions. Once these animals have exhausted their natural foods in a wilderness region that is within reach of an agricultural area, they turn to field crops, while doing so crossing busy highways and causing many serious automobile accidents. On the other hand, in areas where agriculture is at a minimum, overpopulated deer (and moose, elk, and caribou) eventually run out of food and so, obeying natural laws, begin to decline. When this occurs, government-employed wildlife managers either advocate a closed hunting season (if they are enlightened), or, as is occurring in British Columbia and Alberta at the present time, urge the elimination of the predators so that hunters can continue to kill the predators' prey and thus benefit the local economy. In time, such short-sighted practices will surely lead to the extinction of the species that is supposedly being protected as well as to a number of other species that are dependent on a healthy environment.

▲ **The chimneys** of Canadian and American industrial plants have been belch-
ing poisonous fumes into the atmosphere for many years. Numbers of lakes
have already been killed by acid rain in Ontario and Quebec; now the maples
in both provinces are believed to be dying because of such pollution.

▲ **Sometimes called the "fool hen"**, the spruce grouse has little fear of man. Because it is so easily killed, it disappears quickly with the advance of settlement.

During the 1960s, in one region of Ontario, overpopulated deer went into sudden decline because of lack of food, especially in winter, when the animals browse on the tips of deciduous and evergreen trees almost exclusively. A committee composed of local residents blamed the decline on predation by wolves and urged the Ontario government to eliminate *all* wolves in the province. The government listened to these preposterous demands and determined to act on them. The whole affair was conducted in secret. But, at the point when a widespread wolf extermination program was going to be made law, the news leaked. I was highly critical of the proposed legislation; so were many other conservationists. The protests were numerous and loud and the politicians listened; the proposal was defeated.

Soon afterwards, the Outdoor Writers of Canada asked me to chair a wolf-versus-deer debate during the association's annual general meeting. Speaking in favour of maintaining a viable wolf population was Dr. Nicholas Novakowski, a biologist who was then with the Canadian Wildlife Service; speaking against the continued existence of wolves was a physician from the area in question.

When the debate concluded it was clear that Dr. Novakowski had scored the most points and that the majority of those present were at least prepared to tolerate the continued presence of wolves in the wilderness environment. One individual, however, rose at the last moment and stated: "I don't give a *damn* about wolves! I just want to shoot deer!"

Silence greeted this outburst as the meeting broke up. But I have never forgotten that man's words. They represent an attitude that still dominates among those who see the wilderness as their personal killing ground, a place where only the "good" animals may live until they are killed in the name of sport or for their fur, and one in which the "bad" species should not be tolerated. This attitude also prevails among those who exploit the environment for economic reasons, who count only the dollars represented by a standing tree, an underground supply of oil or gas, a coveted mineral, or a piece of forest adjacent to a growing municipality that, when cleared, will provide sites for new houses.

The economic health of a nation is, of course, of prime importance to all its people, and I am not here suggesting that it is wrong to take from the land those resources without which the Canadian economy would undoubtedly collapse. What is at issue, however, is not so much the *use* of such resources as the manner in which they are being *abused* in this country and elsewhere in the world.

Even a casual study of human history reveals that as mankind continued to overpopulate, our societies put more and more pressure on the natural environment. Several centuries ago, when the word "biology" had not yet been coined, destruction of habitat and species was of no consequence to the people of the day. Europe, where technology advanced rapidly, was led into the Industrial Revolution by Britain during the 1760s. Hand tools were replaced by power-driven machines and more and more natural resources were converted into manufactured goods. It was not long before European nations began to exhaust their own resources and began to exploit the "riches" in distant lands, such as those in Asia, Africa, and the American continents. By the end of the eighteenth century, many parts of the world had been devastated. Some two decades into the present century, mass-production went into full swing and pollution spread, but this modern plague was not considered dangerous, or even objectionable, until the middle of the present century. Even then, the stench of the smog produced by factory chimneys was often labelled "the sweet smell of success".

Towards the end of the Second World War, chemistry produced the organo-phosphate poisons — DDT and many others. The use of pesticides and herbicides soared almost overnight; and they continue to do so, even to the point where agriculturalists sincerely believe that crops can no longer be produced without them. At about the same time, synthetic fertilizers were added to the environment, while those historic growth promoters, the manure of cattle, sheep, goats, and chickens, were allowed to accumulate to the point where they became harmful to the environment, in many cases leaching into the waterways and in equally numerous locales pooling on the land. Disposal of these "wastes" continues to be a problem.

When mankind lived within nature, obeying the natural laws, the environment remained healthy and yielded all the produce necessary for the survival of people as well as that of the animals and plants that it contained. Human wastes were all biodegradable and returned regularly to the environment, enriching it. No possible source of energy was lost to the biological system. Since then, burgeoning populations in ever-growing urban centres and the world-wide systems of transportation and commerce — especially the trade in raw or manufactured natural resources — have created serious imbalances. Today, plants, oil, minerals, and animals (for their fur and for use as exotic foods or as aphrodisiacs) that are taken from one part of the biosphere are most frequently used in far-away cities that are densely populated. Waste products, both natural and synthetic, are rarely recycled, nor are they returned to the ecosystem from which they were taken (as trees or animals, or as minerals or oil) in their natural states. What is happening now is that the world's metropolitan centres have become sinks into which nature's raw materials are being funnelled and where the vital energy contained in natural wastes is not only lost, but is converted to pollution because it is unused and concentrated. More and more Canadian cities are looking for more and more garbage-dump sites; more and more land is being filled with non-disposable leftover materials; the sewage from millions of people, although treated, at least in most cases, makes enormous demands on the water supply (18 L [4 gal.] of water are used every time a toilet is flushed).

No natural system can function indefinitely in a healthy state if its products (the plants, animals, the air, and the water it contains) are used up or poisoned at a rate exceeding its survival demands. Over-harvesting will of itself lead to ecological disaster, but when a weakened system is further burdened by massive amounts of urban and industrial pollution, chaos will ensue in due course.

Much has been said of late about acid rain, a catch-phrase that covers a multitude of pollutants that do not always fall as rain, but also descend onto the land during low-cloud levels and, when particles are large enough, hit the earth as fall-out. In my book *The Poison Makers*, which was published in 1967, I documented this so-called acid rain, among the most harmful agents of which are sulphur oxides. Like Rachel Carson before me, whose book, *Silent Spring*, was published in 1962, I was ignored. Now, when the North American environment is in crisis because of acid rain and other contaminants, many words are being uttered regarding the problem, but few actions against pollution are being taken, mainly because to put the proper controls into effect will cost a great deal of money.

Meanwhile, although DDT has been banned in North America, a host of other chemical poisons continue to deluge the environment. In more recent years, because it is deemed to be cheaper to use 2,4–D (2,4–dichlorophenoxy acetic acid) to clear brush from highway and utility-line rights-of-ways than to clear by hand, vast amounts of this chemical are being sprayed under official sanction on roadsides, in wild areas that are traversed by power lines and, for weed-control purposes, on agricultural croplands, usually by aerial spraying. This latter method deposits only a small percentage of the chemical on the target plants and allows most of it to drift over the surrounding environment. Additionally, this chemical is now being widely used to control the weeds in domestic gardens.

Scientists opposed to the indiscriminate use of 2,4–D have conducted studies, the results of which strongly indicate that it is an agent of cancer, birth defects, and other ailments in humans; scientists who deem the chemical safe have conducted studies that deny the harmful effect to humans. The jury is still out on this issue, despite the fact that while 2,4–D in its pure form may, or may not be safe, the chemical breaks down in the soil to dichlorophenol. This proven poison affects animals and humans and is four times more harmful than its parent, for it is a powerful corrosive that is extremely water-soluble; 2,4–D kills "undesirable" broad-leaf plants by acting on the foliage and travelling downwards into the root systems, thence into the soil. When it breaks down to dichlorophenol, it also kills soil bacteria necessary for the health of all plants, including evergreens. Over a period of time, forest margins near sprayed areas decay and the ecosystem dies.

The major problem facing conservation biologists today is how to stop the population declines of animals *and* plants that are being caused by habitat destruction, pollution, and habitat alteration wherein some species of plants or animals are removed, and other, alien, species are introduced and are allowed to colonize the ecosystem. Two other problems are less obvious. The first poses the question of how to determine which species are going to be affected first. There is no clear-cut answer to this question at present; it can only be *presumed* that the species most stressed will go first, but there is evidence to suggest that some species are far more resistant to stress than others. The second problem pertains to the fact that some species dieoffs can come suddenly and as a complete surprise, even after long-term healthy levels. It is common practice among those who are involved in removing animals and plants from any ecosystem to speak about "maximum sustainable yield", assuming that such MSY levels often occur naturally. But a comparison between natural and human-manipulated trends has repeatedly been shown to be invalid and the truth is that those who advocate such harvesting have been wrong more often than they have been right. During the past hundred years, marine fish stocks have seriously declined — in some cases species have become extinct — and many land species have either died off or are now endangered.

Traditionally, politicians and many of the biologists who work for governments (with the notable exception of those employed by the Canadian Wildlife Service) have seen themselves as servants of the industrial-hunting-recreation lobbies and so manage the land for these consumer groups, while those members of the public who do not agree with the exploitation of the environment are rarely listened to. Ironically, the latter are far more numerous than the former! Why, then, is the majority being ignored? The answer is that conservationists are not organized: *they do not speak in one voice.* Elected officials depend on votes. Strong lobbies fielded by hunters and industrialists are listened to; their will is being done.

What is needed in Canada, and indeed, on the North American continent, is a unified conservation movement, an umbrella organization

▲ **Although this Arctic fox** is not yet considered at risk, seven other Arctic species, ranging from the bowhead whale to the wolverine, are considered so by the Committee on the Status of Endangered Wildlife in Canada.

Other than man, bears have few ▶
natural enemies. The spread of settlement and hunting have reduced
the ranges of these magnificent animals, particularly the grizzly.

representing all naturalist associations and one that will assuredly be
backed by millions more votes than those fielded by all the other lobbies put together.

The Bureau of Outdoor Recreation of the United States in 1974 noted
in its report *The Recreation Imperative* that "83 million Americans
enjoy walking and related activities" for an average of 24 days a year.
The report projected an increase to 192 million outdoor enthusiasts by
the turn of this century. An earlier survey by the U.S. Fish and Wildlife
Service summarized outdoor use by almost 7 million hunters,
4.5 million bird-watchers, and 27 million nature photographers. At that
time, the birders and photographers outnumbered the hunters more
than four to one. Clearly, if those bird-watchers and photographers had
joined forces and had spoken in one voice, the politicians in the United
States would have been forced to heed the protests of more than 30
million voters!

Thus, to those many people who have asked me: "What can *I* do?"
I reply: join a conservation organization (see page 295) and urge its
executive officers to co-operate with all other similar organizations, so
that one single umbrella agency will lobby for all those who are concerned with the preservation of the environment. When that happens,
the politicians will listen and true conservation practices will be
generated.

Meanwhile, the individual can become informed. It is good to keep eyes and ears tuned to the media, but because of lack of air-time, or newspaper space, many issues are dealt with in such a cursory fashion that confusion can often result. The study of nature is one of the most important life sciences and although it would not be reasonable to expect lay people to spend time reading the often confusing prose with which biological texts are so frequently filled, there are many lay-oriented books that will fill the gaps of knowledge. A list of these is given on page 303.

Once informed, the individual should make his or her views known to government. In this way it may be possible to avert the repeat of tragedies such as that which took place in British Columbia, where the government permitted the cutting of irreplaceable fir trees on the south part of Moresby Island and on Lyell Island. Some of those trees were 1000 years old. In that case, the Canadian government managed to halt the exploitation by paying a large sum of money to the B.C. government and then declaring the area a national park. In British Columbia, also, as well as in Alberta, government biologists are slaughtering wolves so that hunters may kill more "big game" animals, populations of which are low not because of wolf predation, but as a result of human exploitation of their numbers and their environment, and, perhaps, because of natural population fluctuations. Such "harvesting" can only be labelled *exploitation biology;* it will surely lead to devastation of the regions concerned.

Although I am personally opposed to hunting for sport — I simply cannot see how one can derive pleasure from killing — I recognize that in some areas of North America hunting has become a necessary practice. By altering habitat, removing predators, and allowing certain species to overpopulate, we have created the need to control runaway numbers. There are undoubtedly better ways of exerting such control, but until more enlightened management policies make room for their introduction, hunting will continue to be necessary. Also, and in fairness to hunters, it must be stated that the study of nature was actually encouraged when it was recognized that hunting and fishing had emerged as a form of recreation. The financial benefits derived from hunting and fishing are undoubtedly large and tangible. Hunters and fishermen have subscribed a great deal of money that has supported, and continues to support, wildlife management. Often the hunters and

OVERLEAF   **An example of "clear cut" logging** near Quesnel Lake, British ▶
Columbia.

▲ **Elk, or wapiti**, were once distributed across most of the northern world but are now restricted to pockets of wilderness.

anglers are the ones who oppose the destruction of the environment more loudly than do the conservationists. Nevertheless, I submit that the time has now come to manage nature's affairs from a far wider and far more important perspective: the survival of the environment. It is no longer appropriate that those responsible for regulating Canada's natural environment should do so only from the standpoint of those who want to continue to abuse that environment.

Today, fortunately, there is a growing public awareness of the value of the wild environment, especially of its aesthetic value. We humans, despite our runaway technology, need the solace of nature, of which we are an integral part. It is neither fitting nor fair that the wild world should be managed only for the hunters, the industrialists, or the developers. Endangered species should be encouraged to make a comeback; in areas where species have been eradicated, they should be reintroduced. There should be large expanses of Canada where nature is allowed to prosper without the intervention of the gun, the trap, the oil rigs, and the bulldozers, where the wolf should have as much right to live as the deer and where the forest will prosper in tranquility, without the snarls of the chain-saw.

The real value of nature is that people may enter it for a time, enjoy its beauty, its animals, and its plants, and return home renewed without having taken anything away from the environment. Treated in this way, the wild world will give much pleasure and satisfaction to our people; and it will continue to endure so as to offer the same privileges to future generations.

Although this book specifically addresses the biology of Canada, it should not be supposed that the problems discussed here are unique to our nation. On the contrary. They are international in scope and in a great many other parts of the world have reached a point of crisis.

At this writing, it has been announced that the world's population has reached the 5 billion mark and that the birth rate is considerably larger than the death rate. Humans, although frequently supposed to be above the natural laws, are biological organisms who are for the most part physically and emotionally controlled by biological forces. This means that their numbers would, in a primitively natural sense, be controlled by their environment. This was, indeed, the case during the first 1650 years AD. During year One, based upon historical writings and general estimates, the world population totalled 250 million. By 1650, this number had doubled to 500 million. By 1850, 200 years later, there were one billion people living on our planet. Only 80 years later this number had doubled to two billion, in 1930; in 1975, the number had again doubled. But the time interval had been dramatically reduced, taking only 45 years to reach four billion. Twelve years later another one billion people had been added to the total. At this rate of acceleration, there will probably be ten billion people struggling for survival on our planet by the second decade of the twenty-first century.

Collectively, the dry parts of our world total 14.5 billion ha (35.8 billion acres). Something on the order of half this land is uninhabitable, consisting of ice, desert, or mountains. Thus, if the population reaches the ten-billion mark, and if every metre of *habitable* land can be used, the resulting 7.25 billion ha (17.9 billion acres) would have to accommodate one person per 0.725 ha (1.6 acres) spread evenly across the face of the earth. In reality, however, it would mean that great urban centres would result, giant cities sprawling across the best land where overcrowding would reach proportions undreamed of to date by city planners. In all probability, it would also mean that the great majority of all natural species would become extinct and that the use of "natural" resources would come to a virtual end.

Clearly, the growth of human numbers is a subject that must be examined fearlessly and in detail if the realities of conservation (and this also means *human* conservation) are to be addressed, assessed, and met. Yet, this is not a new concept. More than two thousand years ago Aristotle (384–322 BC) saw the threat and warned in his treatise, *Politics,* that the "neglect of an effective birth-control policy is a never-failing source of poverty which, in turn, is the parent of revolution and crime." Some five hundred years later, Tertullian (150–230 AD), a theologian of the Latin Church, noted that "pestilence, famine, wars and earthquakes have come to be regarded as a blessing to crowded nations since they serve to prune away the luxurious growth of the human race." The English economist Thomas Robert Malthus (1766–1834) warned that in the absence of human birth-control measures, populations would rise to the limits of the capacity of food production. In such an event, he stated, hunger and poverty would be a permanent condition throughout the world.

Aristotle, Tertullian, and Malthus were not biologists and thus did not address the impact that burgeoning human numbers were to have on the natural environment.

We humans are natural organisms; if we reject our biological heritage (and the fundamental laws of nature that govern our bodies and a large part of our minds), we do so at our peril and without regard for future generations of our own kind or for the health of our world and its nature. Yet, I end this book with hope by quoting again the writings of Michael Soule, published in the first edition of *Conservation Biology,* the journal of the Society for Conservation Biology.

Explaining the origins of the society, Dr. Soule concludes:

> The Society is a response by professionals, mostly biological and social scientists, managers and administrators to the biological diversity crisis that will reach a crescendo in the first half of the twenty-first century. We assume implicitly that we are in time, and that by joining together with each other and with other well-intentioned persons and groups, that the worst biological disaster in the last 65 million years can be averted. We assume implicitly that science and technology are neither inherently good nor evil, but are tools that can benefit or harm. We assume implicitly that environmental wounds inflicted by ignorant humans and destructive technologies can be treated by wiser humans and

wholesome technologies. Although we have varying personal philosophies, we share a faith in ourselves, as a species and as individuals, that we are equal to the challenge.

As conservation biologists, our major role in this unprecedented movement is a scientific one, though some of us may take on other jobs in the conservation movement — as publicists, as advocates, as activists, and mentors. But as members of the Society, as students, scientists, managers and administrators, we have particular and unique responsibilities. These include 1) the modeling and analysis of population, community, ecosystem, and planetary processes; 2) basic field work, including inventories and systematics; 3) experimentation to test hypotheses; 4) development and evaluation of technological and management interventions that maintain and restore diversity and function; 5) the communication of results to facilitate their application; and 6) the integration of this knowledge and technology with complementary human activities, from agriculture to anthropology. For these reasons we join together in professional alliance in the service of each other, but also in the service of the less articulate members of our evolutionary tree.

We are not the only organization with these goals. The objectives of many professional groups, societies, foundations and other entities are shared and overlapped with ours. But conditions change, and now they require a new kind of organization. Let us hope that we can be as effective as our sister organizations for the benefit of all beings.

▲ **Jaeger**

▲ **A western painted turtle** emerges from the water. Painted turtles occur across Canada, feeding in lakes, rivers and ponds on small fish, water plants and carrion. During summer they can often be seen lined up on floating logs, sunning themselves.

CONSERVATION ASSOCIATIONS

THE FOLLOWING ASSOCIATIONS ARE RECOMMENDED TO THOSE READERS WHO MAY want to contribute to the conservation of Canada's natural environment. The list includes provincial conservation associations as well as national and international groups. It should be noted that in addition to this list there are a great number of regional conservation associations, clubs, and groups active in Canada, but space does not permit a complete listing:

Canadian Nature Federation
453 Sussex Drive
Ottawa, Ontario
K1N 6Z4

Canadian Parks and Wilderness Society
Suite 1335
160 Bloor St. East
Toronto, Ontario
M4W 1B9

Ecology North
Box 2888
Yellowknife, Northwest Territories
X1A 2R2

Federation of Alberta Naturalists
Box 1472
Edmonton, Alberta
T5J 2N5

Federation of British Columbia Naturalists
321 - 1367 West Broadway
Vancouver, British Columbia
V6H 4A9

Federation of Ontario Naturalists
355 Lesmill Road
Don Mills, Ontario
M3B 2W8

Federation of N.S. Naturalist
c/o The Nova Scotia Museum
1747 Summer Street
Halifax, Nova Scotia
B3H 2A6

International Union for
Conservation of Nature
and Natural Resources
World Conservation Center
Avenue du Mont-Blanc
CH-1196 Gland, Switzerland

International Wildlife Coalition-Canada
P.O. Box 461
Port Credit Post Station
Mississauga, Ontario
L5G 4M1

Manitoba Naturalists Society
128 James Avenue
Suite 302
Winnipeg, Manitoba
R3B 0N8

National Wildlife Federation
1400 16th St. NW
Washington D.C.
20036-2266

Natural History Society of
Newfoundland and Labrador
Box 1013
St. John's, Newfoundland
A1C 5M3

Natural History Society of
Prince Edward Island
Box 2346
Charlottetown, Prince Edward Island
C1A 1Y6

Nature Canada
Box 4348
Regina, Saskatchewan
S4P 3W6

Nature Conservancy of Canada
110 Eglinton Ave. W.
4th Floor
Toronto, Ontario
M4R 2G5

Nova Scotia Bird Society
c/o The Nova Scotia Museum
1747 Summer Street
Halifax, Nova Scotia
B3H 3A6

Union québécoise pour
la conservation de la nature
160, 76 rue Est
Charlesbourg, Quebec
G1H 7H6

Western Canada Wilderness Committee
9526 Jasper Ave.
Edmonton, Alberta
T5H 3V3

World Wildlife Fund
90 Eglinton Ave. E.
Suite 504
Toronto, Ontario
M4P 2Z1

Yukon Conservation Society
Box 4163
Whitehorse, Yukon Territory
Y1A 3T3

INDEX

SELECTED READING LIST

ALLARD, R.W. *Principles of Plant Breeding*. New York: Wiley, 1960.

ALLEN, DURWARD L. *The Life of Prairies and Plains*. New York: McGraw-Hill, 1967.

BANFIELD, A.W.F. *The Mammals of Canada*. 2nd ed., rev. Toronto: University of Toronto Press for National Museums of Canada, 1977.

BATES, MARSTON. *The Forest and the Sea*. New York: Vintage Books, 1960.

BROOKS, DANIEL R., AND WILEY, EDWARD O. *Evolution as Entropy*. Chicago: University of Chicago Press, 1986.

BUCHSBAUM, RALPH; BUCHSBAUM, MILDRED; PEARSE, JOHN; AND PEARSE, VICKI. *Animals without Backbones*. 3rd ed., rev. Chicago: University of Chicago Press, 1987.

BURTON, ROBERT. *Bird Behaviour*. London: Granada, 1985.

CAIN, S.A. *Foundations of Plant Geography*. New York: Harper Bros., 1944.

CALVIN, JACK, AND RICKETS, EDWARD F. *Between Pacific Tides*. 4th ed., rev. 1968 by Hedgpeth, Joel W. CA: Stanford University Press, 1939.

CARSON, RACHEL. *The Edge of the Sea*. Boston: Houghton Mifflin, 1955.

CARSON, RACHEL. *Silent Spring*. Boston: Houghton Mifflin, 1962.

CASE, T.J., AND DIAMOND, J.M. *Community Ecology*. New York: Harper and Row, 1985.

CLEMENS, W.A., AND WILBY, G.V. *Fishes of the Pacific Coast of Canada*. Ottawa: Fisheries Research Board of Canada, 1967.

COUDSLEY-THOMPSON, S.L. *Animal Behaviour*. Edinburgh: Oliver and Boyd, 1960.

COUNCIL OF ENVIRONMENTAL QUALITY AND THE DEPARTMENT OF STATE, USA. *The Global 2000 Report*. London and New York: Penguin Books, 1982.

EISENBERG, JOHN F. *The Mammalian Radiations*. Chicago: University of Chicago Press, 1981.

FEDER, MARTIN E., AND LANDER, GEORGE F., ED. *Predator-Prey Relationships*. Chicago: University of Chicago Press, 1986.

FRANKEL, O.H., AND SOULE, M.E. *Conservation and Evolution*. MA: Cambridge University Press, 1981.

GODFREY, W. EARL. *The Birds of Canada*. 2nd ed., rev. Ottawa: National Museums of Canada, 1986.

GRIFFIN, DONALD R. *Animal Thinking*. MA: Harvard University Press, 1984.

HANDLER, PHILIP, ED. *Biology and the Future of Man*. London and Toronto: Oxford University Press, 1970.

HEEZEN, BRUCE C., AND HOLLISTER, CHARLES D. *The Face of the Deep*. London and Toronto: Oxford University Press, 1971.

HOSIE, R.C. *Native Trees of Canada*. 7th ed. Ottawa: Canadian Forestry Service.

HUXLEY, JULIAN. *Evolution in Action*. New York: Harper and Row, 1958.

LINDSEY, C.C., AND McPHAIL, J.D. *Freshwater Fishes of Northwestern Canada and Alaska*. Ottawa: Fisheries Research Board of Canada, 1970.

MARGALEF, R. *Perspectives in Ecological Theory*. Chicago: University of Chicago Press, 1968.

McHUGH, TOM. *The Time of the Buffalo*. New York: Alfred A. Knopf, 1972.

MILNE, LORUS AND MILNE, MARGERY. *Water and Life*. New York: Atheneum, 1972.

SOULE, MICHAEL E., ED. *Conservation Biology*. Sunderland: Sinauer Associates, 1986.

THOMAS, LEWIS. *The Lives of a Cell*. New York: The Viking Press, 1974.

WEIZ, PAUL B. *Elements of Biology*. New York: McGraw-Hill, 1969.

WILSON, EDWARD O. *Biophilia*. MA: Harvard University Press, 1984.

PHOTO CREDITS